THE

HISTORICAL ATLAS

OF

THE AMERICAN REVOLUTION

THE

HISTORICAL ATLAS

OF

THE AMERICAN

REVOLUTION

IAN BARNES

Consultant Editor

Professor CHARLES ROYSTER

ROUTLEDGE

A member of the Taylor & Francis Group

NEW YORK

Published in 2000 by
Routledge
29 West 35th Street
New York, NY 10001

A member of the Taylor & Francis Group

10 9 8 7 6 5 4 3 2 1

Library of Congress Cataloging-in-Publication Data

Barnes, Ian, 1946–
    The historical atlas of the American Revolution / Ian Barnes; Charles Royster,
  consulting editor.
      p. cm.
    Includes bibliographical references and index.
    ISBN 0-415-92243-7 (alk. paper)
    1. United States—History—Revolution, 1775–1783. 2. United
States—History—Revolution, 1775–1783—Maps.   I. Royster, Charles.   II. Title.

E208 B36 2000
973.3—dc21

99-059920

TO
VIVIENNE, ROBIN, AND AMBER
WITH LOVE AND THANKS

Contents

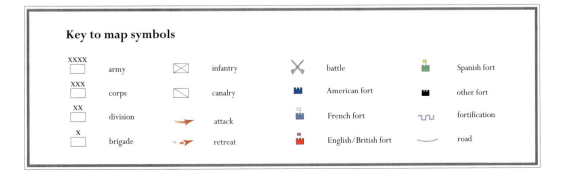

Key to map symbols

XXXX	army		infantry		battle		Spanish fort
XXX	corps		canalry		American fort		other fort
XX	division		attack		French fort		fortification
X	brigade		retreat		English/British fort		road

Foreword

Many writers have reminded us that the War of American Independence—known in Britain at that time as "the American War"—was not the same as the American Revolution. The revolution entailed innovations in government and new political ideas and institutions changing the role of the citizen, the nature of legislative representation, the power of the executive, and the relations between national and local governments. The war, on the other hand, was waged in a manner readily recognizable to veterans of previous conflicts, especially the Seven Years' War, which began twenty years earlier. The War of American Independence was not "revolutionary" in military ideas or practice.

In the Seven Years' War, Britain had dismantled much of France's overseas empire. In the War of American Independence, France, by allying with the Americans, took its revenge, though at a heavy cost, which brought unexpected consequences upon the old regime. Americans, proud of their dedication to republicanism and liberty, nevertheless needed the army, the navy, the munitions, and the money of King Louis XVI in order to win independence from King George III. Americans claimed to have created a new kind of soldier for a new kind of war: a patriot, not a hireling, a thinking fighter, not an automaton. Yet the successes of George Washington's Continental Army depended in large part upon his efforts to make it as reliable as the disciplined regular forces of European monarchs.

The War of American Independence lasted more than eight years, from the first shots in Massachusetts to the treaty of peace in France. The British cabinet led by Frederick North did not mount a sustained offensive for the duration of the war. At one time or another, British forces occupied every significant American city, but 95 percent of Americans did not live in cities, and their resistance, though fluctuating in its scale of effort, continued. The British tried first to isolate a supposed minority of rebellious agitators in the northeast. Then they tried to rally a supposed majority of loyal subjects in other parts of the continent. Neither effort succeeded because both were based upon false assumptions. The Royal Army and Navy repeatedly defeated the American forces or drove them to retreat. Yet these victories did not conquer a continent. And the crucial British defeats—Trenton, New Jersey, at the end of 1776, Saratoga, New York, in the autumn of 1777, and Yorktown, Virginia, in the autumn of 1781—thwarted major offensives and, in the last two cases, lost entire British armies. The North administration took Britain more and more deeply into debt with fewer and fewer successes to justify these large expenditures. At last, North lost his majority in the House of Commons, and George III acknowledged in December 1782 that the treaty of peace must recognize the independence of the United States.

The American Revolution depicted and summarized by this historical atlas was, we can see, more than the military engagements of the War of American Independence. To understand that war and its outcome, the reader needs to know not only the dispositions of forces and materiel in combat, but also the motives underlying Americans' effort to win independence and the difficulties inherent in the North administration's attempt to compel thirteen colonies to remain within the British Empire. For that reason, this historical atlas adopts a wide-ranging approach to its subject and strives to be as comprehensive as possible within the limits of its length.

It begins with a portrait of British North America and with the rivalry between Britain and France for control of North America. And it carries the story of American Independence into the first half of the nineteenth century. The revolution did not end with the departure of British troops. Americans had not yet fully agreed upon what kind of country they had created. Was its federal government perpetual and supreme or temporary and contingent? Would the nation continue human slavery indefinitely or confine and end it? Americans failed to resolve these questions through the mechanism of republican self-government which they so proudly created during the American Revolution. Instead, they found themselves fighting another war—this time not against British enemies but against one another.

The War of American Independence consisted not only of armies' campaigns and naval engagements but also of a transatlantic struggle over trade and supplies. American privateering vessels and, eventually, the navies of France and Spain disrupted Britain's commerce and supply lives. The British Navy tried to impede the flow of munitions and other goods from Europe to the Americans, by way of islands in the Caribbean. The armies fighting in North America were parts of vast and complex networks of logistics which made the Atlantic Ocean both a highway and a battlefield. In this contest, Britain failed. Americans kept their armies in the field until the North administration abandoned its effort to defeat rebellion.

The historical atlas which places the American Revolution in its broadest context—chronologically, geographically, culturally—best serves those readers seeking an introduction to the history of the period and those who use the atlas as a work of reference.

Professor Charles Royster
Louisiana State University

IN CONGRESS, JULY 4, 1776.

The unanimous Declaration of the thirteen united States of America,

When in the Course of human events, it becomes necessary for one people to dissolve the political bands which have connected them with another, and to assume among the powers of the earth, the separate and equal station to which the Laws of Nature and of Nature's God entitle them, a decent respect to the opinions of mankind requires that they should declare the causes which impel them to the separation. —— We hold these truths to be self-evident, that all men are created equal, that they are endowed by their Creator with certain unalienable Rights, that among these are Life, Liberty and the pursuit of Happiness. —— That to secure these rights, Governments are instituted among Men, deriving their just powers from the consent of the governed, —— That whenever any Form of Government becomes destructive of these ends, it is the Right of the People to alter or to abolish it, and to institute new Government, laying its foundation on such principles, and organizing its powers in such form, as to them shall seem most likely to effect their Safety and Happiness. Prudence, indeed, will dictate that Governments long established should not be changed for light and transient causes; and accordingly all experience hath shewn, that mankind are more disposed to suffer, while evils are sufferable, than to right themselves by abolishing the forms to which they are accustomed. But when a long train of abuses and usurpations, pursuing invariably the same Object evinces a design to reduce them under absolute Despotism, it is their right, it is their duty, to throw off such Government, and to provide new Guards for their future security. —— Such has been the patient sufferance of these Colonies; and such is now the necessity which constrains them to alter their former Systems of Government. The history of the present King of Great Britain is a history of repeated injuries and usurpations, all having in direct object the establishment of an absolute Tyranny over these States. To prove this, let Facts be submitted to a candid world. —— He has refused his Assent to Laws, the most wholesome and necessary for the public good. —— He has forbidden his Governors to pass Laws of immediate and pressing importance, unless suspended in their operation till his Assent should be obtained; and when so suspended, he has utterly neglected to attend to them. —— He has refused to pass other Laws for the accommodation of large districts of people, unless those people would relinquish the right of Representation in the Legislature, a right inestimable to them and formidable to tyrants only. —— He has called together legislative bodies at places unusual, uncomfortable, and distant from the depository of their public Records, for the sole purpose of fatiguing them into compliance with his measures. —— He has dissolved Representative Houses repeatedly, for opposing with manly firmness his invasions on the rights of the people. —— He has refused for a long time, after such dissolutions, to cause others to be elected; whereby the Legislative powers, incapable of Annihilation, have returned to the People at large for their exercise; the State remaining in the mean time exposed to all the dangers of invasion from without, and convulsions within. —— He has endeavoured to prevent the population of these States; for that purpose obstructing the Laws for Naturalization of Foreigners; refusing to pass others to encourage their migrations hither, and raising the conditions of new Appropriations of Lands. —— He has obstructed the Administration of Justice, by refusing his Assent to Laws for establishing Judiciary powers. —— He has made Judges dependent on his Will alone, for the tenure of their offices, and the amount and payment of their salaries. —— He has erected a multitude of New Offices, and sent hither swarms of Officers to harrass our people, and eat out their substance. —— He has kept among us, in times of peace, Standing Armies without the Consent of our legislatures. —— He has affected to render the Military independent of and superior to the Civil power. —— He has combined with others to subject us to a jurisdiction foreign to our constitution, and unacknowledged by our laws; giving his Assent to their Acts of pretended Legislation: —— For Quartering large bodies of armed troops among us: —— For protecting them, by a mock Trial, from punishment for any Murders which they should commit on the Inhabitants of these States: —— For cutting off our Trade with all parts of the world: —— For imposing Taxes on us without our Consent: —— For depriving us in many cases, of the benefits of Trial by Jury: —— For transporting us beyond Seas to be tried for pretended offences: —— For abolishing the free System of English Laws in a neighbouring Province, establishing therein an Arbitrary government, and enlarging its Boundaries so as to render it at once an example and fit instrument for introducing the same absolute rule into these Colonies: —— For taking away our Charters, abolishing our most valuable Laws, and altering fundamentally the Forms of our Governments: —— For suspending our own Legislatures, and declaring themselves invested with power to legislate for us in all cases whatsoever. —— He has abdicated Government here, by declaring us out of his Protection and waging War against us. —— He has plundered our seas, ravaged our Coasts, burnt our towns, and destroyed the lives of our people. —— He is at this time transporting large Armies of foreign Mercenaries to compleat the works of death, desolation and tyranny, already begun with circumstances of Cruelty & perfidy scarcely paralleled in the most barbarous ages, and totally unworthy the Head of a civilized nation. —— He has constrained our fellow Citizens taken Captive on the high Seas to bear Arms against their Country, to become the executioners of their friends and Brethren, or to fall themselves by their Hands. —— He has excited domestic insurrections amongst us, and has endeavoured to bring on the inhabitants of our frontiers, the merciless Indian Savages, whose known rule of warfare, is an undistinguished destruction of all ages, sexes and conditions. In every stage of these Oppressions We have Petitioned for Redress in the most humble terms: Our repeated Petitions have been answered only by repeated injury. A Prince whose character is thus marked by every act which may define a Tyrant, is unfit to be the ruler of a free people. Nor have We been wanting in attentions to our Brittish brethren. We have warned them from time to time of attempts by their legislature to extend an unwarrantable jurisdiction over us. We have reminded them of the circumstances of our emigration and settlement here. We have appealed to their native justice and magnanimity, and we have conjured them by the ties of our common kindred to disavow these usurpations, which, would inevitably interrupt our connections and correspondence. They too have been deaf to the voice of justice and of consanguinity. We must, therefore, acquiesce in the necessity, which denounces our Separation, and hold them, as we hold the rest of mankind, Enemies in War, in Peace Friends. ——

We, therefore, the Representatives of the united States of America, in General Congress, Assembled, appealing to the Supreme Judge of the world for the rectitude of our intentions, do, in the Name, and by Authority of the good People of these Colonies, solemnly publish and declare, That these United Colonies are, and of Right ought to be Free and Independent States; that they are Absolved from all Allegiance to the Brittish Crown, and that all political connection between them and the State of Great Britain, is and ought to be totally dissolved; and that as Free and Independent States, they have full Power to levy War, conclude Peace, contract Alliances, establish Commerce, and to do all other Acts and Things which Independent States may of right do. —— And for the support of this Declaration, with a firm reliance on the protection of divine Providence, we mutually pledge to each other our Lives, our Fortunes and our sacred Honor.

Button Gwinnett
Lyman Hall
Geo Walton.

Wm Hooper
Joseph Hewes,
John Penn

Edward Rutledge.

Thos Heyward Junr.
Thomas Lynch Junr.
Arthur Middleton

John Hancock

Samuel Chase
Wm Paca
Thos Stone
Charles Carroll of Carrollton

George Wythe
Richard Henry Lee
Th Jefferson
Benja Harrison
Thos Nelson jr.
Francis Lightfoot Lee
Carter Braxton

Robt Morris
Benjamin Rush
Benja Franklin
John Morton
Geo Clymer
Jas Smith.
Geo Taylor
James Wilson
Geo Ross
Caesar Rodney
Geo Read
Tho M:Kean

Wm Floyd
Phil. Livingston
Frans Lewis
Lewis Morris
Richd Stockton
Jno Witherspoon
Fras Hopkinson
John Hart
Abra Clark

Josiah Bartlett
Wm Whipple
Saml Adams
John Adams
Robt Treat Paine
Elbridge Gerry
Step Hopkins
William Ellery
Roger Sherman
Saml Huntington
Wm Williams
Oliver Wolcott
Matthew Thornton

Introduction

To celebrate Thanksgiving and the Fourth of July is to commemorate, first, the survival of a new society built upon the Mayflower Compact, an early form of the social contract and a social and political innovation. Second, the Declaration of Independence set in motion events leading to the 1787 Constitution, a document rooted in the Enlightenment with a separation of powers between the executive, legislative, and judiciary. Inspired in part by Montesquieu's *L'Esprit des Lois*, the American experience certainly affected and stimulated ideas in France, with the "comparable" Declaration of the Rights of Man and Citizen, one basis for the French Revolution. The American Constitution has ever since occasioned debate around the world, and many liberal political thinkers in Great Britain admire the notion of a Bill of Rights, rather than the current British situation, which allows subjects—notice, not citizens—the right to do anything not covered by the law. In Britain, Parliament is sovereign, not the law, and people can be subjected to political control and disenfranchisement by the dominant party's political whim. For example, the Greater London Council, established in 1965, was abolished in 1986 after acrimonious disputes between its leader, Ken Livingstone, and the Conservative government. Ironically, this man is now the new Mayor of London. In 1991, the population of Greater London was approximately 6,680,000. Hence in 1986, a slightly smaller number lost their electoral vote for local government. How many U.S. states have a population of this size? Taking a long historical view, Americans fought for rights, in the War of Independence, that British subjects have not yet fully gained, and criticisms of arbitrary government and "tyranny" can still be levelled at the British political system.

This Atlas seeks to open up these important issues by considering the background causes of the American Revolution together with some historiographical debates in American history. Editorial constraints mean that immense detail, discussion, and cartographic coverage are impossible. Thus, the resultant work is selective and is intended as an introduction to a dynamic period of American history. To American citizens, new developments in cartographic techniques will introduce novel, exciting three-dimensional maps which will embellish existing understanding of the Revolution. Hopefully, this will whet the appetites of non-Americans and kindle an interest in an important and interesting set of events—a period that has since proved to be an outstandingly important one for the growth of political ideas and concepts of freedom and citizenship, and introducing the world to a country that has become the most significant and powerful state in the world.

History recounts how the early New England colonies were based upon people with dissenting religious ideas outside the remit of the orthodox and state-founded Church of England. The Atlas demonstrates the importance of the Church as a religious, social, and political forum but also points out a debate suggesting that religious influence did decline and became less significant than previously thought. The economic importance of the colonies suggests that they rapidly became linked into patterns of existing world trade and helped develop the wealth of the metropolitan state by constructing an Atlantic economy. A symbiotic relationship between the American colonies and Great Britain grew to such an extent that the severing of such ties would damage the interlocking economies. Consideration is given to the impact of Europeans meeting Native Americans and the consequences in terms of death by disease, enslavement, and colonial–Indian wars. The feelings and mood of the Native Americans are introduced and become a constant theme throughout the Atlas and provide a basis for a reader's later personal exploration of this example of "ethnic cleansing," an experience that devastated Europe during the Second World War and more recently during the war in Yugoslavia and Kosovo.

Early British colonization of North America is placed within the context of a global European imperial growth. Spain, France, the Netherlands, and Sweden all founded colonies, the most important being the Spanish possessions in Florida and Mexico and the French in Mississippi and Canada. The Swedish experience on the Delaware was brief while the Dutch are known for a series of wars with Native Americans: Kieft's War (1639–45), the Peach War (1655–57), and the Esopus Wars (1659–60 and 1663–64). More important, New Amsterdam became New York and was ceded to Britain in 1674 by the Treaty of Westminster. A remaining tie between New York and the Dutch heritage is Brooklyn and its early equivalent little bridge over a canal in Amsterdam. Conflict between the European powers led to a series of colonial wars between Britain and France; the American theater of war was just one battleground in a worldwide series of operations. These wars continued for a hundred years, involved Native Americans on each side, and were characterized by violence and mutual butchery. Eventually, the British preponderance in terms of population transcended internal divisions and overcame the more centralized French colonial regime and Britain acquired Canada in 1763.

The Atlas points out the debate over whether Americans were Englishmen abroad or, alternatively, Americans, and what this concept meant. Here, the migrant ethnic mix is shown, as is the religious upheaval known as the Great Awakening between 1720 and 1740. The consequent internecine religious divisions led to a greater religious plurality, tolerance, and democracy and stimulated a feeling of independence which fuelled the fervor initiating and sustaining the American Revolution. The notion of democracy is highly significant because colonial societies practically ruled themselves and acquired "democratic" institutions which were decentralized away from the British Parliament. The ideas of independence, self-confidence, and democracy were vital ingredients in combatting Britain, and the various introductory essays in the Atlas develop these ideas.

The Atlas outlines the general causes of the American Revolution and Britain's desire for the colonies to pay for their own defense. Consequently, the Stamp Act and Coercive Acts form a logical continuum from the 17th-century Navigation Acts, and their significance is assessed. The detested Québec Act receives treatment, as do colonial responses in terms of settling Indian Territory and the Boston Tea Party. The subsequent British attempts to punish Massachusetts are evaluated as a stage in the drift to war.

The outbreak of war in 1775 introduces a series of maps and accompanying texts which explain the military campaigns and battles of the War of Independence. The texts assess the skills or otherwise of contending military commanders and their accompanying strategic plans and battle tactics. This series of maps show the chaos and fog of war and displays the fortitude of Washington and his regular Continental troops. Foreign aid in terms of technical help from Marquis Marie Joseph de Lafayette and Frederich William von Steuben is assessed, as is the involvement of French troops on American soil. The campaigns are divided into the Northern and Southern states' experience. Considerable interest is shown in the campaigns and generalship of Nathaniel Greene who, despite defeats in battle, so weakened the British forces that the British had to withdraw from the interior of the Carolinas with many troops eventually incarcerating themselves in Yorktown.

The War of Independence is examined as a civil war between Patriots and Tories and the Battle of King's Mountain, North Carolina, in October 1780, receives a map of its own. The oceanic dimension of the American revolutionary war was linked with European conflicts being fought in the Mediterranean Sea and the Indian Ocean, the Caribbean, and Central America, together with struggles on the Spanish-Florida frontier. War on the frontier with Native Americans is given considerable prominence and the subsequent experience of Native Americans after the U. S. victory is shown as precursor events to Native Clearances and the Trail of Tears.

The aftermath of the war is demonstrated in terms of writing a constitution and its ratification together with the growth of political parties and the first constitutional amendments. Early foreign policy is explored, especially unsatisfactory American-British relations whereby Britain refused to withdraw from outposts on the Great Lakes. Spanish-American relations are considered, as are those with France, including the Quasi War and the Louisiana Purchase. The opening of the West and initial territorial expansion are placed in the context of further warfare against Native Americans and of the Lewis and Clark expeditions.

The Atlas ends with two significant developments. First, American-British relations reached a low point in the War of 1812–14. This unnecessary and unfortunate conflict had benefits in that the two states afterwards learned to co-exist; British overall maritime power was recognized, but British respect grew for American naval gunnery after several ship-to-ship frigate actions in which British ships were taken. The second, more important, result was the realization that mutual economic ties were essential and beneficial, especially as the exploitation of cotton was tied to British manufacturing. The Atlas examines in sum, the origins, events, and outcomes of the War of Independence, so let the maps speak for themselves.

Dr Ian Barnes

Chronology

1584   Colony founded at Roanoke Island (North Carolina) under Sir Walter Raleigh; the colony failed.

1606   London and Plymouth Companies established to send settlers to North America.

1607   May, Jamestown Colony, Virginia, founded by Captain John Smith.

1612   Tobacco cultivation began in Virginia.

1620   November. Arrival of the Pilgrim Fathers in the *Mayflower* at Cape Cod; colonists sign the Mayflower Compact, an early political constitution to ensure the new colony's welfare.

1622   Opechancanough, Chief of the Powhatan Indian Confederacy attacked Virginian towns.

1629   March. Massachusetts Bay Company chartered. John Winthrop governor of the Massachusetts Colony. Towns built at Boston, Mystic, Watertown, Roxbury, Lynn, and Dorchester by 1630. By 1634, a representative system of government was established.

1630–42 The Great Migration brought 16,000 settlers from England to Massachusetts.

1632   Maryland Charter granted. St. Mary's colony founded (1634)— a Roman Catholic sanctuary.

1636   Rhode Island founded at Providence by Roger Williams.

        Connecticut founded, comprising towns of Hartford, Windsor, and Wethersfield.

        Harvard College founded at New Towne (Cambridge).

1637   Pequot tribe destroyed by colonists and Narragansett allies.

1638   New Haven theocratic colony established by John Davenport and Theophilus Eaton.

1644   Powhatan Indians assault Virginia again killing 500 settlers. Opechancanough captured and murdered while a prisoner in Jamestown.

1651–73 Navigation Acts passed to protect British trade.

1663   Carolina granted to eight proprietors, separation into North and South by 1713.

1664   New Netherlands seized from the Dutch and New Amsterdam becomes New York.

        Connecticut and New Haven established a union lest the latter was taken by New York.

1672   Royal Africa Company chartered. Slave trade developed.

1676   Bacon's rebellion in Virginia against Governor's failure to prevent Indian raids.

1681   Charter of Pennsylvania signed and Philadelphia laid out in 1682.

1689–97 King William's War.

1690   11 May. Port Royal captured by Sir William Phips, French and Indians raid and kill colonists at Schenectady, Salmon Falls, and Casco Bay. Attack on Quebec fails.

1697   Treaty of Ryswick failed to address Franco-British issues in America.

1702–13 Queen Anne's War.

1704   French and Indian attacks in Connecticut Valley.

1707   British expedition against Port Royal failed.

1710   Colonists with British ships seize Acadia and Port Royal.

1711–13 Tuscarora War, after defeat, many Tuscarora fled to the Iroquois.

1713   Treaty of Utrecht. Britain secures Acadia and Newfoundland.

1715   Yamasee War. South Carolina severely damaged. Start of the Creek threat.

1732   22 February. George Washington born.

1733   Georgia founded.

1743–48 King George's War.

1745   16 June. Capture of Louisbourg by troops from Massachusetts, New Hampshire, and Connecticut led by William Pepperell.

1748   Treaty of Aix-la-Chapelle failed to delineate American and French- Canadian border.

1752   *Sanderson* voyages from Rhode Island, to West Africa, Barbados, and home.

1754   3 July. Washington surrenders Fort Necessity marching out with honors of war.

1754–63 French and Indian War.

1755   19 June. Bay of Fundy expedition captures Forts St. John and Beausejour.

        9 July. Battle of the Monongahela. General Braddock defeated.

        8 September. Battle of Lake George. Johnson defeated a French, Canadian, and Indian force and built Fort William Henry.

1756   Seven Years' War commenced in Europe.

1757   9 August. Montcalm took Fort William Henry. Indians massacre many British soldiers.

1758   8 July. Abercrombie defeated by Montcalm in Battle of Fort Ticonderoga.

27 July. Louisbourg captured by Amherst opening the St. Lawrence.

27 August. Fort Frontenac seized by Colonel John Bradstreet.

1759 26 July. Fort Ticonderoga captured, the day following capture of Fort Niagara.

13 September. Battle of the Plains of Abraham; Montcalm and Wolfe mortally wounded in British victory.

1760 8 September. Canada surrendered thereby ending French control of Canada.

1763 10 February. Treaty of Paris gave Britain Canada and New France east of the Mississippi except for New Orleans.

May–November. Pontiac's uprising.

Proclamation of Indian territory.

1764 Sugar and Currency Acts.

1765 Stamp Act.

1766 Stamp Act repealed. Declaratory Act.

1770 March. Boston Massacre.

1773 16 December. Boston Tea Party.

1774 Administration of Justice Act. Quartering Act. Québec Act.

5 September. First Continental Congress.

1775 19 April. Battles of Lexington and Concord.

10 May. Ethan Allen's Green Mountain Boys capture Fort Ticonderoga.

12 May. Crown Point taken by American forces.

15 June. Washington given command of the Continental Army by the Second Continental Congress.

17 June. Battle of Bunker (Breed's) Hill, a tactical, Pyrrhic British victory.

3 July. Birth of the Continental Army.

31 December. Benedict Arnold fails in assault on Québec.

1775–76 Siege of Boston.

1776 17 February. Captain Hopkins' American squadron attacked New Providence, in the Bahamas.

27 February. Battle of Moores Creek. North Carolina patriots defeat Tories.

17 March. Howe evacuated Boston and sailed to Halifax.

28 June. Battle of Sullivan's Island. Clinton persuaded to abandon designs on Charleston and Carolinas, left in peace from Britain for two years.

June–July. American retreat from Canada.

4 July. American Declaration of Independence.

July–August. Howe concentrated British and mercenary forces on Staten Island.

27 August. Battle of Long Island.

6–7 September. "American Turtle" submarine used off Staten Island.

12 September. Washington abandoned New York.

16 September. Battle of Harlem Heights.

11 October. Battle of Valcour Island.

28 October. Battle of White Plains.

16 November. Fort Washington captured by British.

20 November. Americans evacuate Fort Lee.

November–December. Washington retreated through New Jersey to Pennsylvania.

26 December. Battle of Trenton.

1777 2 January. Washington secretly leaves Trenton after facing Cornwallis.

3 January. Battle of Princeton.

5 July. British capture Fort Ticonderoga.

7 July. Battle of Hubbardton.

23 July. Howe sailed from New York to the Chesapeake to attack Philadelphia.

6 August. Battle of Oriskany.

16 August. Battle of Bennington.

23 August. Benedict Arnold relieves Fort Stanwix.

11 September. Battle of the Brandywine.

19 September. Battle of Freeman's Farm.

21 September. Night action at Paoli. Anthony Wayne's brigade routed.

26 September. Philadelphia occupied by Howe.

4 October. Battle of Germantown.

7 October. Battle of Bemis Heights.

17 October. Burgoyne surrenders to an American army at Saratoga.

1777–78 Americans suffer poor winter quarters at Valley Forge.

1778 January–June. Von Steuben instills tactics, drill, and discipline into Continentals.

6 February. Franco-American treaties.

April–May. John Paul Jones in USS *Ranger* harrassed Irish Sea and took HMS *Drake*.

17 June. France and Britain go to war.

18 June. British evacuate Philadelphia and march toward New York.

28 June. Battle of Monmouth.

3 July. Wyoming Valley Massacre.

4–9 July. George Rogers Clarke takes French Western towns, Kaskaskai and Cahokia.

27 July. First Battle of Ushant, indecisive French-British naval action.

August. An American-French amphibious operation at Newport failed after battle for Rhode Island.

11 November. Cherry Valley Massacre.

29 December. Clinton captures Savannah.

1779 14 February. Andrew Pickens defeated Tory force at Kettle Creek.

25 February. George Rogers Clarke captured Vincennes.

3 March. Americans defeated at Briar Creek, thus attempt to retake Augusta stopped.

21 June. Spain declares war on Britain.

15–16 July. Wayne captures Stony Point.

19 August. Lee captures Paulus Point.

August–September. Sullivan, James Clinton, and Daniel Brodhead campaigned against the Iroquois in northwestern New York destroying villages and crops.

3 September–28 October. Franco-American siege of Savannah failed after French left.

7–30 September. Spanish forces under Bernardo de Galvez captured British West Florida posts at Manchac, Baton Rouge, and Natchez.

23 September. Battle of Flamborough Head. John Paul Jones in USS *Bonhomme Richard* captured HMS *Serapis* despite his own ship sinking.

26 December. Clinton sailed from New York to attack Charleston.

1780 16 January. British Admiral Rodney's naval victory over Spanish squadron in the "Moonlight Battle."

11 February–12 May. Siege of Charleston ended with Lincoln's surrender.

28 February. Russia inaugurates League of Armed Neutrality.

14 March. Galvez took Mobile, capital of British West Florida.

April. Three indecisive naval actions between Rodney and French Admiral de Guichen.

29 May. Banastre Tarketon's Tories massacred an American force at Waxhaw Creek.

May–August. American guerrilla activity against British in the South.

1 June. USS *Trumbell* fought a drawn engagement with HMS *Watt*.

16 August. Battle of Camden.

18 August. Action of Fishing Creek. Sumter's guerrillas broken by Tarleton.

September. Rodney seizes Dutch smuggling islands of St. Eustatius and St. Martin.

23 September. Benedict Arnold's treason discovered.

7 October. Battle of King's Mountain destroys large Tory unit.

20 December. Britain declares war on the Dutch.

30 December–26 March 1781. Arnold fights for British in Virginia.

1781 January. Galvez launches raid capturing Fort St. Joseph on Lake Michigan.

17 January. Battle of Cowpens.

January–February. Greene and Morgan retreat to the Dan.

15 March. Battle of Guilford Courthouse leads Cornwallis to march north to Virginia.

19 April. Battle of Hobkirk's Mill.

29 April. Lafayette arrived in Virginia from New York.

9 May. Campbells surrenders Fort St. George, near Pensacola to Spanish forces.

22 May–19 June. Siege of Fort Ninety-six was unsuccessful and Greene retreated.

29 May. USS *Alliance* takes British sloops, HMS *Atlanta* and HMS *Trepassy*.

May–July. Lafayette and Cornwallis march and countermarch around Virginia.

4 August. Cornwallis enters Yorktown.

5 August. Battle of the Dogger Bank. British naval victory over the Dutch.

13 August. French Admiral de Grasse sails from West Indies to the Chesapeake.

21 August. Washington marched south to join de Grasse and Lafayette.

30 August. De Grasse arrives off Yorktown and lands French troops.

5–9 September. Battle of the Capes leaves French in control of Chesapeake.

8 September. Battle of Eutaw Springs.

14–26 September. Washington and Rochambeau arrive with troops at Williamsburg.

September–October. Siege of Yorktown.

19 October. Cornwallis surrenders at Yorktown.

November. Washington returned to New York.

12 December. Second Battle of Ushant. British naval victory over France.

1781–82 Greene besieged Charleston and pacified Georgia.

1782 February–April 1783. Suffren's operations in the Indian Ocean.

March. Gnaddenhutten Massacre of Moravian Delawares in Pennsylvania.

12 April. Battle of the Saintes. British naval victory over France.

May. Bahamas handed to Spain.

13–14 September. Franco-Spanish attack on Gibraltar failed in this siege from 1779 to 1783.

30 November. Treaty of Paris. U.S. Independence recognized.

1783 Treaty of Augusta.

15 April. Congress ratified the Treaty of Paris.

25 November. British evacuated New York.

1784–87 Northwest Ordinances.

1787 25 May. Constitutional Convention begins.

17 September. Constitution signed.

December–1790. Constitutional ratification.

1789 4 March. First Congress met in New York.

30 April. Washington inaugurated as President.

1790 18–22 October. General Harmar entered the Ohio Valley to

punish Indians for raiding and was defeated by Miami war chief Little Turtle, near Fort Wayne, Indiana.

1791 4 November. General St. Clair defeated by Little Turtle who led a coalition of Wyandots, Iroquois, Shawnees, Miami, Delawares, Ojibwas, and Potawatomis.

December. Bill of Rights amendments to the Constitution.

1794 20 August. Battle of Fallen Timbers. General Wayne defeats the Maumees.

19 November. Jay Treaty with Britain.

1795 3 August. Treaty of Greenville assured peace in Ohio Valley.

27 October. Pinckney Treaty with Spain.

1797 4 March. John Adams becomes President.

1798 Naturalization Act. Alien Act. Sedition Act. Alien Enemies Act.

1798–1800 Quasi War with France. U.S. navy engaged various French vessels with success.

1800 Thomas Jefferson becomes President.

Gabriel's Rebellion.

1803 30 April. Louisiana Purchase from France.

1803–04 Decatur blockaded Tripoli.

1804–06 Lewis and Clark Expedition up the Missouri to reach the Pacific via the Columbia River.

1807 Embargo Act.

1809 Non-Intercourse Act.

1811 7 November. Battle of Tippecanoe against the Shawnee.

1812–14 War of 1812 with Britain.

1813 5 October. Battle of the Thames, Ontario. Tecumseh killed.

1814 27 March. Battle of Horseshoe Bend. Jackson defeated the Creeks, allies of Britain.

9 August. Treaty of Fort Jackson with Creeks.

24 December. Battle of New Orleans. Treaty of Ghent ended War of 1812.

1816–18 First Seminole War.

1819 Florida ceded by Spain to the United States.

1820 3 March. Missouri Compromise.

Chapter One
British North America

"We do by these presents solemnly and mutually in the presence of God and one of another, covenant and combine ourselves together into a Civil Body Politic, for our better ordering and preservation...." Mayflower Compact, 1620.

England's first attempt (1584) to colonize Virginia failed under Raleigh and the next effort was made in 1606. Other colonies were founded in Massachusetts, first at Plymouth (1620) and then

Winthrop established a covenant, an agreement for the new settlement to live under God's law.

Between 1630 and 1642, the Great Migration to Massachusetts Bay Colony brought in some 22,000 immigrants enabling the establishment of other towns such as Boston, Dorchester, and Roxbury. The new settlements pursued similar patterns of politics and administration, each possessing a meeting house and a large measure of autonomy. The family constituted the major social

British North America
1775

Britain and its North American Empire

elsewhere in that colony, followed by settlements in Maryland (1632), Rhode Island (1636), and Connecticut (1636). Migrants from Massachusetts moved to New Haven (1638) and New Hampshire (1638). The background to this rash of foundations can best be explained by differences in religious and economic behavior. A major Royal Charter was granted to the Massachusetts Bay Company (1629), and John Winthrop was elected governor. On the *Arabella*, during the voyage to America, Winthrop stressed the communal character of the postulated North American colony, setting out the submission of the individual to the collective good. Charity and amity were to be pillars of the community and

unit, but the distribution of land was inegalitarian. The best and largest sections of pasture, field, and woodland were given to the most important people, including the minister. The New England communities developed into: interior agricultural regions; coastal towns, such as Boston and Salem, seaports and entry points for newcomers; while, areas such as the Connecticut Valley commercialized agriculture, selling a food surplus onwards. Some settlers, such as William Pynchon, became immensely wealthy, while others like John Harvard bequeathed cash and books to a college founded in 1636. Massachusetts Bay was governed by a General Court held at Boston and no one could be admitted to the corporation lest they were a member of a church in the colony. After 1634, a representative system grew up at the Court because the demographic growth prevented the attendance of all freemen.

In 1638, a local dissenter, Anne Hutchinson, discussed the covenant of grace, a gift of salvation, with men and women, and believed in direct communication with God rather than through ministers. She threatened the orthodox order and the supreme role of men and was consequently banished with her followers. She settled on Aquidneck Island, later Rhode Island, and founded Portsmouth, which was followed by Newport (1639). Other Separatists, such as Roger Williams, championed Native Americans and criticized the monarch's right to give away their land and said that church and state should be separated. He founded Providence, after being banished from Salem, and the town adopted religious toleration. Other people were unhappy with the ideals of Puritanism; they preferred profits to the Bible. Some, sponsored by Lords Saye and Sele, established Fort Saybrook at the mouth of the Connecticut River; others established Hartford, Windsor, and Wethersfield in a search for better land. The Fundamental Order governing these three settlements, known as Connecticut, created an annual assembly or legislature with an elected governor with representatives from each town. Thus, from their origins, the New England colonies established a controversy between religious idealism and secular materialism. By the 1650s, English settlers, together with those of France, Spain, Holland, and Sweden competed on the North American Atlantic seaboard while all Europeans clashed with Native Americans using weapons or spreading disease as they settled more Indian land. The Pequot War in 1637 between the Pequots and the Connecticut towns virtually wiped out the tribe and the Narragansett suffered later.

After Massachusetts Bay Colony was founded, the monarchy issued no more charters for colonization. However, Maryland (1632) was chartered as a sanctuary for Roman Catholics and others, and further new colonies were administered and organized by proprietory charters. The inhabitants of these new areas received certain legislative privileges, but authority over the new colonies was vested in the owners. The king gave them nearly complete freedom to construct any form of government, as well as the right to distribute, sell or gift the lands within the colony to whomever they chose. In 1663, eight noblemen, including the Earl of Clarendon, were granted the Carolinas. After the Tuscarora War (1711) and the Yamasee conflict (1715), the province was reorganized into north and south (1719–29). The British Board of Trade, after the poor showing in the last conflict, provided a royal government for both North and South Carolina. New Netherland, a Dutch possession straddling British north-south communications, was seized in 1664, despite a final Dutch inter-regnum (1673–74), and renamed New York after its new proprietor, James, Duke of York. His annual rent was forty beaver skins to his brother, the king. Constituted out of territories originally captured by the Dutch from Sweden, New Jersey was split into East and West, the latter being settled by Quakers. Parts of the former Swedish lands around Fort Christina founded in 1638, became part of New York, and was administered as part of Pennsylvania from 1682. After 1704, this area of Delaware possessed its own legislature. Elsewhere, in 1682, William Penn, a Quaker and son of an admiral who had served Charles II, received a charter for an ill-defined area between New York in the north and Maryland in the south. Penn promised religious toleration and guaranteed many British legal liberties (bail and trial by jury). His Frame of Government promised a representative assembly, to be elected by the colony's freeholders. A council was given the sole power of initiating legislation, the assembly being able to

On accession to the throne in 1760, George III displayed little interest in colonial affairs but thought colonies were necessary for economic reasons and essential for great power status.

approve or veto bills presented by the council. This form of government was changed in 1682, 1696, and 1701 witnessed a Charter of Privileges. Pennsylvania became a most dynamic colony with an expanding population, increasing from around 3,000 people in 1683 to 12,000 in 1688. Philadelphia developed as a major port, rivalling Boston, and exported food to the West Indies. The colony's very success attracted large numbers of Scots-Irish, Germans, and Swiss; many such moved to the Pennsylvania backcountry and pushed the boundaries of settlement towards the west leading to clashes with Native Americans. This boded ill for Penn's aspirations to treat Native Americans fairly by land purchase, trade regulation, and banning the sale of alcohol.

The colonies were subjected to the political vagaries of the English conflict between monarchy and parliament. Cromwellian authority over the colonies was based upon mercantilist thought and enshrined in the Navigation Acts, passed between 1651 and 1673. These required that colonial exports and imports be carried in British vessels, that certain American goods could only be sold in Britain, and foreign products could only be shipped to the colonies via England and subject to its import duties. In reality, the acts generated a trading milieu and great opportunities and wise British governments left the Americas to their own devices and ignored smuggling and other forms of illegal trade, which rapidly became accepted customs. The Dutch West Indies was soon a favorite spot, especially Curaçao, to sell listed goods and buy untaxed foreign products. When caught, smugglers tended to be treated leniently, and the customs service, finally established in 1671, had little impact on smuggling. The colonies became locked into an important trans-Atlantic web of commercial contacts and traded with the West Indies, the Madeira Islands, southern Europe, and Britain, naval stores being vitally important to the latter. Grain, wood, dried fish, livestock, tobacco, indigo, and rice were all important products with America receiving manufactured goods, slaves, molasses, and spices. Consequently, Boston, Philadelphia, Newport, New York, and,

eventually Charleston, transmuted into bustling ports and ship-building centers.

Upon his restoration in 1660, King Charles II took very little interest in the colonies but his successor, brother James II (1685–88) wished to impose his style of overt control on British colonies, which led to immense resentment. The reign of William and Mary next sought to eradicate maladministration and chaos, and attempted to incrementally reduce the privileges acquired in the previous royal charters. Under Charles II, Connecticut was granted a charter in 1664 and Rhode Island and Providence in 1663, with minor adjustments to the area of Connecticut (plus New Haven, 1664). The year 1684 witnessed the annulment of the Massachusetts Charter after London traders claimed that the colony was ultra vires in the use of its terms. In fact, the late seventeenth century had seen most American colonists exercising much local autonomy. Town meetings in New England handled local affairs and these were attended by most free male adult residents. Elected selectmen in the north and judges of the country court in the Chesapeake ran daily affairs. The New England colonies were virtually independent politically, being outside real proprietorial or royal control. Furthermore, voting was based on a property qualification and a large proportion of males possessed the franchise even if they did not use it; estimates suggest that between 50 percent to 80 percent of adult white males had a vote. Hence, the growth of democracy in America was much in advance of England where most men were tenant-farmers or agricultural wage labourers with no hope of a voice in local political or economic affairs.

Such liberal developments in America were anathema to James II. The Navigation Acts were more vigorously enforced on the assumption that New England was a snakepit full of smugglers. To impose greater authority, James established the Dominion of New England, comprising New York, New England, and New Jersey. The assemblies were dissolved by Governor Andros, but he needed the consent of a nominated council to make laws and collect taxes. However, the Glorious Revolution of 1688 led by William of

Orange and his wife, Mary, daughter of James, overthrew this autocratic Stuart who had incensed parliament by levying taxes without its sanction. New Englanders, New Yorkers, and Marylanders overthrew their hated government, but the new monarchs wanted to enforce strict authority. Massachusetts became a royal colony, like many other provinces, with a governor and court; legislation could be vetoed by the former, but the franchise was also extended. Pennsylvania's 1701 Charter granted the lower house all legislative power, the council being appointive and advisory. Hence, despite royal interference, large measures of liberal and democratic development did exist with a strong legacy of self-rule and this situation was helped by the nature of British government. A whole range of institutions muddled and conflicted with each other, such as the Board of Trade and Plantations, which could evaluate colonial legislation and advise governments but had no real power. A variety of governors, assemblies, the customs service, and ministers for the colonies, together with army garrison commanders, all had their say. Thus, gentlemanly bedlam, decentralization, and calculated forgetfulness allowed the colonies to flourish. However, these soon faced the expense of costly Franco-British colonial wars in the Americas.

The eighteenth century witnessed extensive settlement along the entire Atlantic seaboard with New England, the Middle Colonies, and the South being differentiated in economic and trade terms. Furthermore, a large measure of similar political representation and property enfranchisement existed with the bulk of the population being American-born or recently arrived non-English speaking immigrants. In the decades preceding the Revolution, certainly Massachusetts and its Puritan mentality distrusted British institutions and evolved a tradition of independence but also of intolerance towards others. The colony constantly re-examined its charter of 1629 and claimed that William and Mary's version of 1691 had extinguished their rights and freedoms as English citizens, and this was discussed again in 1775. Massachusetts citizens looked back to the Cromwellian period of paternal neglect as a golden age of de facto independence and

argued against the British view that colonists took no sovereign power with them to America, but Great Britain had seized sovereignty from Indian tribes and nations. Thus, parliament had acquired authority from the Native Americans by conquest, and local laws and assemblies could not alter this. By 1776, Massachusetts was demanding satisfaction of inalienable rights and government by contract. Thus, covenant theology theory became a construct through which colonials viewed British policy. Similarly, New York developed a non-conformist character as evidenced in artisan dissatisfaction and political assertion during the 1689 Leisler revolt against Andros, which led to Leisler's later death by hanging. The growth of mob politics, and socio-economic (class) cleavages became prevalent as colonial economies developed from semi-feudal, agricultural to capitalist ones during the early stages of modernization. American artisans also differed from the British variety in that labor was scarce and valuable and artisans used this as an economic and political lever to acquire higher wages, and they refused to accept a subordinate status or subscribe to British deference patterns.

Therefore, underlying American colonial growth was submerged a measure of intransigence and resentment. In political terms, local representative, actually delegative, assemblies could not pursue local interests in the face of executive power delegated to executive governors by the monarch. Governors, in turn, were relatively weak and constrained by overseas directives that limited cooperation and negotiation with local representatives. Failed or deadlocked town meetings could generate riotous action by artisans. Bacon's Rebellion, New York land riots, squatters, frontiersmen demonstrating in Philadelphia (1764), and North Carolina Regulator activity were all, arguably, instances of citizens demanding redress of grievances or solutions to problems. Hence, mob reactions against the 1765 Stamp Act followed a tradition of American political participation and radical street action and led to further arguments against the Townshend Acts. Thus, American history and development inculcated those traits which proved so formidable in laying the groundwork and legitimacy for later Revolution.

The Colonies

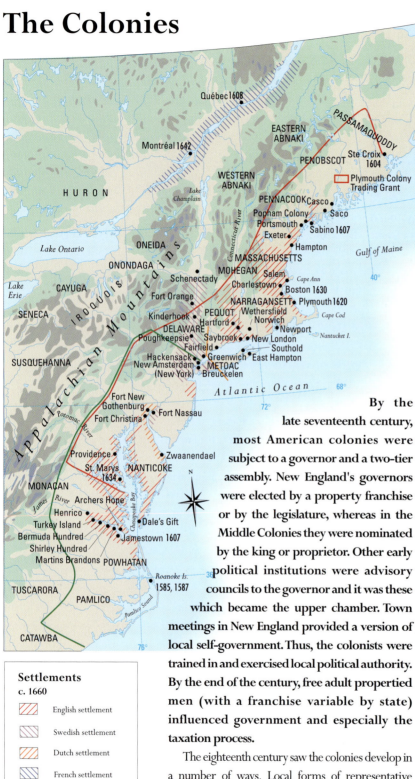

philosophers, such as John Locke and Montesquieu, were debated. This elite became progressively well-educated after higher education expanded with the foundation of Harvard in 1636, the College of William and Mary (1693), Yale (1701), through to Rutgers in 1766.

Early colonists brought English values to America in terms of customs, dress, agricultural techniques, and architecture, thereby changing the American landscape.

By the late seventeenth century, most American colonies were subject to a governor and a two-tier assembly. New England's governors were elected by a property franchise or by the legislature, whereas in the Middle Colonies they were nominated by the king or proprietor. Other early political institutions were advisory councils to the governor and it was these which became the upper chamber. Town meetings in New England provided a version of local self-government. Thus, the colonists were trained in and exercised local political authority. By the end of the century, free adult propertied men (with a franchise variable by state) influenced government and especially the taxation process.

The eighteenth century saw the colonies develop in a number of ways. Local forms of representative government were subject to experiment and were controlled by an expanding political elite. This "aristocracy" was the beneficiary of a developing local and overseas trade, the commercialization of agriculture, and the plantation system. Polite society toyed with political ideas and European political

The population expanded rapidly as settlers married out of economic necessity and bred large families. An influx of non-English Europeans and slave labor expanded colonial numbers to one and a half million people in 1750. Rather than creating an ethnic melting pot, the colonies became disunited and quarrelsome. Increasing diversity followed economic development with four regional economies being created: New England, the Chesapeake, the Middle Colonies and the Lower South. Combined with the ethnic mix, America had to build its own culture and identity. Some historians have argued that English settlers took an English culture across the Atlantic to make the colonies provinces of England. However, over time they became more self-sufficient despite being dependent on English imports in the form of, items like, books and furniture. In reality, early colonists were transformed into colonials and assumed different characteristics to their English counterparts. Tidewater aristocrats occupied mansions similar to

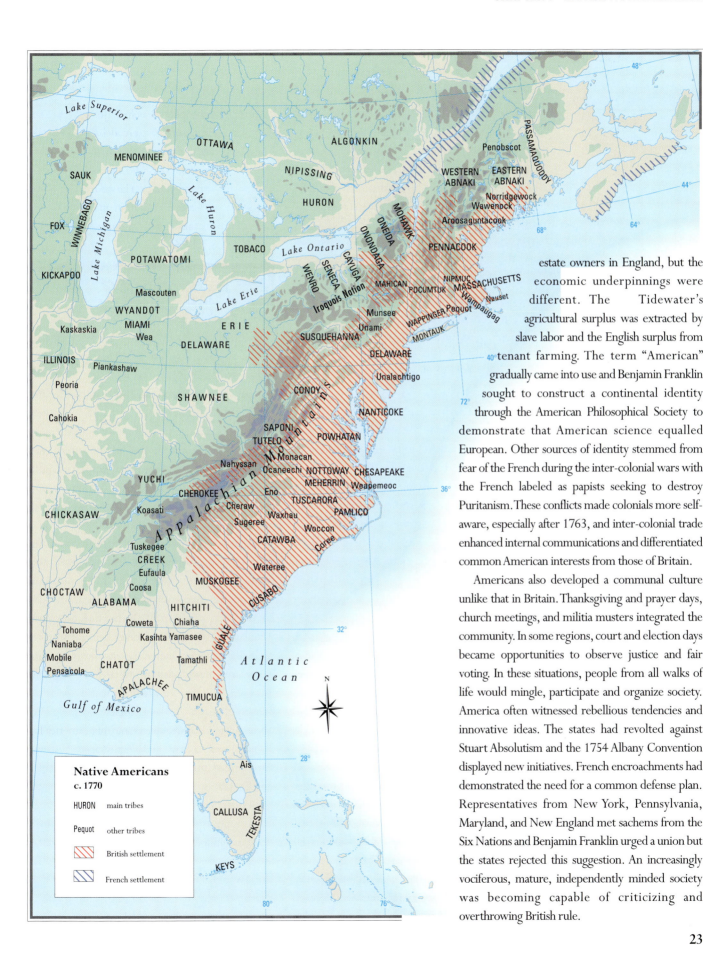

Native Americans
c. 1770

HURON   main tribes

Pequot   other tribes

British settlement

French settlement

estate owners in England, but the economic underpinnings were different. The Tidewater's agricultural surplus was extracted by slave labor and the English surplus from tenant farming. The term "American" gradually came into use and Benjamin Franklin sought to construct a continental identity through the American Philosophical Society to demonstrate that American science equalled European. Other sources of identity stemmed from fear of the French during the inter-colonial wars with the French labeled as papists seeking to destroy Puritanism. These conflicts made colonials more self-aware, especially after 1763, and inter-colonial trade enhanced internal communications and differentiated common American interests from those of Britain.

Americans also developed a communal culture unlike that in Britain. Thanksgiving and prayer days, church meetings, and militia musters integrated the community. In some regions, court and election days became opportunities to observe justice and fair voting. In these situations, people from all walks of life would mingle, participate and organize society. America often witnessed rebellious tendencies and innovative ideas. The states had revolted against Stuart Absolutism and the 1754 Albany Convention displayed new initiatives. French encroachments had demonstrated the need for a common defense plan. Representatives from New York, Pennsylvania, Maryland, and New England met sachems from the Six Nations and Benjamin Franklin urged a union but the states rejected this suggestion. An increasingly vociferous, mature, independently minded society was becoming capable of criticizing and overthrowing British rule.

Native Americans

Early Indian-European relations were characterized by several stages. First, exchanges were made in crops, such as maize and squash, while Europeans introduced livestock, horses, and new forms of weapons technology. Second, the Europeans met many native peoples in the Eastern Woodlands: Abnakis and Narragansett in New England; Delaware and Susquehannock in New Jersey and Pennsylvania; Iroquois in New York; Cherokees in Tennessee and the Carolinas, as well as Creeks, Choctaws, Chickasaws, Catawba, and Yamasee towards the South. Many of these peoples suffered a biological holocaust when European and African diseases and germs cut swathes of death through infection by smallpox, plague, measles, yellow fever, pneumonia, tuberculosis, diphtheria, and influenza. Added to this debacle was the impact of alcohol and European disparagement of Indian cultures, which regarded Indian religion, ritual, and customs as barbaric. Third, the development of the fur trade—in which Indians exchanged pelts for European goods—made the Indians dependent on modern weapons such as metal axes, knives, and muskets.

The final stage of the Indian-European encounter was settler encroachment on Indian territories by force or by purchase. Whichever method was used, the Indians realized that tribal lands once held in common were now owned by foreigners who felled forests and imposed an alien European landscape upon native peoples thereby destroying their lifestyle. The end result was the use of coercion and war which occurred when Indian peoples were themselves experiencing internal flux. Between 1642–53 and 1665–66, the Iroquois Confederation destroyed their Huron trade rivals and pushed survivors into Ontario and the Ohio Valley where sundry remnants, victims of war, lived with other peoples or formed new communities. Another dislocation happened when, in 1711, the Iroquoian

The torture and burning of surveyor-explorer John Lawson, in 1711, after he had traversed 600 miles of Indian trackways and after he was captured by Tuscaroras in the interior of the Carolinas.

Tuscaroras attacked the Swiss-German settlement of New Bern in the Carolinas, which had stolen Indian lands; two hundred settlers were massacred. Tribes that had been victims of the Tuscarora slave trade united with Swiss and English colonists in a two-year conflict that resulted in the enslavement of a thousand Tuscaroras and the defeated tribe was pushed northward to join other Iroquoian peoples. Yet another group of native people was forced to migrate. The Yamasees joined with the Creeks to attack English settlers (1715) in response to the colonial slave trade in Indians. Northern reinforcements and a Cherokee alliance defeated the enemy, and the Yamasees were forced into Spanish territories and Creeks moved westward.

The Middle Colonies experienced warfare, too. In 1622 Opechancanough, Powhatan's brother, launched a campaign on James River settlements in Virginia. Twenty-five percent of the colony was slaughtered. The survivors were reinforced from England and counterattacked the Indians. A 1646 treaty, after another failed Indian onslaught, forced the Indians to accept European authority.

Bitter conflicts occurred in New England. The Pequot Indians traded with the Dutch on Manhattan to the annoyance of the English in Connecticut. Following the murder of a Boston trader (1636), an English-Narragansett punitive expedition virtually wiped out the Pequots on the Mystic River, with the survivors becoming slaves. The Pequot war ushered in uneasy and tense relationships in New England. European settlements steadily absorbed Indian hunting grounds and some Indians were being Christianized. In response, Chief Metacomet (King Philip) of the Wampanoags constructed an alliance of most Indians from Maine to Connecticut, including the Nipmucs and Narragansetts. Twenty settlements were destroyed and five hundred European men killed or captured, 10 percent of Massachusetts men were slaughtered. The power of the New England tribes was destroyed after a massive European counterattack in 1676. Thereafter, colonial settlements advanced, helped by Indian tribal disunity and the settlers' superior numbers and weapons.

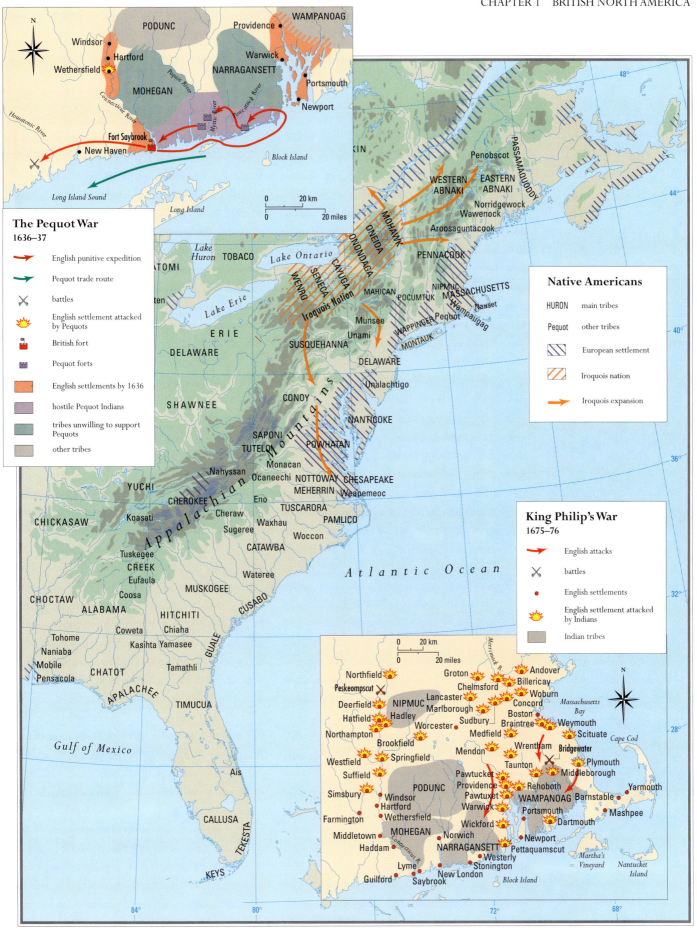

The Pequot War
1636–37

→ English punitive expedition

→ Pequot trade route

✗ battles

💥 English settlement attacked by Pequots

🏰 British fort

🏯 Pequot forts

English settlements by 1636

hostile Pequot Indians

tribes unwilling to support Pequots

other tribes

Native Americans

HURON   main tribes

Pequot   other tribes

European settlement

Iroquois nation

→ Iroquois expansion

King Philip's War
1675–76

→ English attacks

✗ battles

• English settlements

💥 English settlement attacked by Indians

Indian tribes

Church Formation

In 1656, Quakerism was the largest and fastest growing radical, dissenting sect in England. The colonial elites were aware of these "wicked and dangerous seducers," as they liked to call them, and found them guilty of the sin of pride.

Eighteenth-century colonial America's largest religious denominations were Congregationalism in New England and Anglicanism with a large presence in the South but existing elsewhere. These Churches were financed by taxes and possessed a legal monopoly over religious activities. Other denominations included Baptists, Quakers, Dutch Reformed, Roman Catholics, and Lutherans. New England settlements were dominated by the meeting-house, which became the political, educational, and social focus of the inhabitants and was where a town's magistrates would debate. By 1780, 749 Congregational churches existed, often characterized by white-painted, wooden architecture; New England was thoroughly gospelized. Rhode Island was an exception; it became a sanctuary for dissenters of all types, such as Quakers, Anabaptists, Arminians, and Ranters. Eighty-five percent of colonial churches existing in 1775 were founded after 1700 and some 60 percent of these after 1740.

The first surge in church expansion occurred between 1680 and 1710. Anglican campaigns established churches in Virginia, and when Maryland became a royal colony in 1692, the Church of England rapidly moved in to assume the position of the official church, despite the fact that Maryland was founded by English Roman Catholics in 1634. South Carolina also became Anglicanized and with New York and North Carolina created ninety congregations between 1680 and 1710, helped by the Society for the Propagation of the Gospel. Despite the activities of private societies, Anglicanism never gained the status or establishment of the Congregationalists who themselves built sixty new congregations during the same years, either in new towns or where older congregations needed to divide in accordance with settlement changes. These two churches overshadowed all others which tended to be small or highly regional such as the Dutch Reformed in New York and New Jersey. Elsewhere, William Penn's

Pennsylvania became a haven for Dutch, Swiss, and Amish Mennonites; Moravians; Dunker Brethren; Scots Presbyterians; Welsh Baptists; German Catholics; and German Lutherans.

The second wave of growth occurred between 1740 and 1770. This Great Awakening with its evangelical radicalism drew on Calvinist traditions, and the Methodist preacher George Whitefield, preaching from Georgia to Maine, was important in the movement. Hundreds listened to a religious calling and joined a new community of evangelicals which cut across gender, class, and race. Baptists were the major beneficiaries, but Congregationalists and Presbyterians were also revitalized by Jonathan Edwards and Jonathan Dickinson, respectively.

Between 1740 and 1770, two hundred Presbyterian churches and two hundred Baptist congregations were founded in Philadelphia, Charleston, and Rhode Island. In combination with German Lutherans and the German Reformed Church, they founded 1,200 congregations in the colonies. New England remained dauntingly Congregationalist, but the southern colonies were more mixed with 33 percent Anglican, 30 percent Baptist, and 25 percent Presbyterian. The Middle Colonies were even more heterogeneous: one third of the churches were German-speaking (Amish, Mennonite, Moravian, and German Baptist). English-speakers were Presbyterians, Quakers, Baptists, and Anglicans. Twelve Roman Catholic churches were established there, a springboard for later expansion. By 1790, some fifteen hundred Jews, mainly Sephardic, had migrated from Spain and Portugal to the Netherlands and onward to Dutch American colonies. They founded synagogues, especially in New York and Newport.

Arguably, the years prior to the Revolution witnessed the weakening of government-supported Congregationalist and Anglican churches as well as the rapid expansion of dissenting faiths and sects. This rich ethnic and religious mix created by questioning and radical minds characterized a colonial society which was soon to examine the established political order.

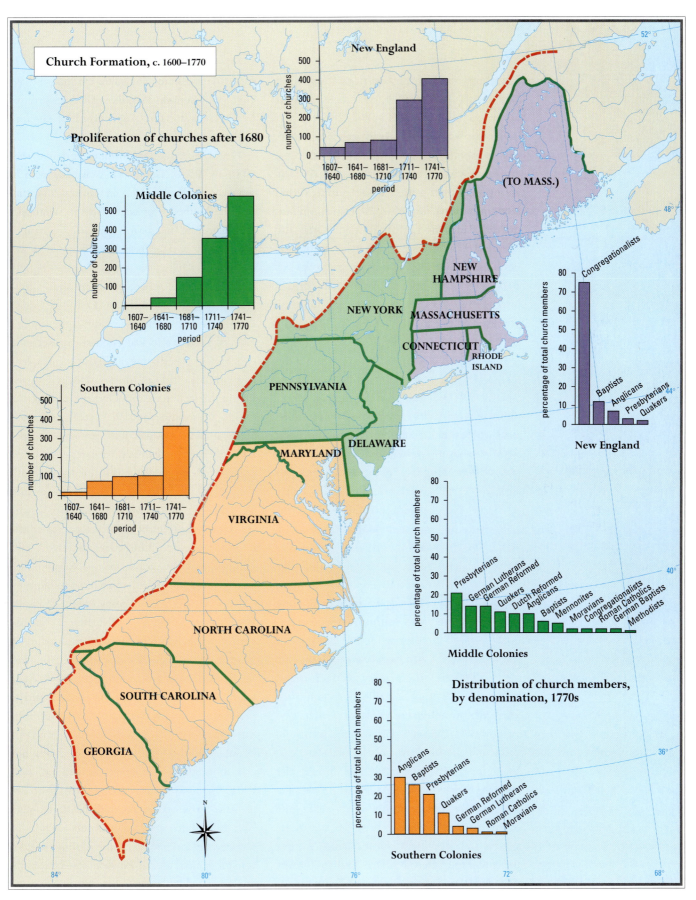

Church Formation, c. 1600–1770

Proliferation of churches after 1680

New England

number of churches

1607–1640 1641–1680 1681–1710 1711–1740 1741–1770
period

Middle Colonies

number of churches

1607–1640 1641–1680 1681–1710 1711–1740 1741–1770
period

Southern Colonies

number of churches

1607–1640 1641–1680 1681–1710 1711–1740 1741–1770
period

(TO MASS.)

NEW HAMPSHIRE

NEW YORK

MASSACHUSETTS

CONNECTICUT

RHODE ISLAND

PENNSYLVANIA

DELAWARE

MARYLAND

VIRGINIA

NORTH CAROLINA

SOUTH CAROLINA

GEORGIA

percentage of total church members

Congregationalists

Baptists Anglicans Presbyterians Quakers

New England

percentage of total church members

Presbyterians German Lutherans German Reformed Quakers Dutch Reformed Anglicans Baptists Mennonites Moravians Congregationalists Roman Catholics German Baptists Methodists

Middle Colonies

Distribution of church members, by denomination, 1770s

percentage of total church members

Anglicans Baptists Presbyterians Quakers German Reformed German Lutherans Roman Catholics Moravians

Southern Colonies

Church and Politics

Myth suggests that the American Revolution was a rebellion of natural law against common law, a rebellion of Protestant dissenters against Anglican predominance, and that religious and political rebellion were identical. This hostility targeted the English monarchy which held political and religious hegemony in North America. Arguably, a basis here is found in the 1620 Mayflower Compact that government was established by the covenant of the people in the interests of the people. By 1775, the British government had broken faith and Thomas Jefferson embodied these ideas in *A Summary View of the Rights of British America.* **He argued that the original colonists were individuals, not agents of the British government. They formed colonial governments embodying the natural rights of expatriates from one country to choose the terms of their subjection to a new ruler. Colonial assemblies shared power with the British Parliament until British tyranny broke any governmental contract. Hence, Jefferson used a "historical" view to legitimize a rebellion against a government attempting to enslave the colonies.**

However, although the Puritan spirit did command the allegiance of the early settlers, by 1775 fewer than 20 percent of the population was linked to a church in any real fashion. The construction of churches and congregations existed to help early settlers survive and to provide a focus for family life in the community. Between 1630 and 1660, New England church membership was between 70 and 80 percent of the adult population. By 1690, these ritualist and "tribal" communities were diminishing to 15 percent during the Salem witch trials. The Middle and Southern colonies' churches had even lower membership rates. Evidence demonstrates that 85 percent of white babies in Charles Parish, Virginia, remained unbaptized between 1650 and 1680. One estimate in 1780 suggested that church attendance in Boston, New York City, and Philadelphia failed to reach 17 percent, and probably only 10 percent in the latter two cities. Anglican ministers in Delaware stated that of those eligible to receive communion, only 20 percent did in 1740, but this declined to 8 to10 percent in the 1770s.

Arguably, church membership did not reflect society at large. Women formed the main membership; in 1680, women constituted 60 percent of the membership and even increased male membership rates during the Great Awakening failed to sustain themselves. By 1775, some 70 to 90 percent of European colonists were unattached to any church. So, how did religion characterize the Revolution? Congregationalist and Presbyterian churches were interested in home-rule and self-rule and opposed foreign control. Many Methodists and Baptists enlisted with German and Dutch dissenters in the patriot cause, but this religious breadth did not occasion the Revolution. To argue that Southern Loyalists were Anglican means little when Anglicanism had been Americanized there and Anglicans supported the colonial cause and were essential to it. However, Middle state and New England Anglicanism was more firmly linked to British policies. What must be remembered is that churches provided social, cultural, and political power via the pulpit and the meeting-house. Propaganda and information could be gathered at church, and hence churches possessed an impact beyond their mere membership figures.

George Whitefield was a key figure in the Great Awakening and visited America more than once. He said, "Don't tell me you are a Baptist, an Independent, a Presbyterian, a dissenter, tell me you are a Christian." To achieve conversions, he wrote some 18,000 sermons during his lifetime.

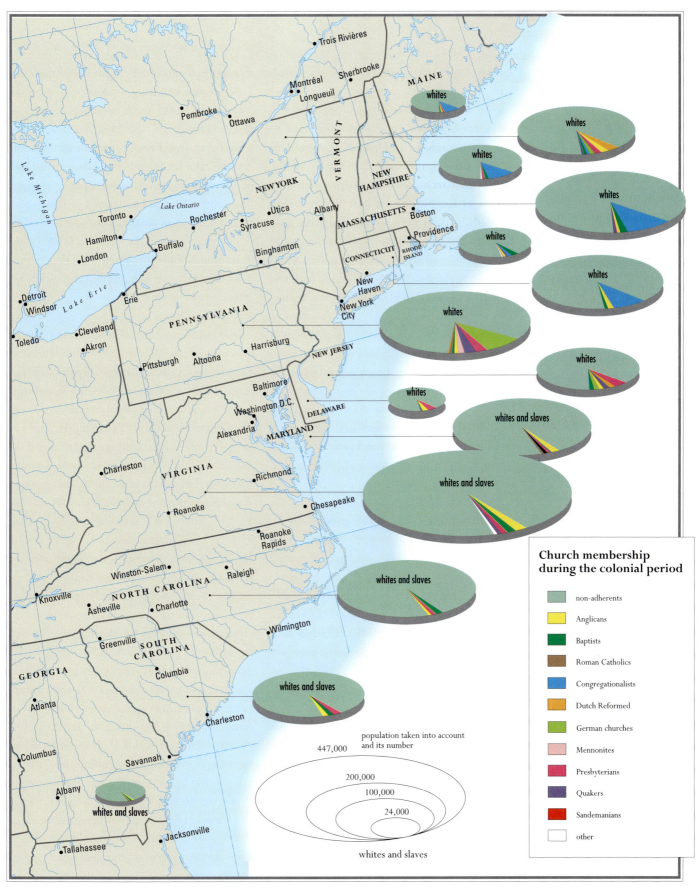

Church membership
during the colonial period

non-adherents
Anglicans
Baptists
Roman Catholics
Congregationalists
Dutch Reformed
German churches
Mennonites
Presbyterians
Quakers
Sandemanians
other

population taken into account
and its number

447,000
200,000
100,000
24,000

whites and slaves

Trade and Industry

American economic activity traveled through certain identifiable periods. Prior to the English Civil War (1642-46), the fur trade paid for needed British goods, and a stream of migrants bought up surplus colonial necessities. After the Great Migration, the 1640s witnessed the farming of grain, the birth of the lumber industry, and the growing fishing trade. Salt fish could be sold in the West Indies and barrel staves to the Madeira Islands, which produced wine. Into this system fitted the "triangular trade." Highly important was the export of tobacco, naval stores, rice, indigo, and skins to Great Britain in return for manufactured products. Similarly, goods from Spain, such as fruit and wine, went to Britain, while the Iberian peninsula imported meat, fish, rum, timber, and grain from the Americas. By 1770, the North Atlantic was locked into a mutually profitable economic system, with Boston, Newport, New York, Philadelphia, Norfolk, and Charleston developing as the principal American ports.

In fact, America was an important source of raw materials and re-exports, and the early 1770s saw the Thirteen Colonies receiving 37 percent of all British exports thereby underpinning a commercial system created by the Navigation Acts which were considered essential for British prosperity and, indeed, power. The Acts, passed between 1651 and 1673, required that only English or colonial ships could trade with the colonies, that certain American goods (such as wool, sugar, tobacco, indigo, ginger, dyes, rice, naval goods, copper, and furs) could only be sold in Britain, and that foreign goods targeted at American markets must be shipped via Britain and these faced import duties. Finally, the colonies were not supposed to make or export products that would compete with similar British items (woollens, hats, milled iron). Benefits accrued to colonial ship-builders in New England, and the Middle Colonies produced goods for export which were not subject to these mercantilist Acts. Some colonials engaged in smuggling to circumvent the

Acts, with strong links to the Dutch West Indies.

The eighteenth century witnessed the growth of internal communications as settlements increased in size and number and a coastal trade developed with many ships engaged in this business rather than sailing overseas. By 1775, the largest American industry was in iron-making and forging with eighty-two furnaces and one hundred and seventy-five forges making America a bigger iron producer than England. This industry was mainly based in Maryland, Pennsylvania, and New Jersey. The inter-colonial wars benefited some areas with Boston acting as a major privateering center with its vessels interdicting foreign West Indian trade.

Regionally, New England mainly exported dried fish, livestock, and wood to the West Indies; dried fish to southern Europe; and mainly whale oil to Britain. The Middle Colonies developed commercial farming in Pennsylvania and New York with bread and grain as major trading products being exported to the West Indies, southern Europe, and the Madeiras. War and poor harvests in Britain increased agricultural prices and colonial profits, but peace saw recessions in ship-building. Peace also saw colonials counting the dead, especially in Boston and elsewhere in Massachusetts, which bore the brunt of the casualties as well as the expense of many campaigns in the West Indies and Canada .

Increased demand for grain led some Chesapeake planters to diversify their crops by turning over some tobacco fields to wheat and other grains. The area's main foreign market was Britain which absorbed mainly tobacco, while grains were sent to the West Indies and southern Europe. Enlarged grain production increased wealth allowing the growth of towns such as Baltimore. The southern states exported a more varied range of goods to Britain, including rice and indigo, naval stores, deerskins, and corn. However, dependence on foreign markets caused a depression during King George's War, but the adverse effects changed to prosperity in the 1760s. In sum, American economic health depended upon fluctuating market conditions in Europe and the West Indies.

Opposite: American ports became centers of trade, commerce, and culture. Boston pursued maritime industries; New York linked riverine, coastal, and ocean trade; and Philadelphia produced iron and textiles. Nantucket became the center of the whaling industry. The cities also became centers of education with the foundation of Harvard and King's College (Columbia) in New York.

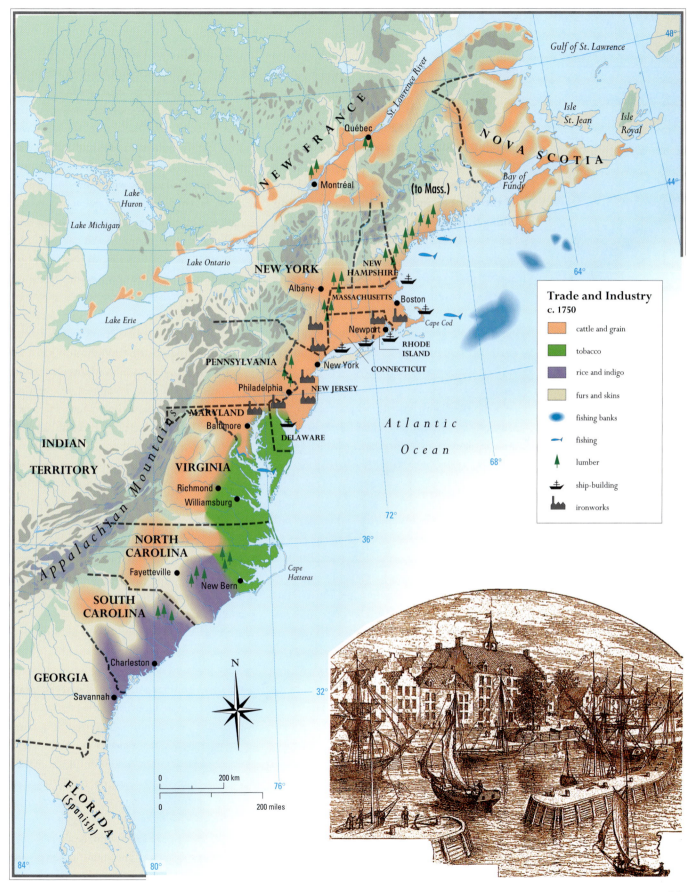

48°

Gulf of St. Lawrence

Isle St. Jean

Isle Royal

N O V A   S C O T I A

N E W   F R A N C E

St. Lawrence River

Québec

Bay of Fundy

44°

Montréal

(to Mass.)

Lake Huron

Lake Michigan

Lake Ontario

64°

NEW YORK

NEW HAMPSHIRE

Albany

MASSACHUSETTS

Boston

Lake Erie

Cape Cod

Newport

RHODE ISLAND

PENNSYLVANIA

New York

CONNECTICUT

Philadelphia

NEW JERSEY

Trade and Industry
c. 1750

▮ orange	cattle and grain
▮ green	tobacco
▮ purple	rice and indigo
▮ tan	furs and skins
● blue	fishing banks
🐟	fishing
🌲	lumber
⚓	ship-building
🏭	ironworks

MARYLAND

Baltimore

DELAWARE

Atlantic Ocean

68°

INDIAN TERRITORY

Appalachian Mountains

VIRGINIA

Richmond

Williamsburg

72°

NORTH CAROLINA

36°

Fayetteville

Cape Hatteras

New Bern

SOUTH CAROLINA

N

32°

GEORGIA

Charleston

Savannah

0   200 km

76°

0   200 miles

F L O R I D A
(Spanish)

84°

80°

Origins of Settler Population

British colonization of America commenced with the foundation of the Jamestown Colony, which ultimately led to young unmarried men traveling to the tobacco and sugar plantations of the South and West Indies. However, between 1630 and 1642, a great migration took place to the Massachusetts Bay Colony with some sixteen thousand settlers. Entire families moved to America, the Bermudas, Nevis, Antigua, and Montserrat. Historians have since questioned why migrations took place and from where in England.

Most migrants left England from Yarmouth and Ipswich in East Anglia; from Southampton in the south; or from Bristol, Weymouth, and Plymouth in the West Country. Therefore, most migrants originated in the south of England from land which is either low-lying or characterized by low rolling hills. The counties of Norfolk, Suffolk, and Essex provided the greatest percentage of colonists, and this was the very heartland of where Cromwell raised recruits for the Roundhead Puritan army from the Eastern Association of these counties. During the sixteenth and seventeenth centuries, Puritanism spread through the east and into Northamptonshire and Rutland, and some historians argue that migrants from these areas wanted religious freedom. Other arguments are plausible. The Puritan region was suffering from land enclosures and new modes of economic production. This process caused dislocation, especially among those in the cloth industry, which suffered from an economic depression during the 1640s. Many people were dispossessed by sheep as wool became more important than people. Hence, economic distress fuelled migration. Possibly, many factors caused the first wave of migration, but later arrivals probably differed in their reasons. The Commonwealth period of British history virtually ended British migration. However, subsequent Stuart monarchs rewarded supporters with vast tracts of territory in New York, New Jersey, Pennsylvania, and the Carolinas. Some proprietors were successful in recruiting settlers, and New York and New Jersey grew rapidly, which also incorporated a Dutch population from the former New Amsterdam, now New York. A small remnant population from a former Swedish settlement on the Delaware was also acquired. Elsewhere, William Penn, a Quaker, was granted Pennsylvania, which he envisaged as a sanctuary for other Quakers. Likewise, Maryland became a haven for Roman Catholics. The Carolinas developed differently. North Carolina became a virtual economic outgrowth of Virginia, but South Carolina was founded by white Barbadians leaving their overpopulated island and bringing a slave culture with them.

The origins of migration are complex but are undoubtedly linked to economics, politics, religion, and slavery. The history of North Carolina is a microcosm of America, and the state's ethnic mix and origins provide further reasons for migration. In 1730, the population was probably no more than thirty thousand whites and six thousand blacks on the Coastal Plain. By 1775, the population had spread through the Piedmont to the Blue Ridge Mountains with over 265,000 inhabitants. The original settlers were of English descent, but in 1740 Scots Highlanders arrived, mostly entering at Wilmington. Persecution of the clans drove them from Scotland, but, ironically, they generally remained loyal to Britain during the Revolution. Oaths of loyalty bound some while others profited from producing naval stores for Britain in the Cape Fear region. The Scots-Irish from Ulster was another migrant group. These Presbyterians dissenters from the Anglican Church, supplied large numbers of troops for Washington during the Revolution. Other incomers were German Lutherans and members of the German Reformed Church, and they peopled the backcountry. One highly coherent German group were the Moravians whose unique community at Salem was neutral during the Revolution.

Predominant Immigrant Groups, c. 1750

- English
- Scots-Irish
- Highland Scots
- Dutch
- French
- Germans
- Africans
- Native Americans
- ✡ Jews
- □ Swedes
- △ Welsh
- ◇ French Huguenots
- HURON Native American tribe

QUÉBEC

ACADIA

NOVA SCOTIA

St. Lawrence River

Québec

Montréal

HURON

MAINE

ABNAKI

NEW HAMPSHIRE

PENNACOOK

Lake Ontario

IROQUOIS

NEW YORK

Albany

MASSACHUSETTS

Boston

Cape Cod

Connecticut R.

POCUMTUK

CONN.

Newport

RHODE ISLAND

Lake Erie

ERIE

SUSQUEHANNA

Hudson R.

Susquehanna R.

New York

PENNSYLVANIA

DELAWARE

Philadelphia

NEW JERSEY

SHAWNEE

MARYLAND

Baltimore

DELAWARE

CONOY

NANTICOKE

Chesapeake Bay

James R.

VIRGINIA

Richmond

Williamsburg

Appalachian Mountains

TUTELO

YUCHI

POWHATAN

CHEROKEE

CATAWBA

TUSCARORA

NORTH CAROLINA

Fayetteville

New Bern

SOUTH CAROLINA

Savannah R.

Atlantic Ocean

Charleston

GEORGIA

Savannah

N

FLORIDA

0   100 km

0   100 miles

After the failure of the Jacobite rebellion in 1745, Scots were banned from speaking Gaelic and wearing tartans. Early Highland Clearances replaced people with sheep and many villages were depopulated. Many Scots paid for fares to America or, in some cases, their landlords paid. The North Carolina mountains became a home to many.

The Slave Triangle

The Americas witnessed some ten million enslaved people arriving between 1492 and 1770. Most of these went to Brazil; to Spanish possessions in South America; and to the British, French, Dutch, and Danish West Indian islands. By 1775, some 260,000 had entered the Thirteen Colonies. Many of the slaves were sold by the kingdoms of West Africa, especially in Guinea and the Bight of Benin. In the beginning, slaves sent to America were wartime captives, criminals, and the obstreperous. As demand grew, however, coastal African kingdoms raided the interior for slaves.

In 1672, Charles II chartered the Royal African Company, which gained the monopoly of trade with sub-Saharan Africa. The company built several forts in West Africa and developing trade carried English manufactures to Africa after which some 120,000 slaves were sent to Britain's Caribbean and North American colonies.

Slave ships packed in their cargo like sardines. The Adventure *sold 64 slaves for 37 pounds sterling in June 1774.*

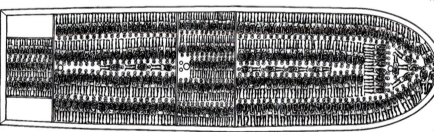

Slave ships were notorious for their atrocious conditions. Packed in like sardines, up to 20 percent of the slaves would die en route to the Americas. Sometimes disease would kill more. This Middle Passage was meant to be part of the so-called slave triangle. Allegedly, ships sailed from Newport and Boston laden with rum, iron bars, and other trade goods to destinations such as Elmina or Cape Coast Castle on the slave coast. These products paid for slaves to be transported to the West Indies and exchanged for molasses and sugar. Returning to New England, molasses was distilled into rum, which re-commenced the triangle. Much evidence to support the triangular

trade concept is based upon the voyage of the *Sanderson*, which departed from Newport, Rhode Island, in March 1752 starting a ten-thousand-mile voyage which took fourteen months. The cargo comprised iron bars for an African medium of exchange and 8,220 gallons of rum. Arriving at Cape Coast Castle, the *Sanderson* exchanged its goods for fifty-six black slaves, forty-eight ounces of gold, and 908 pounds of pepper. The ship sailed to Barbados, sold its slaves, and returned to Newport with fifty-five hogsheads of molasses, three hogsheads of sugar, and £412.3 shillings worth of bills of exchange on Liverpool.

In reality, the triangular trade was part of a larger set of complex trade relations which linked the Atlantic states into a trans-Atlantic economy. Often, slaves sold to the Spanish possessions would be sold on to Jamaica, Cuba, and Virginia.

Britain, too, was directly involved in the slave trade, and its industries provided the weapons which were in such demand in West Africa.

London, Bristol, and Liverpool thrived on the slave trade. On arrival in the Thirteen Colonies, slaves were normally used as domestic servants and hired out in trade; in the Middle Colonies and on plantations in the Southern colonies they were used as agricultural labor. In Newport and New York City, black slaves comprised more than 10 percent of the population.

The South Carolinian slave experience is interesting. Southerners believed the African heritage suited Africans to the climate and the general environment, including the transferable skills of killing crocodiles to hunting alligators and fishing. Eventually, plantations grew indigo and rice. Africans possessed the ability to grow the latter because rice was commonly cropped in the coastal swamps of present-day Gambia, Senegal, and Guinea. The slave labor system became the foundation of the Southern colonial economy, establishing the "peculiar institution" called into question during the U.S. Civil War.

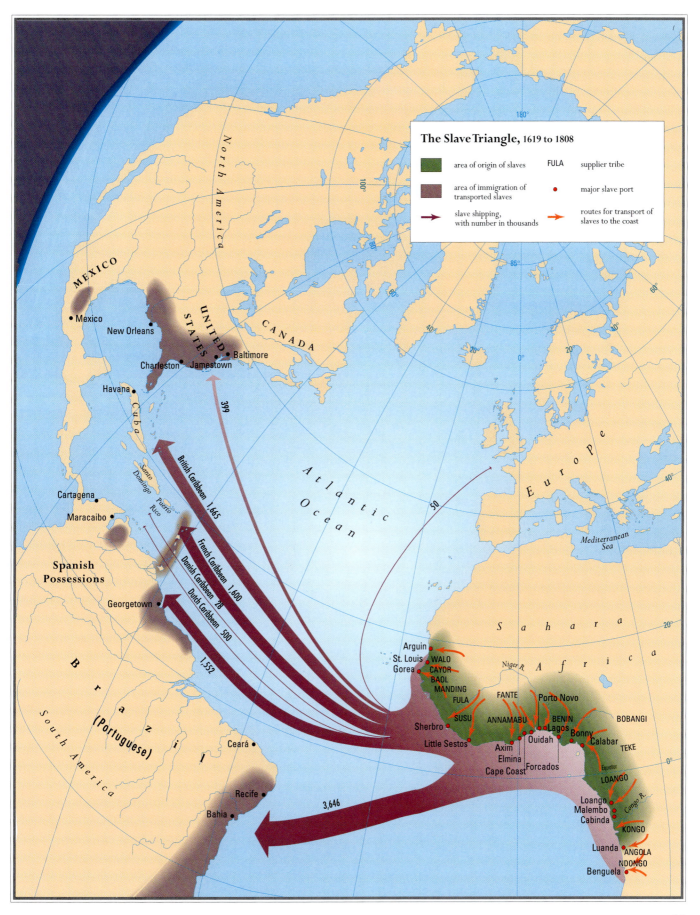

The Slave Triangle, 1619 to 1808

- ▇ area of origin of slaves
- ▇ area of immigration of transported slaves
- → slave shipping, with number in thousands
- FULA   supplier tribe
- ● major slave port
- → routes for transport of slaves to the coast

North America

MEXICO

• Mexico

New Orleans

Charleston   Baltimore
Jamestown

Havana •

Cuba

UNITED STATES

CANADA

Cartagena •

Maracaibo •

Santo Domingo

Puerto Rico

Spanish Possessions

Georgetown •

Brazil (Portuguese)

Ceará •

Recife •

Bahia •

South America

Atlantic Ocean

Europe

Mediterranean Sea

Sahara

AFRICA

Niger R.

399

British Caribbean 1,665

French Caribbean 1,600

Danish Caribbean 28

Dutch Caribbean 500

1,552

50

3,646

Arguin •
St. Louis • WALO
Gorea • CAYOR
BAOL
MANDING
FULA

FANTE   Porto Novo

SUSU   ANNAMABU   BENIN   BOBANGI

Sherbro •   Lagos •   Bonny •
Little Sestos •   Ouidah •   Calabar •   TEKE
Axim •
Elmina •   Forcados
Cape Coast
LOANGO

Loango •
Malembo •
Cabinda •   Congo R.
KONGO

Luanda • ANGOLA
NDONGO
Benguela •

Equator

Density of Population Settlement

By 1775, the Thirteen Colonies boasted some two and a half million souls. About half were of English origin; the character of the population differed from Britain, and each colony was different. Demographic studies of early America are difficult because censuses were seldom held. For example, Pennsylvania never counted its population, Virginia failed to conduct any census after 1703, whereas New York and Rhode Island have adequate statistics. Hence, other databases have to be used such as tax and militia lists, and details of births, marriages, and deaths.

This label for Virginia Tobacco, London, c. 1700 displays colonial elites enjoying pipes of tobacco and glasses of rum punch while in the background slaves labor in the fields to maintain sufficient profits to sustain this lifestyle.

The colonial population was low and thinly spread but commenced a rapid increase in the middle of the seventeenth century ensuring that the colonies would survive. By 1770, the New England and Middle Colonies had roughly equal populations, but the South contained almost half the population by the time of the Revolution. Simultaneously, figures suggest that New York, New Jersey, and Pennsylvania were increasing their populations rapidly. Significance might be attached to the fact that half the population was under sixteen years at the end of the eighteenth century. By 1775, evidence demonstrates that the colonial population was developing a non-English character. Twenty percent of Americans had African roots while Germans, Irish, Scots, and Welsh swarmed in after 1700. An orthodox view estimates that about thirty percent of white settlers were from England. Also, differences existed between states. The white population of New England was seventy-five percent English but south of New York, non-English were in a majority. The Pennsylvania inhabitants were 19.5 percent English, 33.3 percent German, and 42.8 percent Celtic.

The majority of colonials were farmers but urbanization took place as trade increased in the major ports where merchants congregated around seats of colonial government. The urban population tended to be more aware of political developments and more directly tied to the British Empire with its changes in colonial policy. By 1770, the most important cities were Boston, Newport, New York, Philadelphia, and Charles Town. Philadelphia was the largest with about 28,000 inhabitants and the first to be built upon a grid pattern.

Americans were increasingly aware of their numbers in an age which considered population to be an attribute of wealth and power. Benjamin Franklin remarked upon this growth and extrapolated that Americans would outnumber the English; this had implications for political representation and republican ideas. The British government, too, realized the problems associated with demographic expansion, especially after 1763. Should the population be encouraged to disperse to fragment unity and self-help or should the population be kept east of the Alleghenies? The latter would allow easier political control and policing as well as providing a more concentrated market for British goods.

Early colonial populations were restricted to the coastal plains and the piedmont because the Appalachian and Blue Mountains formed a barrier to large-scale population movements until the eighteenth century when men such as Boone tried to settle what became Kentucky.

English settlement
to 1780

- settled by 1700
- settled by 1740
- settled by 1760
- settled by 1780
- modern borders

The American demographic increase was the result of declining mortality, younger ages of marriage than in Europe by four or five years, a large scale of food production and a high nutrition rate, all allowing men to be about three to three and a half inches taller than their British cousins.

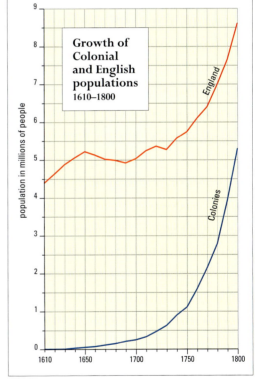

Growth of Colonial and English populations 1610–1800

The restrictive policy won but active and independent colonials moved into the Ohio Valley and into present Tennessee. Settlers disapproved of George III establishing royal provinces and an Indian Reserve from former French possessions and from Spanish Florida (1763/64). Promoters tried to establish Vandalia, but the British government did not consent. Transylvania was proclaimed by Richard Henderson and other speculators. They were never recognized by either British or American officials and these failed after independence in the face of territorial claims by older colonies. The Québec Act (1774) also caused resentment and was visualized as constituting part of the Coercive Acts. Finally, the size of the population had a psychological impact on Americans who realized that their numbers meant that they were able to fight against oppression and resistance was possible.

Chapter Two
Prologue to Dissent

"Society in every state is a blessing, but government even in its best state is but a necessary evil; in its worst state an intolerable one…" Tom Paine, *Common Sense,* **1776.**

The seventeenth century witnessed statesmen and political philosophers debating the nature of the balance of power. Hence, Habsburgs and Ottomans balanced each other in the Danube Valley while France and Denmark (1645) sought a Baltic and North Sea equipoise, which meant a close look at the status of potential competitors—the Dutch, Swedes, and Russians. The 1660s saw English thinkers envisaging France as a new major power in Europe, and French enemies saw England as a counterweight to France. When Louis XIV fought the War of Devolution (1667–68), he sought to acquire lands from the Spanish Netherlands in order to confound the Habsburgs and spread French influence throughout Europe. In 1672, England deserted its erstwhile ally, the Dutch Republic, and helped Louis XIV, in order to capture Dutch mercantile trade. The trait of joining a winning side gradually destabilized any notion of a balance of power. This concept argued that it was morally right to prevent any state from expanding territorially to

such an extent that its newfound strength might be a danger to others or develop regional hegemony.

The latter years of the seventeenth century saw not just philosophizing about the virtues of a balance but encountered two new important factors which required assimilation. First, European states were acquiring colonial empires in the Americas, on the African coast, in India, and in the East Indies. There was a development in colonial trade, so much so that the entire network of Atlantic trade was essential to the economic well-being of the Atlantic European states. Europeans, especially the British and French, began to evaluate the worth of colonies in their respective assessments of their power and strength. Another factor was the diminution of Swedish Baltic power and the rise of Russia as a major power in its own right, which was seeking Baltic and Black Sea influence on the periphery of Europe. Russia also aimed at leverage in the Balkans and Near East while projecting a spearhead of Cossack power across Siberia. Russia had now to be built into the European system of states, and its impact, as in Catherine the Great's League of Armed Neutrality, upon western European state politics had to be taken into careful consideration.

French and British colonial aspirations were evidenced, first, in France's desire not for further, expensive European expansion but in aggressive, colonial acquisitions, which would provide substance to Colbert's earlier mercantilist ideas. Their goals included an expanded Canadian colony and moves into the Mississippi basin. New France, as it was known, became a French royal province dominating the St. Lawrence River with its main population centers at Québec and eventually Montréal, the focus for the western fur trade. In 1699, Biloxi was founded on the lower Mississippi to prevent Spanish or British encroachments on the area, and Louisiana became the subsequent colony; in 1702, the station was moved to St. Louis on

Revivalist preachers spread a radical message attacking established authority, and this religious confrontation spread into politics as those finding fellowship in religion sought to spread this fervor against political authority.

Washington pursued strict moral and physical codes which required him to "adhere absolutely to truth, to practice rigid honesty, to do his full duty, to put forth his largest effort, to maintain uniform courtesy and, above all, to deal justly. ... He seemed young when his elders looked at him, but not when they listened to him."(Biographer, Douglas Southall Freeman)

Mobile Bay. In 1710 and 1718, Mobile was founded and New Orleans was built; Detroit had already been founded (in 1701) by Antoine de Cadillac. In 1667, the population of New France had reached some 6,000 in a society replicating the seigneurial and patronage economic and political systems of *ancien régime* France. Meanwhile, tension with Britain grew as the chartered Hudson Bay Company (1670) was given a trade monopoly and the right to govern all territories draining into the Bay while its trading posts competed with those of New France. Furthermore, a British presence had penetrated the Hudson Valley in alliance with the Iroquois, formerly the friends of the New Amsterdam Dutch whose colony had been captured by Britain (1664).

Into this situation was inserted Frontenac, a wayward and belligerent old man just entering his second incumbency as governor of New France in 1689. His reappointment coincided with the onset of King William's War (War of the League of Augsburg, 1689–97), and he dispatched Indian raiders into New England and New York.

Countering the threat of Protestantism, revenge upon the Iroquois, and fear of British trade expansion motivated the French. The British captured Port Royal, threatened Acadia, failed in an attempt on Québec while British posts in Maine and the Hudson Bay were lost. All conquests were returned by the Treaty of Ryswick (1697) but the status quo meant that each side would again test the resolve of the other. Both the French and British realized the benefits of the fur and skin trade. British views mirrored the French that a well-managed and expanded trade would ensure wealth and strength, as argued by a British mercantilist in 1696.

Queen Anne's War (War of the Spanish Succession, 1701–13), witnessed French-encouraged Abnaki Indians conducting border raids, but the British government reinforced the colonies which allowed the capture of Acadia, but an attempt on Québec failed. Nevertheless, the Treaty of Utrecht compelled the French to recognize British sovereignty over the Hudson Bay, Newfoundland, and Nova Scotia (Acadia), which allowed Britain to threaten the Gulf of St.

By 1776, black Americans constituted about 20 percent of America's population. Mostly slaves, these downtrodden people were the mainstay of rural society, especially the plantation system. Ironically, colonial white Americans condoned slavery while praising liberty as their own goal against the metropolitan British government.

Lawrence. Hence, the French built the fortress of Louisbourg on Cape Breton Island, which they retained with Prince Edward Island. Further expansionist tendencies were curbed by the British construction of Fort Oswego on Lake Ontario which stimulated the French to erect forts at Crown Point and Ticonderoga. Hence, each side sought to threaten the other while protecting its own fur trade. New France had plugged the Hudson River and Lake Champlain route to Canada, but Britain possessed an overall advantage in terms of colonial population numbers and, ultimately, Indian allies. However, competition spread westward with the French reaching the Saskatchewan River and the British the foothills of the Rockies.

By 1743, with the outbreak of King George's War (War of the Austrian Succession, 1743–48), Britain realized its maritime strength, the value of its international trade, and the possibility of holding the balance of power in European wars. Hence, French resources could be sapped in the Americas and elsewhere, while the main brunt of war could be borne by British allies in Europe. As usual, frontier warfare became endemic while simultaneously colonial troops and the British captured Louisbourg and attacked French and Spanish Caribbean possessions. The subsequent peace treaty at Aix-la-Chapelle restored the

colonial status quo despite the number of Massachusetts militiamen who had died around Louisbourg and in an onslaught on Canada.

The failure to solve the French threat became enmeshed in concerns about colonial trade and how the capture of enemy colonies could deplete their resources and curtail enemy power. The French feared British naval superiority and later, after the fall of Québec, French Foreign Minister Choiseul felt that the loss of American colonies and trade reduced France from a first- to a second-rate power. Meanwhile, after Aix-la-Chapelle, in 1749, Halifax was founded with 2,500 settlers, which would confront Louisbourg. In the Ohio Valley, Virginian, and Pennsylvanian merchants were moving towards the Mississippi Indian villages with settlers building a post at Draper's Meadow on the Greenbrier River in 1748. In 1749, the Ohio Company, organized by Virginians and English, won a grant of 500,000 acres in the Ohio Valley. American expansionist dreams were evident and the French responded by establishing forts such as Fort Rouillé (Toronto) to capture the fur trade from Oswego. The construction of a chain of French forts in the Ohio valley was a major precursor and cause of the French and Indian War (Seven Years' War, 1755–63). Despite initial French successes in the capture and destruction of British forts and trading stations at Oswego and in New England, the New French military leader, Montcalm, was unable to translate local successes into a continental victory. The huge preponderance of American over French settlers militated against France as did Québeçois corruption, and differences with Governor de Vaudreuil, hampered Montcalm. The British, however, removed some 10,000 Acadians in British territory, as a potential fifth column and dispersed them among the Thirteen Colonies. Furthermore, Britain's colonies were determined to eradicate any French obstacle to expansion, and, backed by the willpower of William Pitt and his application of resources, captured Québec and eventually Montréal.

Britain was partially beset by mercantilist

principles that if Britain could possess the entire American trade, dominate the Caribbean, and seize West Indian sugar production, then French wealth would trickle away as would French strength and power. The growth of British maritime and commercial dominance made France determined to regain its status by establishing a new balance of power. Hence, France encouraged European interests to confront Britain's "exaggerated" maritime power; thus, Britain should be a European target. However important colonies were considered to be, in the final analysis, any balance of power was restored by European resources in terms of demography, minerals, and agricultural production. A major issue facing France during these years was the erosion of its diplomatic position as former allies slipped away leading to a psychological crisis. Tsar Peter the Great defeated the Swedes at Poltava thereby severely damaging the Swedish Baltic Empire. By 1721, Sweden lost the Balticum to Russia and other lands to Prussia, Hanover, and Denmark. Poland, wherein the French had interfered in kingship elections, fell under Russian tutelage. Turkey, too, suffered defeats by the Russians in a 1736–39 war, and

Catherine the Great's war against Turkey (1768–74) resulted in the Treaty of Kuchuk Kainardji (1774) giving Russia interference rights in Moldavia, Wallachia, and even Constantinople. The weakening of older states and the expansion or rejuvenation of countries like Prussia and Russia altered the participants in the balance of power. As always, changes in tradition generated flux, instability and soul-searching. France was sufficiently tormented and humiliated after being thrown out of the Americas (Treaty of Paris, 1763) that Foreign Minister Vergennes was only too willing to redress the balance and seek revenge during the American Revolution.

British success generated confidence and a certain arrogant tactlessness. The acquisition of French territories now meant that Britain sought an imperial policy rather than letting its colonies look after themselves. Britain needed to plan its expansion into its new lands as British power moved inland to the Mississippi and down into the Floridas. Elsewhere, the Thirteen Colonies had developed similar patterns of government with governors, councils, elected legislative assemblies, and a system of English law. A Royal Proclamation sought to establish a systematic

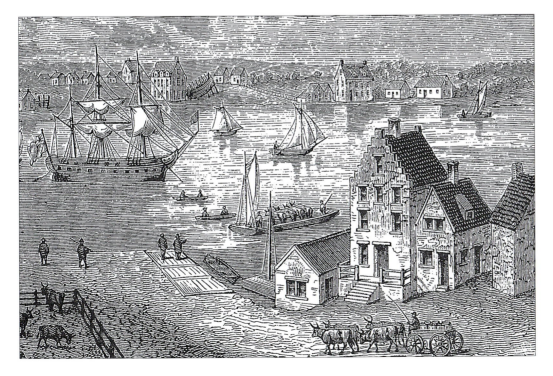

By the mid-seventeenth century, New York was a bustling city with a city hall and great dock, but one-fourth of all New York buildings were beer houses. The population was rapidly advancing towards 20,000 inhabitants.

JOIN, or DIE.

The Rattlesnake image was a powerful symbol in a revolutionary situation. It was used on paper currency, on uniform buttons, and often on flags together with the words: "Don't tread on me." John Paul Jones used a rattlesnake flag on the Alfred, *and South Carolina adopted such a banner.*

growth and population of these areas without eroding the rights of Native Americans. Hence, white settlers could not cross the crest of the Alleghenies and the protected Indians were placed under the Superintendents of Indian Affairs of the British Indian Department, controlled by London. Two regional officers replaced the uncoordinated policies of colonial governors, the most noteworthy officers being William Johnson (1746–74) and Guy Johnson (1774–82) in the north and John Stuart in the south. Indian treaties were to be signed, the fur trade stabilized, and eventual white settlement was envisaged. The Northern Office sought to influence the 8,500 warriors and their families in the Iroquois Confederacy (2,100), the Canadian tribes of the St. Lawrence (800), the Great Lakes peoples (1,200), western tribes (1,250), Ohio tribes (1,100), the Illinois (150) and the Wabash Confederacy (2,000). The Southern Office took in the Five Civilized Tribes: the Cherokee, Choctaw, Creek, Chickasaw, and Catawba (13,000 warriors).

By adjusting the Proclamation Line westward, the superintendents allowed white incursions by various treaties with the Indians between 1768 and 1775. The land companies and settlement projects emanating from ignoring these treaties brought Indian-settler relations to a very low

level. The outbreak of war in 1775 saw British Indian policy providing more trade goods to the Indians in an attempt to secure their neutrality and then alliance as the Indians targeted their major settler enemies.

White colonists regarded victory in the French and Indian War as opening up the Ohio region to settlement and speculation. The removal of the French threat of political and religious control meant that the colonies could exert their territorial claims to the west but were prevented by London. The fact that Britain now wanted to tax the colonies stuck in the colonial craw. The prevention of westward population movement angered Americans, and it seemed that the old French empire was given a new lease on life when the Québec borders were expanded and Roman Catholicism allowed to spread within its confines. The Paris Treaty gave Britain a difficult victory to police; unchained colonials from a foreign threat and the need for a metropolitan protector; and unleashed dreams of migration, personal independence, and local autonomy. The growth of an "American interest" gradually developed and many Americans saw their aspirations as different from and counter to Britain's.

Opposite: Americans resented British taxation and considered that the colonies were being treated as a milk cow. Colonists wanted equality with the English in England who were taxed by decisions affirmed by their elected representatives. However, Soame Jenyns, Dunwich MP, England, wrote in the 1770s, "...every Englishman is taxed, and not one in twenty represented: copyholders, leaseholders, and all men possessed of personal property only, chose no representatives; Manchester, Birmingham, and many more of our richest and most flourishing trading towns send no members to Parliament, consequently cannot consent by their representatives, because they chose none to represent them; yet are they not Englishmen? or are they not taxed?"

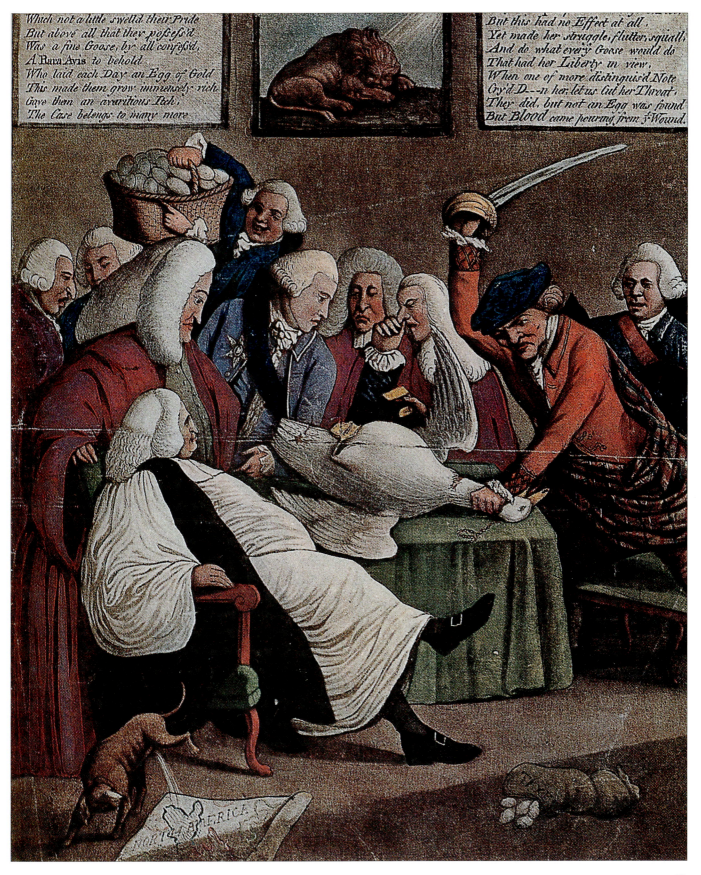

King William's War

During the seventeenth century, increasing rivalry developed between France and Britain for control of North America. This competition became part of a European war when King Louis XIV of France allied himself with the deposed English King, James II. Consequently, England declared war on France in 1689. In Europe, this first inter-colonial war was known as the War of the League of Augsburg, which was fought along the Rhine and in the Netherlands and reached a stalemate by 1697.

In Fall 1696, the Iroquois pleaded for a united attack on Canada: "We are now down upon one knee, but we are not quite down on the ground, lett the Great King of England send the great canoes with seventy guns each, and let the brethren…awake, and we will stand up straight again upon our feet; our heart is yet stout and good; we doubt not but to destroy the enemy."

King William's War witnessed the French with their Abnaki allies fighting the English with their Iroquois friends, the Abnaki being a loose coalition of Malecites, Norridgewocks, Passamaquoddys, and Penobscots from today's Maine, New Brunswick, and Québec. The Iroquois tribal confederation had built economic ties with the English after their previous trading partners, the Dutch, had English authority exerted over the New Netherlands in 1664. A British fear was that despite an Iroquois shield, the Franco-Abnaki alliance, which also included Micmacs and Pennacooks, could cause immense devastation along the frontier. Other worries were that the French might invade New England in a crusading frenzy and use their Indian alliance to enforce Roman Catholicism on the New Englanders.

Prior to the official outbreak of war, 1688 saw colonists attacking the Abnaki in Massachusetts because the Indians were killing their cattle. Abnaki raids occurred in response. Consequently, in April 1688, Sir Edmund Andros, the new governor of the Dominion of New England (all the Northern colonies), attacked and captured a French possession on Penobscot Bay claiming it was British land.

After the European war broke out, the French governor of New France, the Comte de Frontenac, planned a series of counterattacks on New York state and city after American colonists had raided Canada. However, large Iroquois warbands first assaulted the French settlement at Lachine, near Montréal, massacring many of its inhabitants. Frontenac decided that guerrilla warfare would be most beneficial to France and raid and counterraid followed. During late 1689, Frontenac led a force into New England, burning Schenectady and killing many people, and in 1690 attacked Salmon Falls in New Hampshire and destroyed Fort Loyal in Maine. In addition, French privateers harbored in Nova Scotia waged war on New England shipping.

An Abnaki raid at Haverhill in 1697 captured thirty-nine people. Hannah Dustan, who had delivered her eighth child one week earlier was seized with her baby. On route to Abnaki territory, the baby had its brains battered out on a tree and those who were slow were killed. During the latter part of her 150-mile journey, Dustan walked with an Indian family comprising two men, three women, and seven children. One evening with two companions, Dustan seized a hatchet and butchered ten Indians. She returned to Massachusetts with their scalps and received a fifty pound bounty.

In a new strategy, New England colonists built

up an expeditionary force commanded by the new governor of Massachusetts, Sir William Phips, a frontiersman from Maine. His force captured Port Royal in Nova Scotia and attacked Montréal and Québec in 1689. This invasion failed because Phips' command was beset by smallpox and logistical difficulties. On the other side, Frontenac's frontier witnessed (1691) an elderly and virtually immobile Captain Benjamin Church counterattacking the Abnaki scoring some successes, but this failed to deter the continued raiding. In 1692 Wells in Maine and Deerfield, Massachusetts, were assaulted. Raids continued for a number of years. Eventually, the war was ended in 1697 by the Treaty of Ryswick, which returned Port Royal to the French but failed to solve either Franco-British relations in the Americas or Indian depredations. Further colonial wars would have to be fought to ascertain the predominant political power in North America.

In July 1689, 1,500 Iroquois warriors attacked the New French settlement of Lachine killing twenty-four and destroying fifty-six of the village's seventy-seven dwellings thereby stimulating Frontenac to counterattack.

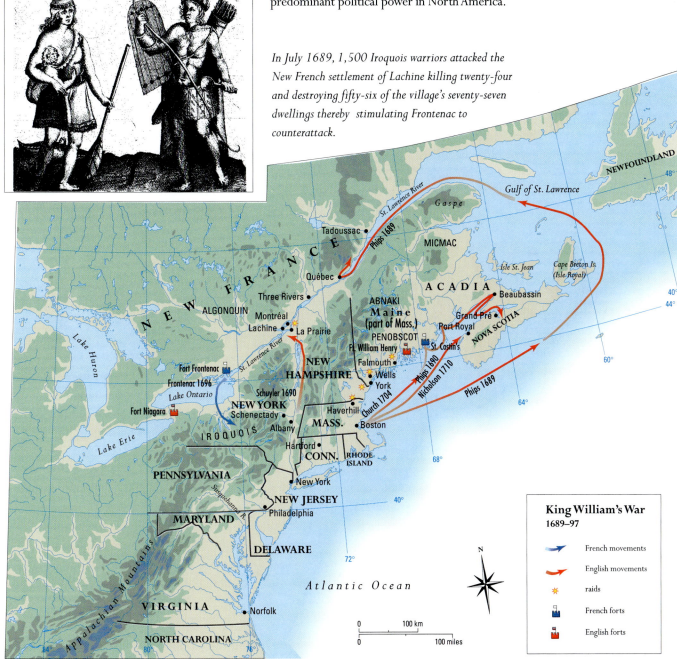

Queen Anne's War

Known as the War of the Spanish Succession in Europe after King Charles II of Spain died childless, Queen Anne's War (1702–13) was the second inter-colonial war fought between England and France. The conflict mirrored the European war in which the alliance of Great Britain, the Netherlands, and the Holy Roman Empire fought Spain and France, the seats of war lying principally in Italy, the Netherlands, and Germany.

England wished to counter French influence after France had colonized parts of Louisiana and built a fort in the Detroit area, thereby worrying both the colonists and the Iroquois. However, action commenced in the south, where in 1702 a British naval expedition assaulted and looted Spanish St. Augustine in Florida. Chickasaw Indians burned the town and then progressed through western Florida destroying thirteen of the fourteen missions there but failed to capture the French forts at Pensacola, Mobile, and Maurepas, despite smashing pro-French Indian resistance along the way. Conflict developed between Indian tribes, with the Creeks and Choctaws allied with the French and the Chickasaws with the British while the Cherokee remained neutral; the Creeks were eventually won over by British bribes.

In 1704, a mixed force of French and Abnakis struck Deerfield, Massachusetts, in the Connecticut Valley and slaughtered many of the inhabitants. Indian raids spread along the frontier even to the outskirts of Boston. In 1704 and 1707 unsuccessful expeditions were mounted by New England troops against French Acadia and Port Royal, Nova Scotia. In return, the French attacked and captured the English settlement at Bonavista in Newfoundland and took St. John's in 1708. French campaigns against Charleston, South Carolina, were unsuccessful.

The year 1710 witnessed 4,000 colonists under Sir Francis Nicholson with a British naval squadron and a marine regiment launch an expedition against Port Royal. Acadia became the British province of Nova Scotia, and Port Royal was renamed Annapolis Royal. However, in 1711, a large British and colonial military and naval campaign against Montréal and Québec failed. Led by Admiral Sir Hovenden Walker and General Sir John Hill, the expedition included seven of the Duke of Marlborough's crack regiments and 1,500 colonials. However, the destruction of ten ships after entering the St. Lawrence compelled Walker to retire, and Nicholson soon followed from Montréal.

The 1713 Treaty of Utrecht ended the War of the Spanish Succession after Philip of Anjou gained the Spanish crown. The treaty gave Acadia and Newfoundland to Britain, and Britain's claims to the Hudson Bay country were recognized, as were claims to Iroquois lands. The French could no longer fish the Acadian coasts but were allowed to retain Cape Breton Island. Additionally, an *asiento*, a monopoly for supplying African slaves to Spanish colonies in the Americas, was granted to the British South Sea Company, allowing 4,800 slaves to be supplied annually. However, such trade was disrupted by war and an unfavorable Spanish trade tax.

A postscript to Utrecht was the War of Jenkins' Ear. Many British merchants found the treaty's provisions unacceptable and resorted to smuggling. One smuggler, Jenkins, had his brig *Rebecca* seized by a Spanish coastguard vessel, and its crew cut off his ear (1738). Used as a pretext for war, Spanish possessions in the Caribbean were attacked, and troops from Georgia, the Carolinas, and Virginia, under Oglethorpe, the founder of Savannah, mounted an expedition against Florida. The attack was unsuccessful. Later, Oglethorpe repelled a Spanish raid on Georgia in 1742 and failed again to take St. Augustine in 1743. Thus ended one more phase in the inter-colonial wars, but competition was soon to erupt again in the War of the Austrian Succession.

Queen Anne's War
1702–13

➤ French movements

➤ British movements

➤ French-Spanish movements

➤ Native American movements

✳ raids

⛫ French forts

⛫ British forts

Aug. 1704

Bonavista ✳ 48°

NEWFOUNDLAND

1708

St. John

Phips 1711

Gulf of St. Lawrence

St. Lawrence River

Gaspé

Tadoussac

MICMAC

Québec

Three Rivers

ACADIA

Beaubassin

Isle St. Jean   *Cape Breton Is.*
                  (Isle Royal)

ALGONQUIN

Montréal

ABNAKI

Grand-Pré

44°

Lachine   La Prairie

Maine
(part of Mass.)

Port Royal

NOVA SCOTIA

40°

Ft. William
Henry

St. Costin's

60°

Fort Frontenac

St. Lawrence River

NEW
HAMPSHIRE

Falmouth

Church 1704

64°

Fort Niagara

Lake Ontario

Wells
York

Nicholson 1710

NEW YORK

Schenectady

Haverhill

Atlantic Ocean

Lake Huron

Lake Erie

IROQUOIS

Albany

Deerfield

MA.

68°

Hartford

Boston

N

CONN.

RHODE
ISLAND

PENNSYLVANIA

New York

0   200 km

NEW JERSEY

72°

0   200 miles

Susquehanna River

Philadelphia

40°

MARYLAND

DELAWARE

VIRGINIA

80°

76°

NORTH
CAROLINA

36°

SOUTH
CAROLINA

YAMASEE

Charleston

Moore 1703–04

Moore 1702

32°

French-Spanish force 1706

Santa Maria

TIMUCUA

St. Augustine

80°

FLORIDA

28°

60°

from Havana

76°

To destroy Canada, New York State
would fight and the Iroquois were
prepared to sacrifice any neutrality.
Philip Schuyler and Robert
Livingstone sent four Iroquois chiefs
to Queen Anne to request aid against
the French. One, a Mohawk chief,
Tiyanoga, or Hendrick, met Queen
Anne in 1710. This colonial
publicity campaign brought several
hundred Iroquois warriors together,
except for the Seneca, but plans to use
them went wrong.

47

King George's War

In 1745, New England troops commanded by William Pepperell landed at Gabarus Bay in order to attack Louisbourg fortress, the apparently impregnable French bastion guarding the approaches to Québec. This mid-eighteenth century engraving commemorates the event in some detail.

In 1740, Charles VI died, extinguishing the ruling Habsburg line in Austria. Although he had sought to ensure the succession of his daughter, Maria Theresa, a variety of claimants for the Austrian inheritance emerged: Charles Albert of Bavaria, Philip V of Spain, and Augustus III of Saxony-Poland. Fluctuating alliance systems during the the War of Austrian Succession (1743–48), known as King George's War in the Americas, ensured that conflict between France and Britain would occur again. In North America, disputes continued over the boundaries of Nova Scotia, northern New England, and territories along the Ohio River. This third inter-colonial war was marked again by raids and counterattacks when the French and their Abnaki and Micmac allies fought the English and their Mohawk friends.

The most important event of the war in America was the capture of Louisbourg, one of the strongest forts in the Americas. Louisbourg was a prime target because it guarded the approaches to the St. Lawrence River and Québec. This bastion had taken twenty-five years to construct and was armed with 116 large cannons. Governor William Shirley of Massachusetts appealed to other colonies for help and assembled some four thousand militiamen from his own colony, New Hampshire, and Connecticut, and placed them under the command of Sir William Pepperell, a merchant from Maine. Transports were provided by the colonies and warships were supplied by the British navy. The expedition arrived off Louisbourg on 30 April 1745 but could not enter the harbor which was protected by three bastions: the fortress itself on the west bank; Island Battery near the bay's entrance; and the Grand Battery of twenty-eight cannons facing the harbor's entrance.

Assessing the situation, Pepperell landed at Gabarus Bay, west of Louisbourg, where French positions were weak and marched overland, dragging cannons across marshland after which they could be aimed at Louisbourg. The French forces at Gabarus Bay retired into the fort. A small British unit seized the Grand Battery, which had been evacuated by the French, who thought it indefensible, leaving some of its 36-pounder cannons imperfectly spiked. These guns were made good and moved to both sides of the harbor; a bombardment destroyed Island Battery and breached Louisbourg's walls after which the French garrison surrendered on 16 June.

The French attempted to retake Cape Breton and Nova Scotia in 1746, but a storm destroyed their fleet. In 1747, a second French fleet voyaging to America for the same reason was caught and annihilated by a British naval squadron. Elsewhere, Sir William Johnson, British Superintendent of the six Iroquois nations failed in an attack on Montréal, which incited the French and their Indian allies to raid the frontier as far south as New York during 1746–48. The campaign against Montréal failed because of logistical breakdowns and the lack of support by colonial militias and Mohawk allies. The Mohawks were wary of fighting since they had suffered severe casualties while attacking

Fort St. Frederic (Crown Point). Yet, the Iroquois remained staunchly loyal to Britain, which supported their land claims against the Delawares.

The war was ended by the Treaty of Aix-la-Chapelle in 1748. Louisbourg was returned to France in exchange for British control of Madras, which was acquired during the Carnatic war, the Indian dimension of the European war. The colonies were extremely angry at the Treaty being based only upon European considerations because the question of colonial control and Indian wars remained unresolved until the later French and Indian War (1754–63). Abnakis continued to raid relentlessly in their personal war against the English. Elsewhere, Nova Scotia, the Ohio Valley, and Cherokee nation country were areas of conflict.

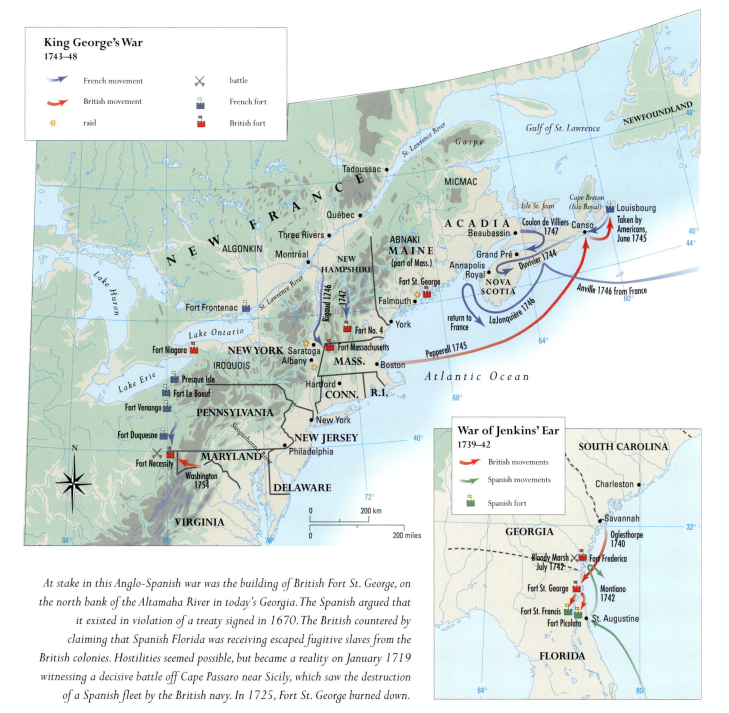

At stake in this Anglo-Spanish war was the building of British Fort St. George, on the north bank of the Altamaha River in today's Georgia. The Spanish argued that it existed in violation of a treaty signed in 1670. The British countered by claiming that Spanish Florida was receiving escaped fugitive slaves from the British colonies. Hostilities seemed possible, but became a reality on January 1719 witnessing a decisive battle off Cape Passaro near Sicily, which saw the destruction of a Spanish fleet by the British navy. In 1725, Fort St. George burned down.

French and Indian Wars

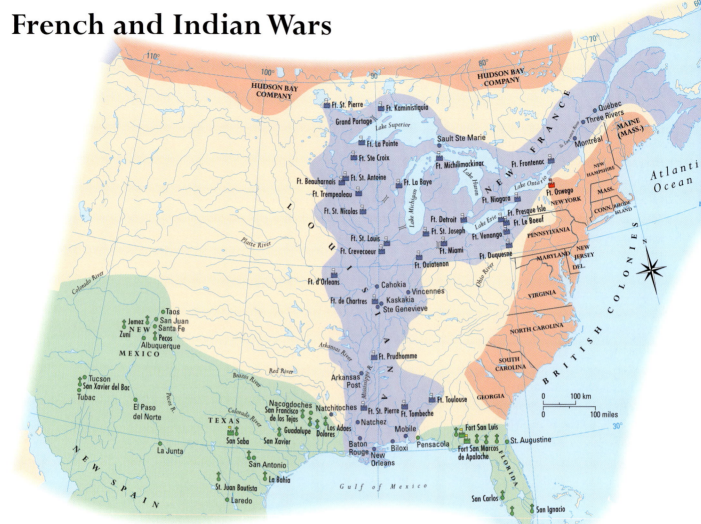

France and Spain
Before 1763

British territory

French territory

Spanish territory

British fort

French fort, settlement

Spanish fort, settlement, mission

portage

After King George's War, Virginians and Pennsylvanians pushed westward into the Ohio Valley and moved as far as the Mississippi River. In 1749, the Ohio Company was organized, granted half a million acres on the upper Ohio, and established a trading center at Cumberland, Maryland. The French response was to build a series of forts at Rouillé, Presque Isle, Le Boeuf, and Duquesne. The French planned to construct a chain of forts along the Mississippi to link their Canadian and Louisiana territories and thereby contain the British inside the Atlantic colonies. In 1754, Virginian troops were sent to build Fort Necessity opposite Fort Duquesne at the fork of the Ohio. This forward policy caused the French to attack Necessity after which the American commander, George Washington, was forced to surrender and retire with the honors of war.

The French and Indian Wars began formally in 1755. Major General Braddock decided to attack the French with four columns. One force sailed into the Bay of Fundy in Acadia and captured Forts St. John and Beausejour in June. Elsewhere, Braddock advanced on Fort Duquesne with 1,400 regulars and 450 militia intending to take control of the Ohio Basin. On 9 July, he was surprised by 900 French and Indians and was killed with half of his force at the Battle of the Monongahela River. European battle tactics proved useless once more during wilderness combat. Washington was a volunteer with the force and he accompanied the remnants of Braddock's force. Between August and September, the third column, under William Johnson, comprising 3,500 colonials and three hundred Indians, advanced from Albany to Crown Point. Ultimately, they met a mixed bunch of 2,000 French, Canadians and Indians under Baron Dieskau at Lake George. The latter was defeated and captured and Johnson built a fort, William Henry, and left a garrison there, and his troops were dispersed home while the French remained north in Fort Ticonderoga.

The final column was led by Governor Shirley of Massachusetts. Comprising fifteen hundred men, the force advanced up the Mohawk Valley to Oswego intending to attack Niagara. Realizing that the task was too dangerous in the face of French reinforcements, Shirley returned to Albany. In May 1756, the Marquis de Montcalm arrived in Canada and took the offensive by capturing and destroying Oswego in August before retiring to winter quarters. Between June and September 1757, the British mounted an expedition against Louisbourg but found a French fleet in harbor and abandoned the attempt after a storm scattered the British fleet. In August 1757, a French force advanced from Ticonderoga and captured Fort William Henry. Despite marching out with the honors of war, Montcalm's Indians massacred many of the surrendered garrison including women and children.

In 1756 William Pitt was appointed British prime minister, and he devised fresh, aggressive plans for the conflict. General Abercrombie was appointed commander-in-chief of British forces; Louisbourg,

Ticonderoga and Duquesne were Pitt's targets. Between May and July, Generals Amherst and Wolfe invested Louisbourg and captured the fort and twelve French warships on 27 July. A battle at Ticonderoga between 12,000 British and colonial troops were defeated by Montcalm's 3,000 men who inflicted 1,600 casualties on the British. Consequently, Abercrombie was replaced by Amherst. In late November, Brigadier General Forbes forced out the French from Fort Duquesne and renamed it Fort Pitt. Fort Frontenac followed when a colonial force under Colonel Bradstreet seized it. Now, the French were squeezed on both flanks while being protected by Ticonderoga in the center. In 1759 Pitt again demanded aggressive campaigns. Fort Oswego was reoccupied and Niagara captured on 25 July, but the British leader, Prideaux, was killed. Ticonderoga and Crown Point fell in late July. On 13 September, British forces mounted an amphibious operation against Québec and Wolfe defeated Montcalm at the Battle of the Plains of Abraham, both commanders dying. Canada was surrendered in 1760. The subsequent Treaty of Paris (1763) gave England Canada, Spanish Florida, and all French territories east of the Mississippi, making England the hegemonic power in North America.

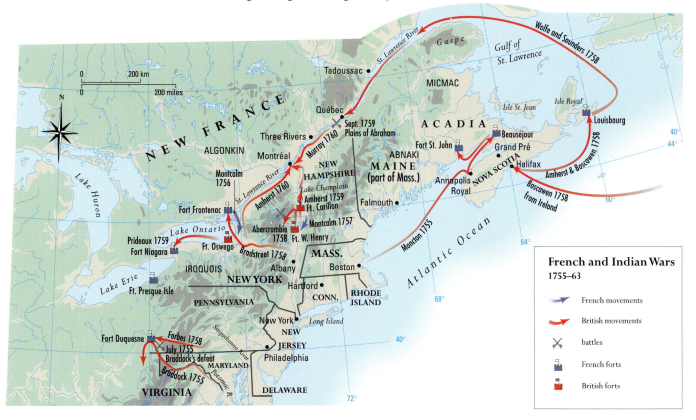

French and Indian Wars
1755–63

→ French movements

→ British movements

✕ battles

🏰 French forts

🏰 British forts

Methods of 18th-century War

Loading and firing sequence for the muzzle-loading musket.

By 1745, soldiers normally primed from a cartridge instead of a powder horn; this increased loading and firing speeds and aided volley firing. Bayonet defense involved two ranks of socket bayoneted muskets.

Use of bayonets in defense.

bullet, which had immense destructive capacity if it found its mark.

Because military conflict could be extremely costly in terms of men and expensive equipment, new military tactics were designed to preserve armies. In Europe, they became increasingly locked up in intricate fortifications often based upon Vauban, Louis XIV's engineering expert. Vauban constructed forts based on a star design allowing all approaches to be enfiladed. The walls would be

Changes in military technology and weaponry took place in the latter part of the seventeenth century. Whereas infantry combat had involved soldiers armed with matchlocks protected by pikemen, the development of the flintlock revolutionized warfare. As the numbers of troops increased, the ability to produce cheap, standardized weapons became increasingly important to equip large armies. In Britain, ordnance officers developed the Tower musket with a forty-six-inch barrel. However wilderness fighting during the French and Indian Wars demanded a shorter and lighter barrel, and in 1768 the forty-two-inch barrel became standard. Known in America as the Brown Bess, the gun used a three-quarter-inch

Use of bayonets in attack.

closely integrated with the landscape and could only be taken by using Vauban's enveloping and zig-zag pattern of siege trenches. Warfare also included campaigns of maneuver and counter-maneuver to gain positions and territory by outflanking marches; a further objective was to

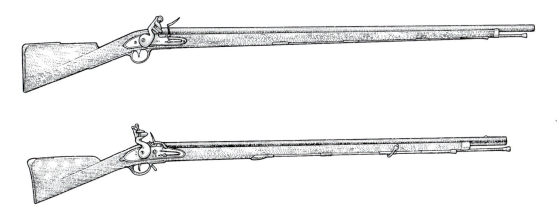

The British Brown Bess musket was the main arm of the British soldier, but the Americans produced a shorter version which facilitated forest fighting because the barrel was less likely to be in the way of trees.

restrict casualties. The European penchant for forts was introduced into the Americas during the inter-colonial wars where they could both defend strategic and assembly points and act as depots. However, their quality was nowhere near as good as in Europe because they were built of inferior materials and they were highly susceptible to artillery bombardment as evidenced in the capture of Fort William Henry (1757) and Louisbourg (1745).

Similarly, infantry tactics developed for open ground warfare proved to be sometimes inappropriate and the British War Office established the Royal Americans, a regiment of light infantry (1755–56). These disciplined troops were important under Colonel Robert Rogers in the 1760 Québec and Montréal campaigns. Later, Rogers commanded the British Queen's Rangers for service around New York during the American Revolution.

The American struggle for independence saw Washington build up a European-style army in order to confront musketeers in open-line warfare. Success was rare until von Steuben retrained the Continentals at Valley Forge. Training in bayonet fighting and charges also served the Americans well at Monmouth, Stony Point, and Paulus Hook. The Americans

also confounded British military traditions by fighting from behind stone walls and fence rails using natural cover as field fortifications, as at Bunker Hill, at Breeds Hill, and during the Saratoga campaign, all of which contributed to the caution of British generalship. The Americans were also helped by Germanic immigrants who crossed the Atlantic with their firearms manufacturing skills. They copied the old Jäger rifle, adapting it to American conditions and produced the Pennsylvania rifle, which was accurate at two hundred yards. Rifle units were especially useful as skirmishers and snipers but were of little use in the battle line where their firing rate was one shot a minute compared with the musket's five. Furthermore, the rifle was not fitted with a bayonet.

The transfer of European warfare to the Americas caused the British problems. The mindset that equated victory with taking cities was not part of the American psyche. The losses of Boston, New York, or Philadelphia were important, but they required garrisons and that tied down troops who could not then campaign in the field. American fluidity, flexibility, and the basic desire to survive were more important militarily.

Artillery pieces required specialist handling, and before 1700 gunners were not regular soldiers. British guns were three-, six-, nine-, and twelve-pounders, while mortars and howitzers had bores of eight- and ten-inches.

George Washington in the West

"Every task was performed as if it were a land survey—step by step, with the closest possible approach to absolute precision." (Douglas Southall Freeman)

This theodolite would have been the type used by Washington and is illustrated in William Gardiner's 1737 book, Practical Surveying.

George Washington (1732–99) has been surrounded by heroic myth and legend; founder of a nation, statesman, and sage, when he died the British Channel Fleet and the Napoleonic armies honoured his memory. What formed this reserved and brave man? The answer must be sought in his formative years as a surveyor and in a military career during the French and Indian Wars.

Washington lived with his brother, Lawrence, at Mount Vernon, Virginia. His early years were spent in planter society where he acquired knowledge of manners, mathematics, surveying, and horsemanship. Eventually, Lord Fairfax who owned some five million acres in northern Virginia and the unsettled Shenandoah Valley decided to survey his lands to regularize into tenants the squatters arriving from Pennsylvania. At age sixteen, Washington was invited to join the surveying party over the Blue Ridge Mountains. His diary mentions sleeping in vermin-infested blankets, encountering Indians, and meeting Pennsylvania Dutch who served wild turkey on large wood chips in lieu of plates. The experience encouraged an enduring interest in the western lands and, in 1749, Washington received an appointment as official surveyor for Culpepper County, but he also worked in Frederick and Augusta counties. His surveying duties beyond the tidewater region taught him endurance in the wilderness, resourcefulness, and determination to overcome any vicissitude.

At age twenty, Washington inherited all the family property on the death of Lawrence and his niece, Sarah. Already Washington was investing in the Ohio Company, which had a large land grant south of the Ohio. However, the area was claimed by the French from Canada. To impose their control, the French constructed a chain of forts from Lake Erie into western Pennsylvania. Dismayed by French territorial aspirations, an Ohio Company investor and major in the Virginian militia, Robert Dinwiddie, lieutenant governor of Virginia, ordered Washington, himself a militia major and adjutant of a Virginia district, to demand that the French withdraw from Virginian land. Advancing with six companions to Fort Le Boeuf, Washington delivered Dinwiddie's note, but the French refused to withdraw. Returning to Virginia, the young major was promoted to lieutenant-colonel and required to find volunteers to confront the French. He left Alexandria with about 150 men and some artillery and advanced to the fork of the Ohio, where he found that the French had seized the Ohio Company fort there and named it Fort Duquesne. Washington attacked a small French advance party, killing or capturing them all. He then built Fort Necessity near the French fort and he was reinforced. Superior French forces arrived and Washington was compelled to surrender after a strenuous fight and was allowed to withdraw with honor.

Although lauded by the Virginia House of Burgesses upon his return, he resigned his commission in 1754 after being underpaid and told that all provincial officers were subordinate to regular officers, whatever the colonial rank. Nevertheless, he volunteered to join Braddock's advance on Fort Duquesne, which ended in ignominious defeat by the French and Indians. After extracting the remaining American and British troops, while having two horses shot beneath him and his clothes cut by four bullets, he was appointed commander of all Virginian troops, despite being only twenty-three years old. Now a full colonel, he was ordered to defend Virginia's four hundred mile western frontier. From 1756 through 1757, the Virginian border was protected from Indian attacks and his Virgina Regiment became a well-disciplined force. Washington joined Forbes in the 1758 renewed campaign against Fort Duquesne, where he led a brigade of seven hundred men drawn from four colonies. After British success, he was elected to the House of Burgesses, and he resigned as an honorary brigadier-general.

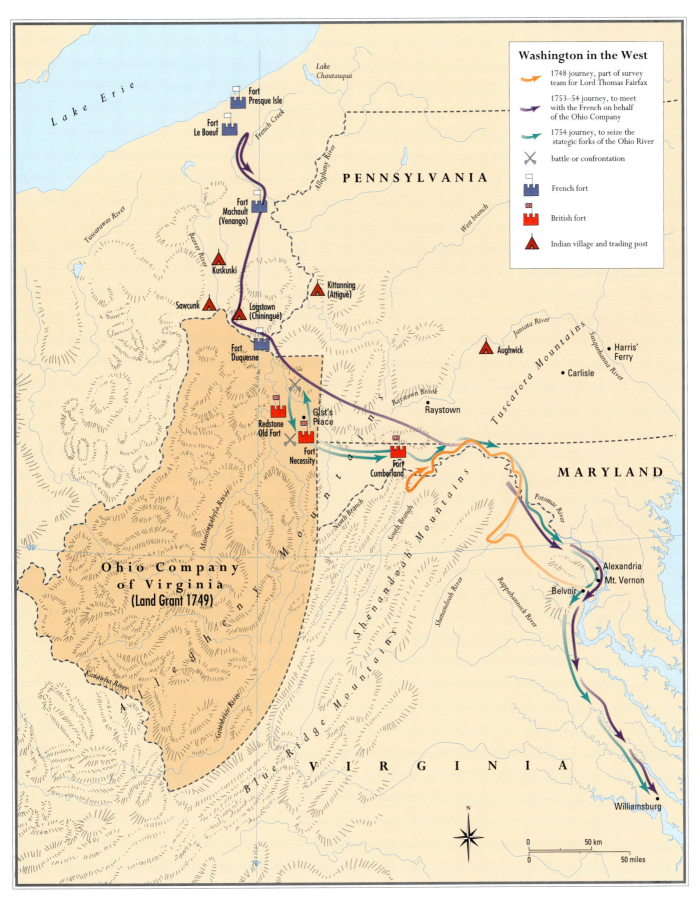

Washington in the West

→ 1748 journey, part of survey team for Lord Thomas Fairfax

→ 1753–54 journey, to meet with the French on behalf of the Ohio Company

→ 1754 journey, to seize the stategic forks of the Ohio River

✕ battle or confrontation

French fort

British fort

Indian village and trading post

Lake Erie

Lake Chautauqua

Fort Presque Isle

Fort Le Boeuf

French Creek

PENNSYLVANIA

Allegheny River

Fort Machault (Venango)

West branch

Tuscarawas River

Beaver River

Kuskuski

Kittanning (Attigué)

Sawcunk

Logstown (Chininqué)

Juniata River

Susquehanna River

Aughwick

Harris' Ferry

Fort Duquesne

Tuscarora Mountains

Carlisle

Redstone Old Fort

Gist's Place

Raystown Brook

Raystown

Monongahela River

Fort Necessity

Fort Cumberland

MARYLAND

North Branch

South Branch

Potomac River

Ohio Company of Virginia (Land Grant 1749)

Allegheny Mountains

Shenandoah Mountains

Blue Ridge Mountains

Shenandoah River

Rappahannock River

Alexandria

Mt. Vernon

Belvoir

Kanawha River

Greenbrier River

39°

70°

VIRGINIA

Williamsburg

N

0   50 km

0   50 miles

Global Implication of American Wars

The four inter-colonial wars were part of the struggle for a balance of power in Europe where Britain sought to curb French and Spanish ambitions. The colonial repercussions dragged in the American colonies and a struggle for India. Colonial campaigns in turn had an impact on Europe because success abroad and territorial acquisitions were viewed as make-weights in the power struggle and at the peace table. The final victory for Britain in its American imperial expansion was that the Thirteen Colonies attracted large numbers of settlers, whereas French and Spanish territories were scantily populated.

After the 1713 Treaty of Utrecht, the Caribbean witnessed smuggling, illegal trade with Spanish territories, and piracy. When British and Spanish relations degenerated into the 1739 War of Jenkins' Ear, British and American attacks on Florida were paired with an unsuccessful 1741 assault on Cuba and a planned but abandoned attack on Panama in 1742. When Frederick the Great of Prussia invaded and occupied Habsburg Silesia in a bid for eastern European supremacy, the eventual outbreak of war between Britain and France linked a battle for Caribbean trade and Silesia into an Anglo-French conflict ranging from North America to India and the West Indies. In India, Dupleix captured Madras from Britain beginning the struggle for India, while British

Admiral Sir Charles Knowles seized Port Louis on Haiti, cannonaded Santiago, and attacked a Spanish fleet off Havana.

The 1748 Treaty of Aix-la-Chapelle failed to resolve imperial tensions. French military superiority manifested itself in a string of forts preventing American expansion, but the Seven Years' War in Europe prevented France from reinforcing its Empire while British fleets controlled oceanic communications. In the Caribbean, the British, led by Rodney, captured nearly every French and Spanish sugar-producing island. These were kept by the 1763 Treaty of Paris in which the British exchanged Guadeloupe for Canada. Admirals Albemarle and Pocock captured Havana in 1762 and occupied the city for six months. British naval victories at Lagos and Quiberon Bay, where Admiral Hawke destroyed seven out of twenty-one French warships, had been vital in securing a British victory.

In India, Anglo-French rivalry continued with each side supporting native rulers to protect both the French and British East India Companies. British sea power enabled constant reinforcements to replenish its forces led by Robert Clive. Clive stemmed earlier French advances by seizing Arcot (1751) and defeated the French-backed claimant to the throne of the Carnatic. This unofficial war merged into the Seven Years' War during which the British seized French Chandernagore (1757) in Bengal. The victory at Plassey (1757) secured Bengal, while victories in the south and the capture of French Pondicherry (1761) eliminated French influence there.

Final British victory at the end of the inter-colonial wars presented certain problems. Indian tribes could no longer force concessions from Britain by threatening allegiance to France and Spain. Because of the lack of foreign competition, British traders raised the prices of trade goods and officials allowed settlers to move into Iroquois and Delaware lands. The subsequent Pontiac uprising showed the difficulty of holding down recalcitrant inhabitants.

Colonial North America
c. 1762

European territorial claims, 1750

- British
- French
- Spanish
- ✕ battle
- British fort
- French fort

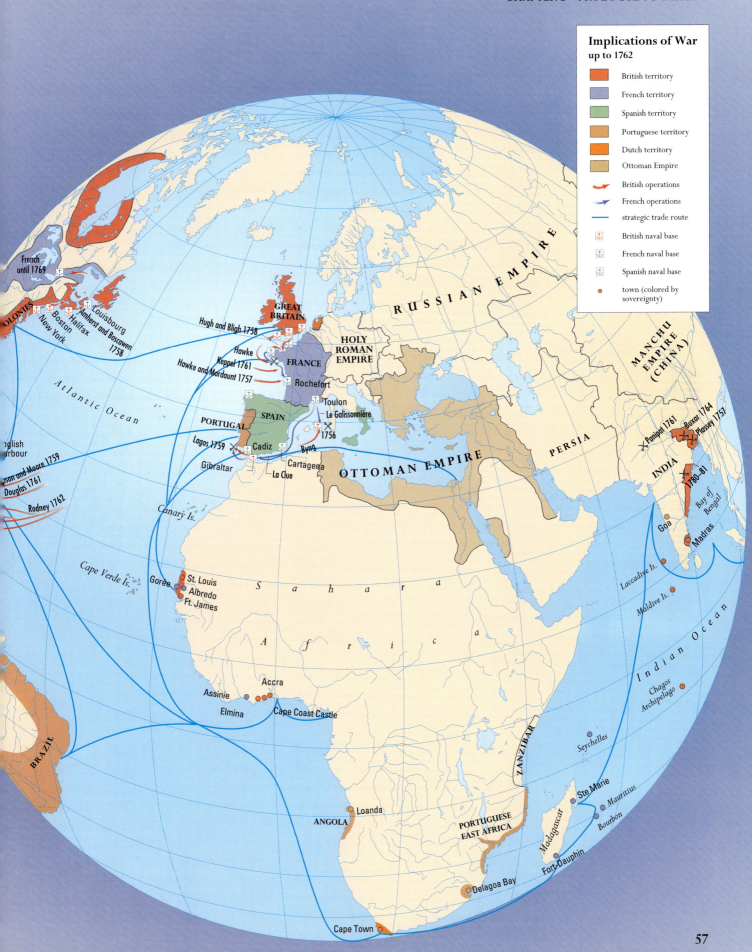

Implications of War
up to 1762

British territory
French territory
Spanish territory
Portuguese territory
Dutch territory
Ottoman Empire
British operations
French operations
strategic trade route
British naval base
French naval base
Spanish naval base
town (colored by sovereignty)

French until 1769

COLONIES
Boston
New York
Halifax
Amherst and Boscawen 1758
Louisbourg

GREAT BRITAIN
Hugh and Bligh 1758

HOLY ROMAN EMPIRE

RUSSIAN EMPIRE

MANCHU EMPIRE (CHINA)

Hawke
Keppel 1761
Hawke and Mordaunt 1757
FRANCE
Rochefort

Toulon
Le Galissonière
1756

PORTUGAL
SPAIN

PERSIA

Panipat 1761
Buxar 1764
Plassey 1757
INDIA
1780-81

Lagos 1759
Cadiz
Byng
Gibraltar
Cartagena
La Clue

OTTOMAN EMPIRE

Bay of Bengal

Atlantic Ocean

English Harbour
son and Moore 1759
Douglas 1761
Rodney 1762

Canary Is.

Cape Verde Is.

Gorée
St. Louis
Albredo
Ft. James

S a h a r a

A f r i c a

Goa
Madras
Laccadive Is.
Maldive Is.

Indian Ocean

Chagos Archipelago

Accra
Assinie
Elmina
Cape Coast Castle

BRAZIL

Loanda
ANGOLA

PORTUGUESE EAST AFRICA

ZANZIBAR

Seychelles

Ste Marie
Mauritius
Bourbon

Madagascar

Fort-Dauphin

Delagoa Bay

Cape Town

57

Native Americans Before the War

Probably born to parents of Ottawa, Chippewa, or Miami origin, Pontiac was the instigator of pan-tribal confederations and was a precursor to Little Turtle and Tecumseh.

Opposite: *A typical Native American village or township with a collection of huts surrounded by a wooden stockade used for defense but insufficient to withstand cannon-fire.*

After 1763, relations between the British and Indians changed. The western tribes had been moved by the British during the colonial wars and had received gifts, liquor, and higher fur prices than those given by the French. After Britain assumed control of new interior lands, General Amherst ended this policy, thus depriving the Indians of a source of goods on which they had come to depend. These products could now only be bought from fur traders. Amherst also ordered severe restrictions on the sale of alcohol and stated that if the Indians misbehaved then they would be punished. The abolition of French trading led to cheating, fraud, and high prices at the hands of the British. Indians were also compelled to sell their furs at forts where they were sometimes mistreated. Furthermore, the Indians witnessed settlers from the east moving into Kentucky, western Pennsylvania, and Tennessee. Rumors abounded that warbelts were passing among the Ottawa, Huron, Potawatomi, and Chippewa tribes in the Lake Superior region. Reports existed of a Delaware-Shawnee link. Maybe encouraged by French inhabitants on the St. Lawrence, warbelts were passed from the Seneca via the Delaware to the Shawnee and the Miami, and from the Seneca to the Detroit Indians.

Accordingly, the Ottawa chief, Pontiac, felt obliged to rise against the British at Fort Detroit, although some historians mistakenly see him as the genius behind some great conspiracy. Fourteen British posts existed near Lake Superior and all except Niagara, Pitt, Ligonier, and Detroit were captured in a May 1763 uprising. According to legend, an Indian woman had a liaison with an officer in Detroit and forewarned him of Pontiac's plot to take the fort. Pontiac laid siege, but reinforcements entered Detroit by the lake. Indians elsewhere were inspired to attack British posts. Chief Minavavana of the Chippewa captured Michilimackinac, while Potawatomi warriors seized Fort St. Joseph. Eventually, Pontiac called off the siege and promised peace. He was murdered by members of the Peoria tribe in 1767. One reason for Pontiac's lifting of the Detroit siege was the news of the Battle of Bushy Run. Here, Colonel Henry Bouquet advanced on Fort Pitt with a relief expedition comprising Royal Americans, the Black Watch, and other light companies (500 men), but he was surprised. Forming a circle around his wagon train, Bouquet drew in the Indians, attacked their flank, and routed them thereby relieving Fort Pitt. Indians, when negotiating with the defenders of Fort Pitt, were given blankets from the smallpox hospital, so ordered by General Amherst.

The British realized that if the Indians could be defeated they would never be submissive, so measures were needed to prevent costly future wars. Accordingly, in 1763 the Proclamation of Indian territory was authorized, whereby the British reserved the trans-Allegheny region for the Indians with limited numbers of British forts to protect them from settler incursions. The Proclamation angered those engaged in land speculation (such as the Mississippi and Ohio Companies) and the colonies, which felt their northern and southern borders extended westward to the Pacific.

War also commenced at the southern end of the Appalachians. The Cherokees had many contacts with the colonists and could raise an estimated 2,750 warriors according to John Stuart, Superintendent of Indian Affairs south of the Ohio in 1764. The Creeks could field 3,600 and in what is now Mississippi; 5,000 Choctaw and 450 Chickasaw fighters could be found. The Cherokee war of 1760 caused much destruction. A column of 1,600 Scots-Highlanders under Colonel Montgomerie marched into Cherokee territory and was ambushed in what is today's Macon county and were defeated. A second force under Colonel Grant with 2,250 men routed the

Cherokee; destroyed their towns, crops, and grain stores; and pushed them into the mountains. The southern colonies had to wait until a meeting (1763) at Augusta, Georgia, ended in a peace treaty. Meanwhile, those Americans wishing to develop western lands regarded the Proclamation line as a British-imposed obstacle to expansion.

Native Americans and white soldiers negotiating through a typical "pow-wow" in a place of significance, under a tree.

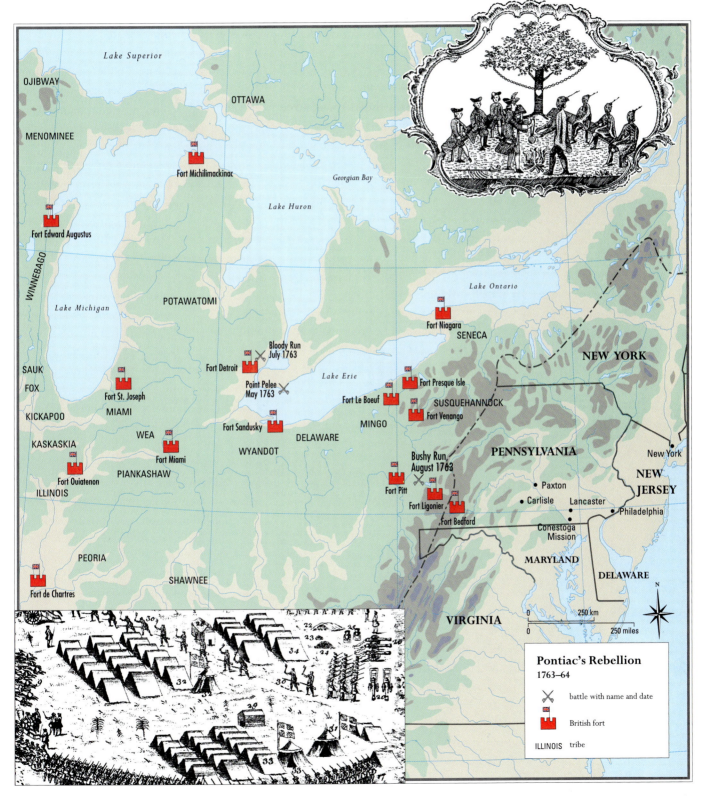

Pontiac's Rebellion
1763–64

✕   battle with name and date

🏰   British fort

ILLINOIS   tribe

Division in Colonial Society

Colonial residents were not unified in the face of encroaching British governmental powers around and after 1763. Tension and conflict existed between colonies, classes, religions, and ethnic groups. In 1760, land riots became common when farmers in what is now Vermont violently attacked proprietors' agents who demanded quitrents. The year 1765 ushered in a time of violence along the Hudson River when poor Dutch and German migrants were charged high rents, and one area of New York saw squatters refusing to leave land they had occupied for thirty years to make space for legal tenants. British troops were sent to crush a revolt which terrorized much of the Hudson Valley. The 1760s were characterized by class tension in the Carolinas.

In 1779, five provincial units were granted places in the newly created American army establishment. The Loyalist Queen's Rangers, noted for their good record, then became the First American Regiment.

A Regulator movement had developed in South Carolina and it spread to North Carolina in the 1770s. Frontier settlers, mostly Scots-Irish, confronted wealthy planters who controlled politics, and the Regulators defied royal ordinances because they felt underrepresented in the colonies' assemblies. The southern Regulators policed their own territories sometimes in their own interests, while the North Carolinian version

faced a militia force dispatched by Governor William Tryon, which defeated the rebellion at Alamance Creek in May 1771. Hence, farmers faced planters in an ethnic, economic, and political furor.

The 1730s had witnessed the arrival of the Methodist George Whitefield from England, who preached from Georgia to New England. He focused his efforts upon large cities in the north and south, such as Charleston, New York, and Philadelphia, creating a religious revival movement. Controversy arose between this new Great Awakening and other sects as old congregations were divided as Methodists and Baptists attracted new worshippers. These god-fearing and dissenting people challenged the old order, as seen in Virginia. Baptists became anathema to members of the plantocracy whose very culture was deemed sinful by these new religious groups. Baptists defended individual and minority group interests against larger communities and could be dubbed subversive of tradition, ranging from aspects of religion through politics and economics. The traditional order was also shaken by waves of immigrants from Germany, Ireland, Scotland, and slaves from Africa. South Carolina's population included about 2,500 blacks in 1700, but this increased to between 80,000 and 90,000 by 1765 with whites outnumbered two to one. Germans, mainly originating from the Rhenish Palatinate, settled in the Middle Atlantic colonies, numbering some 250,000. The Scots and Irish spread through all colonies but tended to move to western areas.

Violence and disturbances grew because of resentment at royal rule and creeping British oppression. The Stamp Act generated such hostility that Boston laborers destroyed an alleged stamp office and a stamp official's home pitting politics and class warfare against wealth. However, merchants, lawyers, professionals, and the educated considered that political debate could best redress grievances. These socio-economic groups wished to unify resistance and focus it through a colonies-wide Sons of Liberty organization. Women, too, entered the fray by establishing the Daughters of Liberty, attacking, in particular, the Townshend duties on tea. Demands for non-importation of British goods and imports followed setting up another division in society. Merchants would suffer from non-importation while artisans and craftspeople would benefit from increased demands for their products. The artisans could mobilize crowds against merchants and government officials.

Inter-colonial conflict is evidenced by conflict between Connecticut and Pennsylvania over the former's settlement in the latter's Wyoming Valley of the Susquehanna. Elsewhere, Lord Dunmore, Governor of Virginia, waged war on the Shawnees and tried unsuccessfully to take land from the Indians in an attempt to break the Proclamation line. The Indians met defeat at Point Pleasant.

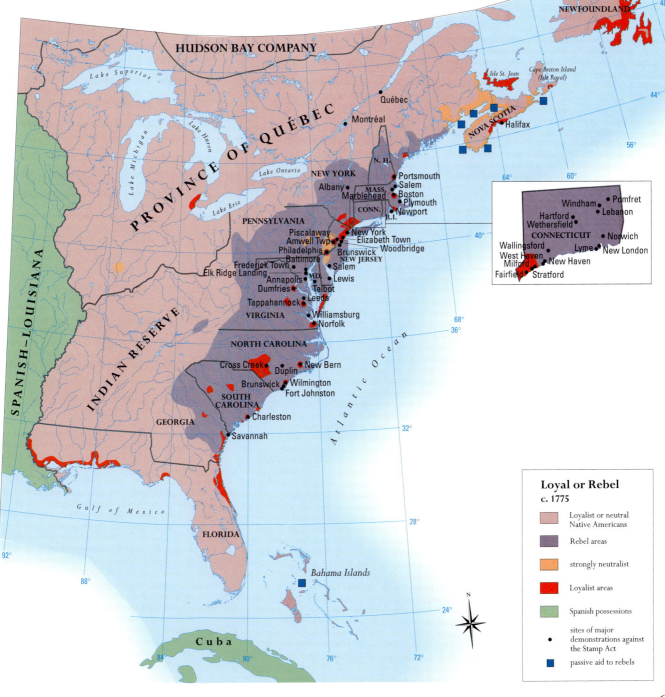

Loyal or Rebel
c. 1775

- Loyalist or neutral Native Americans
- Rebel areas
- strongly neutralist
- Loyalist areas
- Spanish possessions
- sites of major demonstrations against the Stamp Act
- passive aid to rebels

The Québec Act

The Québec Act can be understood as the culmination of oppression, the last in a series of tyrannical policies imposed on America. Despite relating to Canada, colonists saw the Québec Act as a dangerous precedent, especially following so soon after the March 1774 Coercive Acts.

Unwise laws commenced in 1764 with the Sugar and Currency Acts. The first sought to prevent the smuggling trade in molasses, an important American product. The second banned colonial issuance of paper money with the effect of slowing down trade by reducing a useful medium of exchange. Furthermore, these laws occurred during an economic slump, and distress was so great that eight colonial assemblies petitioned for the repeal of the Sugar Act, to no avail.

The next British imposition, the Stamp Act (1765), demanded a tax stamp on most printed materials. That the tax should be paid in sterling was an insult; that violators should be tried by an admiralty court without a jury was a further injury. Additionally, the colonies normally taxed themselves and colonial politicians claimed that the British parliament could not legitimately impose taxes because Americans were not represented in that institution. Opposition became widespread with many riots and demonstrations. Less aggressive responses were meetings held by the Sons of Liberty, the non-importation of British products, and a protest made by an inter-colonial congress meeting in New York. Ultimately, the combination of Americans and British merchant allies helped persuade Prime Minister Rockingham to repeal the Stamp Act in 1766. However, a Declaratory Act approved in the same year maintained that the British parliament possessed the authority to tax and enact laws for America in all cases.

In 1767, the British Chancellor of the Exchequer, Townshend, decided to extract colonial taxes by placing a tax on items such as glass, paper, tea, lead, and painters' colors. From these revenues, fixed salaries would be paid to royal officials in the colonies. A Boston town meeting immediately adopted a non-importation agreement. In 1768, the Massachusetts assembly drew up a petition, wrote to the Chancellor, and sent a circular letter to the other colonies. A two-year campaign against the Townshend Acts followed, ranging from colonial non-importation agreements (Maryland, 1769) to riots against British military repression, such as the Battle of Golden Hill in New York and the Boston Massacre in 1770. A new British Prime Minister, Lord North, repealed all Townshend duties, except that on tea.

December 1773 witnessed the Boston Tea Party, and resistance to the landing of tea sparked the new Ministry of American Affairs to press for the Coercive Acts. The Boston Port Act closed that port raising fears that other ports might be shut down. The Massachusetts Government Act changed the colony's charter and deprived the citizens of most of their rights while increasing the governor's power. Which colony would be the next target? The Justice Act allowed people accused of a capital crime to be tried in England or in another colony. The Quartering Act (1774) gave British officers authority to requisition uninhabited houses, out-houses, barns, and similar structures to make fit for occupancy by troops.

Finally, the Québec Act extended the boundary of that province to include the territory east of the Mississippi and north of the Ohio River. This measure cut across the claims of Virginia, Connecticut, New York, and Massachusetts. Turning the area into Indian territory also prevented white settlement. That the Act tolerated Roman Catholicism in an extended Québec gave rise to apprehensions among Protestants of one denomination or another. In response to apparently planned oppression, the first Continental Congress met at Philadelphia from 5 September to 26 October 1774.

Hudson Bay

HUDSON BAY COMPANY

LABRADOR

60°

56°

52°

48°

Lake Superior

NEWFOUNDLAND

St. Pierre
et Miquelon

52°

PROVINCE OF QUÉBEC

QUÉBEC

Québec

NOVA SCOTIA

44°

Lake Michigan

Lake Huron

Montréal

Lake Ontario

40°

Lake Erie

Boston

THE THIRTEEN COLONIES

SPANISH-
LOUISIANA

New York

VANDALIA

Philadelphia

Atlantic Ocean

36°

TRANSYLVANIA

Norfolk

56°

INDIAN RESERVE

32°

Charleston

Bermuda

The Québec Act
1774

Savannah

WEST FLORIDA
(formerly Spanish)

St. Augustine

92°

28°

EAST
FLORIDA

Gulf of Mexico

88°   84°   80°   76°   72°   68°

Bahamas

	original province of Québec
	Province of Québec after 1774
	the Thirteen Colonies and British possessions
	Indian Reservation open for settlers for the Thirteen Colonies 1767–71
	Spanish Louisiana, secretly ceded by France in 1763
	only French possession after Treaty of Paris, 1763

Chapter Three
The Shot Heard Around the World

"The history of the present King of Great Britain is a history of repeated injuries and usurpations, all having in direct object the establishment of an absolute tyranny over these States." The Declaration of Independence, 4 July 1776.

The Americans initially adopted a defensive strategy hoping to negotiate a settlement with North's government but this quickly changed to a struggle for total independence with a more focused effort on combatting Britain. In June 1775, Congress seized control of the 17,000

Warren helped fight three British attacks before being one of the last to leave his redoubt. After Warren was shot through the head, Paul Revere was able to identify his body by recognizing two artificial teeth he had personally fashioned for the dead hero.

When war broke out, British forces were dispersed around the world and the British government, apart from hiring German mercenaries, merely recruited more men into existing regiments rather than create new ones, lest the French fear the development of a newly aggressive Britain; only the 71st (Fraser's) Highlanders were raised immediately (1775–76). However, when France intervened, Britain expanded its army rapidly. Twelve infantry regiments were raised in 1778 and fourteen in 1779 plus three light dragoon regiments. The British army increased from some 36,000 effectives in 1775 to 110,000 in 1781. In addition, some 70 regiments of militia and fencibles were raised against the possibility of invasion.

colonial troops laying siege to Boston and ordered the creation of an army numbering some 75,000 officers and men, although the new Continental Army was scarcely ever more than 34,000 strong and often suffered up to 33 percent losses each year from casualties, sickness, and desertion. The Continentals were gradually strengthened, trained, and disciplined, and America was eventually considered to be a worthy ally for France.

When France entered the conflict, Foreign Minister Vergennes thought that Britain's international standing would be reduced by the loss of the Thirteen Colonies. Also, Britain's economy would suffer and France could become America's major trading partner, which might help lessen French financial difficulties that had been brought on by the Seven Years' War. Finance Minister Turgot desired internal financial reform not expensive foreign adventures. France also sought to expand its empire at the expense of Britain in the Caribbean, Africa, and India.

On entering the war in 1778, the French population was twice that of Great Britain and Ireland, at approximately 25 million and sustained a peace-time standing army of some 150,000. Additionally, France could rely on its ally in India, Haider Ali of Mysore, to muster about 130,000 infantry and cavalry, augmented by some French regulars. In reply, the British East India Company could raise about 71,000 sepoys, but in 1779, 32 percent of European recruits sent to the Company were under sixteen years old, and many of the rest were actual or suspected criminals, some having their sentence commuted if they served in the East Indies. Hence, regulars were needed, but the dispatch of Scots-Highlanders regiments proved useless because mountaineers from the cold north could not tolerate the heat of the Indian plains. France could also devote all its financial strength to a maritime and colonial conflict and investments in the navy ran to hundreds of millions of livres. The expenditure for both the army and navy was so great that the French taxation system required reform, while any new financial policy ran foul of the entrenched vested interests among the nobility determined to defend their tax exemption privileges, as did the clergy. Furthermore, the aristocracy staffed a top-heavy officer corps, which proved inefficient and expensive.

A second factor benefiting America was the entry of Spain into the war in 1779. The theoretical strength of the Spanish army was 70,000 with 23,000 militia and some colonial-raised troops. In reality, the army possessed less than half this in effectives and the navy was understaffed and in decline. The Spanish inegalitarian taxation system produced insufficient revenue to wage a large colonial war. However, despite weaknesses at home, Bernardo de Galvez fought successful campaigns based in Louisiana. The entry of the Dutch into the fray, caused by a British declaration of war brought a dour, dogged maritime race into the conflict. However, the Dutch Republic had fallen into disrepair and was nowhere as strong as when it fought England in 1652, 1665, and 1672. The army of 100,000 in the War of Spanish Succession had shrunk to fewer than 30,000, severely reducing the Republic's capabilities. The navy was small but could still manage a successful action as at the Dogger Bank in 1781. Given the nature of these protagonists and their different times of entry into the war, the various and changing American and British war strategies require analysis.

The cornerstone of American strategy was Washington, but Nathanael Greene played a vital part in the Southern campaigns. Both men developed strands in strategy and tactics, both being labeled as Fabians who sought a war of attrition, while realizing that they could never face the British on equal terms. Hence, both men knew their inherent weakness in formal battle conditions, so they had to know when to retreat, withdraw from combat, or be prepared to sustain some losses to erode irreplaceable British troops. Washington realized that he must preserve his army and avoid losing a fight even though this defensive strategy might mean never winning a battle. The risk of the latter was too great; preferably, then, actions had to be undertaken to dissipate British strength. Hence, Washington constantly masked and observed major British forces while tormenting them at the end points of their lines, such as attacking Rall at Trenton. Thus, storming peripheral defenses, engaging in forage wars, and counter patrolling were the chosen strategies. In more modern terms, Washington desired patrol superiority, the isolation and capture of outposts and conflict with minor parts of the British army as at Princeton, Germantown, and Monmouth. Even when facing Cornwallis at Yorktown, Washington managed to concentrate American and French troops, courtesy of French local naval superiority, against one part of the British army in the South. British troops from Wilmington, Savannah, and Charleston were not present.

Throughout his campaigning, Washington would advance when the British appeared weak and retreat into defensive positions when facing overwhelming or equal force and then engage in formalized guerrilla warfare by attacking weak outposts. His actions were redolent of Mao Zedong's tactics against the Japanese and Guomindang during the Yennan Soviet years and civil war in China. Apart from almost failing to extricate his nearly entrapped army at New York, Washington kept his army in being until it was trained by von Steuben at Valley Forge. Thereafter, the Continentals performed as well as any regular troops but, furthermore, managed to adapt linear tactics to American geography and its wilderness environment. The Battle of Monmouth (1778) showed American military maturity after which French help ensured a decisive victory somewhere on the American continent. After Yorktown, the British incarcerated themselves in a few remaining garrison cities with Washington observing the major British force in New York. Washington's caution might be partially explained by the loss of French naval superiority after Admiral Rodney defeated Admiral de Grasse at the Battle of the Saintes (1782).

Greene, in the South, waged a strategically brilliant campaign using his Continentals and riflemen together with the guerrilla patriot forces under leaders such as Sumter, Pickens, and Marion. Despite dividing his troops, Greene sought to lure Cornwallis into an error. Eventually, the British pursued Greene while sending Tarleton after Morgan. The latter joined his Continentals to partisans and local militia and smashed Tarleton at Cowpens (1781) totally destroying the myth of his Loyalist Legion's invincibility. Cornwallis then pursued the reunited forces of Greene and Morgan to the River Dan, while partisan forces culled 20 percent of Cornwallis' 2,500 men through harassing attacks. Greene then managed to fight the British who won two Pyrrhic victories. Cornwallis won Guilford Court House but lost so many men that he withdrew to Virginia and then locked himself into Yorktown. Likewise,

Lord Rawdon defeated Greene at Hobkirk's Hill but sustained such casualties that he evacuated Camden. Eutaw Springs had similar results and the British were reduced to holding coastal enclaves, while Greene and partisan units mopped up minor British posts in the interior. Greene never knew when he was beaten and always rapidly rebuilt his forces to fight again. The swift retreat to the Dan saw him advancing again one month later. A constant stream of losses meant that Britain was unable to rebuild its Southern military pressure.

For Britain, the war fell into two parts. Initially, it fought a purely colonial war in an attempt to quash a rebellion and restore law and order. This changed slightly into a policy of destroying American independence until the conflict became a war of survival against the combined might of America, France, Spain, and Holland. Britain was confronted by vast geographic distances and the need to rebuild its fleet and move its reserves out of ordinary, but once at war, the mobilized fleet was outnumbered in ships of the line if the French and Spanish could ever unite or cooperate. Britain also neglected to establish a logical command structure. The army was subject to the authority of both the Secretary of State for War and the Colonial Secretary, Lord George Germain. Furthermore, Carleton commanded troops in Canada, while other generals operated in the colonies, each theater being subject to Germain. Also, the British army had no commander-in-chief for several years; thus, a degree of chaos existed, perhaps best exemplified by the failure of the three British constituent parts during the Saratoga campaign. British bungling existed in other quarters. Contemporaries reckoned a third of Americans supported Revolution, a third were Loyalist, and the remainder were neutral. Britain never developed a campaign to consolidate and mobilize Loyalist support, nor did Britain ascertain how to win over the neutrals. Instead, vicious and licentious soldiery, especially the non-English-speaking Hessians brutalized local populations thereby driving them into rebel arms.

Britain tried a variety of policies. A naval blockade failed because there were insufficient ships to enforce it and privateers could slip out of America quite easily; to chase them meant reducing what blockade existed. The British also tried to eliminate Washington's army, but once he left Manhattan Island, they lost the chance. When the British army was enlarged to a sufficient size to crush the American revolution, a global war commenced leaving many British worldwide interests to be defended. The Saratoga campaign provided an opportunity to isolate New England from the Middle and Southern Colonies. However, Howe failed to complete his part of the plan and Burgoyne took an inefficient route for his march rather than using established roads. Had the Hudson line been secured by the British, further military success might have ensued. The Southern campaign was initially successful, but British policies occasioned local hostility, and Greene found a milieu in which guerrilla warfare could flourish. The final Virginia campaign of "total war" with the destruction of property, crops, livestock; the seizure of horses; and the liberation of slaves resulting in chaos which Lafayette and Wayne could not prevent. Had Clinton not ordered Cornwallis to Yorktown, the continuation of a scorched-earth policy might have opened up many potentialities, especially because the British were mounting troops on captured horses thereby becoming more mobile. Tarleton had previously demonstrated what mobility could achieve, such as the 105-mile ride in 54 hours to destroy Buford's force at the Battle of Waxhaws in May 1780.

The French made British planning difficult because France could choose its point of attack. French policy was based on naval power which envisaged attacks on British West Indian islands, the brilliant actions of Suffren in the Indian Ocean, some failed opportunities in American waters (d'Estaing at New York, July 1778, and Newport, August 1778, and chaos at Savannah in October 1779). Matters only proved successful when Rochambeau landed a proper expeditionary force at Rhode Island, which led to the Yorktown siege and surrender. Threats were also made upon the British Isles. Between June and August 1779, a French and Spanish fleet of 66 ships of the line met near Plymouth in the English Channel with the aim of transporting to Britain 30,000 French troops encamped at Le Havre and St. Malo. By mid-September, the Franco-Spanish fleet sailed home; lack of agreement and cooperation, as well as storm damage, provided the excuses after a British fleet under Hardy failed to engage—a missed opportunity.

In 1781, another Franco-Spanish fleet blocked the Channel approaches in a line from the Scilly Isles to Ushant but failed to achieve anything because of sickness, caution, and lack of cooperation. An attempt on the south coast of England might have repaid dividends. Jersey had proved easy to attack in January 1781. An assault on the Isle of Wight, a common French practice from the Middle Ages onward, could have threatened the naval base at Portsmouth and bottled up a British fleet, but imagination was lacking.

Overall, American strategy during the Revolution was the most carefully devised and focused, whereas all the other countries had so many interests to protect that piecemeal policies achieved little except the financial collapse of France, the trimming of the British Empire, and the exposure of Spain as a power in total decline.

Occupation meant profiteering, goods shortages, lack of fuel, and a decrease in the food supply. A black market flourished and martial law tried to clean up the city. Soldier-civilian relations deteriorated, and courts martial were held daily in an attempt to curb rampant soldiery.

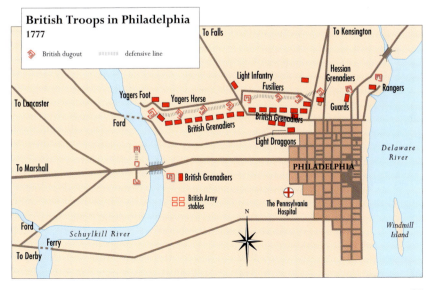

Distribution of Armed Forces in the Colonies

Contemporary pen and ink drawing, attributed to Philip de Loutherbourg. This is one of the best illustrations of military dress at the time, sketched during maneuvers at Warley Common Camp, Essex, England, in October 1778.

At the outbreak of war in 1775, the British army comprised some 36,000 men, although its paper strength approached 50,000. However, these troops were widely dispersed to defend British possessions around the world and Britain itself against foreign invasion. Hence, the British army was stationed in Gibraltar and Minorca in the Mediterranean, in Ireland, in the West Indies, and on the Gold Coast in Africa. India was largely protected by the East India Company's sepoy army numbering approximately 64,000 men. British forces in the American colonies were small at about 8,000 men spread from Canada southward. The British government planned for an army expansion in 1776 to some 96,000, dispersed approximately thus: nearly 25,000 in Britain, 5,500 in the Mediterranean, 8,000 in Ireland, 3,500 in Africa and the West Indies, 40,000 in the Thirteen Colonies, and 14,000 in Canada.

British forces included mercenaries from Germany: treaties negotiated in 1776 with Hesse-Cassel, Hesse-Hanau, Waldeck, and Brunswick were due to raise 18,000, while agreements with Anspach-Bayreuth and Anhalt-Zerbst produced another 3,000. Additionally, Hanover sent several units to Gibraltar and Minorca to relieve British regulars for duty in the Americas. Britain also relied on raising Loyalist forces, but they were never plentiful except in Canada, and Indian allies were of doubtful reliability as proved by the unpredictable nature of Burgoyne's Native American troops. Ultimately, a third of British troops were German mercenaries and their sometimes brutal treatment of colonists drove many Americans to the side of the revolutionaries.

Despite its size, the British army had not seen action since the Seven Years' War and many soldiers had only been involved in police actions in Ireland. Hence, these forces were not entirely suited to their task. Additionally, British generals faced campaigns over some 1,200 miles of Atlantic coastline, while command centers in Britain were several weeks away. The British penchant for seaboard bases, locked garrisons, and foraging for supplies required guard detachments for defense. Accordingly, British field armies were small and, therefore, potentially vulnerable. After France entered the war, reinforcements were few and regiments were sent from America to take part in defending the West Indies. However, Britain had a sizeable navy, which underpinned any seaboard strategy but was unable to blockade the entire coast and was eventually overstretched when the French, Spanish, and Dutch entered the fray.

American military forces were initially entirely different. The Thirteen Colonies had no standing army, as they sometimes regarded such as an agency of tyranny. Instead, separate state militias were used, comprising short-term enlistments that often ran out at critical times. Militias were often ill-led, ill-equipped, and ill-trained, but some proved reliable and capable of defeating British units. Militias sometimes refused to serve outside their own colony. However, they could counter Loyalist activity, engage in guerrilla warfare, gather intelligence, and occasionally act as a makeweight on the battlefield. Other tasks included guarding supply points and prisoners of war. The militia played a significant part in the Revolutionary War and some 250,000 to 375,000 men served in them. Events changed at the Second Continental Congress in May 1775 when George Washington was appointed to command all Continental forces and create a Continental army which would remain in being and not subject to enlistment expiring. Once in place, Washington's task was to keep the new army intact and surrender territory only to survive. Provided that Washington did not lose, a defensive strategy avoiding large battles would erode British strength in a war of attrition. Britain could only win the war if the Continentals were destroyed, which did not happen.

The British Military Presence in the Colonies
1764–66

- British territory
- army garrisons, 1766
- army headquarters, 1764
- naval headquarters
- **HALIFAX** vice-Admiralty Courts, 1764–68
- **Boston** additional Vice-Admiralty Courts, 1768
- New Bern colonial capitals
- anti-customs riots, 1764–74
- formal ports of entry, 1768
- Spanish territory

Lexington and Concord

Open rebellion broke out because of long-standing differences between the Thirteen Colonies and the British government. This irreconcilability was ignited by events after the closure of the Boston port by a coercive act. Colonists began to drill and collect arms near Boston. General Thomas Gage, governor of Massachusetts, sent a column (700 men), commanded by Lieutenant Colonel Smith, to Lexington to arrest the patriot leaders, Samuel Adams and John

rode to warn the Massachusetts minutemen militia. Paul Revere, William Dawes, and Dr. Samuel Prescott rode to give warning. Revere was captured, Dawes turned back, but Prescott reached Concord.

Hearing church bells ringing ahead, Smith sent back a message to Boston requesting reinforcements. The British column reached Lexington at dawn and heard the beating of a drum ahead. The advance guard of light infantry under Major John Pitcairn rushed onto Lexington

In this painting by Howard Pyle, Captain John Parker's company of seventy men gathered on Lexington Common to meet the British advance guard under Major John Pitcairn. An unknown person among the Americans fired the "shot heard around the world," which brought return fire by the British troops, The Americans were obliged to quit the field leaving eight dead and ten wounded.

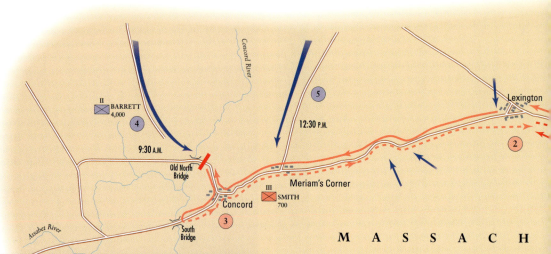

Common by the church and found Captain John Parker with seventy militiamen, half of those summoned. Pitcairn demanded that the militia drop their weapons and disperse. Parker ordered his men to leave because he realized that his small force was outnumbered. Pitcairn shouted that they must leave their weapons. Suddenly, a gun fired, soon followed by two British platoon-strength volleys. No one knows who fired the first shot but the militia was driven from the common with eight killed and ten wounded; one British soldier received a minor wound. Pitcairn and Smith regrouped and marched toward Concord.

Hancock. Leaving under cover of darkness, the capture of the two men and the seizure of military stores at Concord would be assured. However, midnight messengers

News of the Lexington skirmish soon reached Concord and approximately four hundred militia congregated there. When faced by Smith's light infantry, the militia withdrew across the Old North Bridge to Punkatasset Hill. Smith divided his force: one unit marched to the farm of militia Colonel Barrett where it expected to find cannon and stores; three companies guarded the bridge; and the remaining British troops searched the town for hidden supplies. The British soldiers lost control and burned the courthouse and a smithy, which so enraged the militia that they advanced. After delivering a volley, they retreated but remained a threat to Smith's force.

The British decided to return to Boston, but Colonel Smith did not expect to run into snipers. Constantly ambushed, the British bayonet sallies

British withdrew into Charlestown. The combined British force lost seventy-three dead, one hundred and seventy-four wounded, and twenty-six missing; American casualties reached ninety-three. The Americans had managed to combine some 3,500 militia for the ambush and proved that wilderness tactics could combat regular troops trained only for open warfare.

One day later, on 20 April, nearly 20,000 American militia congregated near Boston. Although not all remained, the Massachusetts Provincial Congress authorized the raising of nearly 14,000 militia, with Major General Artemas Ward as its commander. Other militia from Rhode Island,

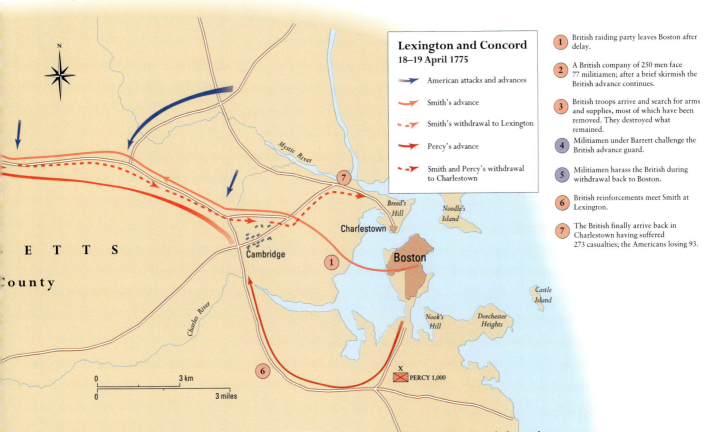

Lexington and Concord
18–19 April 1775

→ American attacks and advances

→ Smith's advance

- -→ Smith's withdrawal to Lexington

→ Percy's advance

- -→ Smith and Percy's withdrawal to Charlestown

1 British raiding party leaves Boston after delay.

2 A British company of 250 men face 77 militiamen; after a brief skirmish the British advance continues.

3 British troops arrive and search for arms and supplies, most of which have been removed. They destroyed what remained.

4 Militiamen under Barrett challenge the British advance guard.

5 Militiamen harass the British during withdrawal back to Boston.

6 British reinforcements meet Smith at Lexington.

7 The British finally arrive back in Charlestown having suffered 273 casualties; the Americans losing 93.

into the trees failed to trap Americans in any significant numbers. The British retreated under fire. Reaching Lexington, Smith met reinforcements under Brigadier-General Percy with a thousand men and cannon. This combined force continued its retreat under fire. When British troops commenced looting roadside homes, American anger grew and sniping was combined with hand-to-hand fighting. The Americans stopped their fire near Harvard College, and the

New Hampshire, and Connecticut sent help, and Boston was placed under siege. American anger and determination was well expressed in a naval officer's report to London: "The Enthusiastic Zeal with which those people have behaved must convince every reasonable man what a difficult and unpleasant task General Gage has before him, even Weamin had firelocks one was seen to fire a Blunderbuss between her Father, and Husband, from their Windows…"

Fort Ticonderoga to Canada

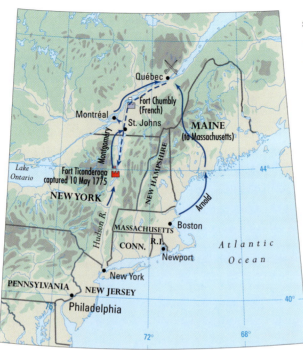

The American approach on Montréal and Québec after the capture of Fort Ticonderoga.

In May 1775, Colonel Benedict Arnold was ordered to capture Fort Ticonderoga. Aided by the jealous Ethan Allen, a combined force overran the unprepared garrison of forty-five men. The fort was considered to be a suitable staging post for an attack on Canada. Command for this project was given to General Schuyler. The Americans were planning to use the traditional route via Lake Champlain and the Richelieu River to enter Canada.

Montgomery, the second in command, heard that the British were building a naval force at St. Johns. Under Schuyler's command, the American force, comprising some fifteen hundred men, advanced down the lake to Crown Point, then to the Isle la Motte, and down the Richelieu River to attack Fort St. Johns. Schuyler's two assaults failed, and he retired sick leaving Montgomery in charge. Montgomery laid siege to St. Johns on 16 September 1775, but the British, led by Major Charles Preston, held until 2 November when their provisions were nearly exhausted and then surrendered his six hundred men. The lengthy

siege weakened Montgomery's force, which now had to face harsh winter conditions. However, he captured seventeen bronze artillery pieces, iron cannon, mortars, howitzers, and cohorns (an early grenade launcher).

Meanwhile, Montgomery had dispatched Ethan Allen northward with some companions in an attempt to recruit Canadian volunteers to join the rebellion against Britain. Allen, and his comrade, Major Brown, won some three hundred supporters, and marched on Montréal. Allen crossed the St. Lawrence at Longeuil. Sir Guy Carleton, the British governor of Canada, sent 250 Loyalist volunteers to oppose Allen who had not been joined by Brown and his force. Allen's group collapsed and he was captured with thirty-five others.

During the St. Johns siege, Montgomery ordered fifty Americans and three hundred Canadians to attack the British post at Fort Chambly. Garrisoned by seventy-eight men under Major Joseph Stopford, the fort succumbed after a forty-eight hour bombardment by two cannons. The fall of Fort Chambly cut British communications with Preston, which was another reason for the surrender of St. Johns. Montgomery was faced by troops who wanted to end the campaign; in addition, some militia enlistments were about to expire. Nevertheless, he persuaded his men to advance on Montréal, which they reached on 12 November. Sir Guy Carleton had only one hundred and fifty men and he evacuated the city, which surrendered on 14 November. Montgomery also captured a river flotilla. Carleton had meanwhile escaped to Québec, and was Montgomery's next target.

Elsewhere, Benedict Arnold and 1,100 volunteers travelled through the Maine wilderness manhandling double-ended boats

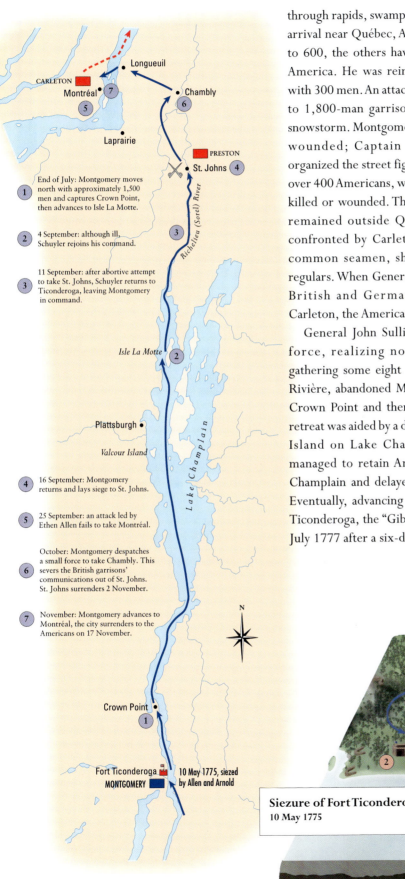

① End of July: Montgomery moves north with approximately 1,500 men and captures Crown Point, then advances to Isle La Motte.

② 4 September: although ill, Schuyler rejoins his command.

③ 11 September: after abortive attempt to take St. Johns, Schuyler returns to Ticonderoga, leaving Montgomery in command.

④ 16 September: Montgomery returns and lays siege to St. Johns.

⑤ 25 September: an attack led by Ethen Allen fails to take Montréal.

⑥ October: Montgomery despatches a small force to take Chambly. This severs the British garrisons' communications out of St. Johns. St. Johns surrenders 2 November.

⑦ November: Montgomery advances to Montréal, the city surrenders to the Americans on 17 November.

Crown Point

Fort Ticonderoga   10 May 1775, siezed by Allen and Arnold
MONTGOMERY

through rapids, swamps, and portages. On their arrival near Québec, Arnold's force had shrunk to 600, the others having died or returned to America. He was reinforced by Montgomery with 300 men. An attack against Québec's 1,200 to 1,800-man garrison followed in a driving snowstorm. Montgomery was killed and Arnold wounded; Captain Daniel Morgan, who organized the street fighting, was captured with over 400 Americans, while some 60 others were killed or wounded. The survivors of this fiasco remained outside Québec for five months confronted by Carleton's force of Loyalists, common seamen, ships' marines, and 100 regulars. When General Burgoyne arrived with British and German reinforcements for Carleton, the Americans withdrew.

General John Sullivan, commander of the force, realizing now that Burgoyne was gathering some eight thousand troops at Trois Rivière, abandoned Montréal. He retreated to Crown Point and then Fort Ticonderoga. This retreat was aided by a delaying action off Valcour Island on Lake Champlain. Here, Arnold managed to retain American control of Lake Champlain and delayed the British for a year. Eventually, advancing British forces took Fort Ticonderoga, the "Gibraltar of the North" on 6 July 1777 after a six-day siege.

① 10 May 3 A.M.: Colonel Arnold crosses Lake Champlain and lands with 83 men and moves on Fort Ticonderoga.

② The British garrison taken by surprise surrenders after a short negotiation.

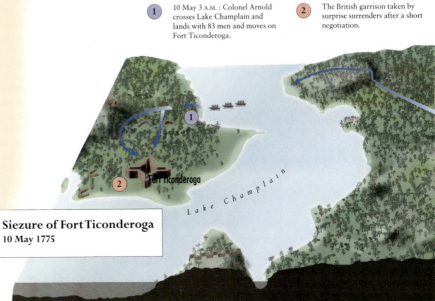

Siezure of Fort Ticonderoga
10 May 1775

Bunker Hill

Boston cooped up British forces, but they remained secure because the Americans could not mount an attack or prepare a proper siege. Some 18,000 colonial militia had successfully surrounded the 6,500-man garrison. The arrival of Generals Howe, Clinton, and Burgoyne impacted upon the Boston commander, Gage. He was advised to take and fortify Dorchester Heights and thereby control Boston Harbor. On learning about this, the Americans sought to fortify the Heights and also Bunker Hill on the Charlestown peninsula.

This painting by Howard Pyle shows American troops held their position through two British attacks only giving way when short of ammunition and enfiladed by cannon fire and under severe pressure of yet another attack.

American commanders, on arriving at Charlestown Neck decided to fortify the lower Breed's Hill instead. Accordingly, 17 June witnessed the construction of an American redoubt defended by about 1,000 soldiers. Gage ordered Howe with 2,500 men to clear the Charlestown peninsula. A British landing took place on Moulton's Point while British warships bombarded the redoubt and also set Charlestown on fire. Meanwhile, the American Colonel Prescott realized that the Breed's Hill position was precarious and ordered Captain Knowlton to defend a rail fence on his left while John Stark was to occupy Knowlton's left and build a stone wall

for protection. Prescott's forces were linked to his now-defended flank by small field fortifications and fronted by a breastwork. The first British attack was mounted against Stark's position. He had placed a stick fifty yards in front of his wall and ordered his men to hold fire until the redcoats reached it. The British soldiers attacked with bayonets and unloaded muskets and suffered Stark's volleys until, leaving dead and dying, they fled. Ninety-six British dead lay on the beach in front of the wall.

Howe next decided to attack the rail fence while Colonel Pigot was to assault Prescott's breastwork and redoubt. Close-range musketry drove the British back again. The losses inflicted were terrible and Howe realized that his troops could not continue fighting for much longer. He regrouped his men and dispatched them with his reserves against Prescott in a third attack. His men dropped their field packs and stormed the hill in a final bayonet charge. Despite the colonial firepower, they eventually drove the defenders off the hill, a consequence of the militia running out of ammunition. Prescott led a retreat over Charlestown Neck while under fire from HMS *Glasgow* and *Symmetry*. Burgoyne commented that the retreat was not a rout but covered with bravery and military skill. Howe's force sustained 1,054 casualties, while the Americans suffered 411 dead and wounded and 30 captured. Howe replaced Gage after these astounding losses, but he never forgot the determination of the entrenched American defender and subsequently all his moves were tinged by caution. These "hordes of peasants armed with old muskets and fowling pieces" could fight. Although the British commanded the field of battle, they had met defeat and the situation at Boston remained unchanged. However, the colonies' morale was boosted and psychologically the Americans felt able to deal with British regular redcoats.

The siege of Boston continued with the Americans developing new fortifications. Despite expiring enlistments and poor winter quarters, the Americans held on even though the Boston garrison was reinforced until it outnumbered the besiegers. Eventually, in November 1775, Colonel Knox was sent to Fort Ticonderoga to collect its artillery. Moving cannons on sledges over snow, Knox brought his artillery to Boston. In early March 1776, Dorchester Heights were fortified and armed with Knox's weapons. Now, Howe was in a dire situation and surrounded by 20,000 Continentals and 6,000 militia. Accordingly, Howe evacuated Boston and sailed to Halifax. Washington immediately commenced moving troops to New York, envisaging that city as the next British target.

Earlier, the Second Continental Congress had met at Philadelphia to commence deliberations on 10 May 1775. By June, Washington was appointed to command a new Continental Army.

In this contemporary painting, British bombard Charlestown and Bunker Hill from Boston Harbor.

The Battle of Bunker Hill
17 June 1775

Charlestown Neck

Mill Pond

Pre-existing British redan

Bunker Hill

Mystic River

STARK
Blockhouse

KNOWLTON

PRESCOTT 1,200

Wall

American Retreat

gunboats

The British immediately launch a second attack heading up Breed's Hill. This attack is also driven off with heavy casualties.

Redoubt

Breed's Hill

MARINES

First Assault
Light Infantry

Second Assault
Grenadiers

Third Assault

marsh

marsh

Moulton's Hill

HOWE 2,200

Moulton's Point

3 During the afternoon the British launch their first attack on American positions. The main thrust makes for the American's left, this attack is driven off with heavy losses.

4

2 British troops land near Moulton's Hill.

Falcon

Glasgow

School Hill

Charlestown

1 17 June at dawn: British ships open fire on American positions.

Lively (Initial Position)

5 After receiving reinforcements and repositioning their artillery the British again attack with bayonets fixed. The American, short of ammunitions and under increasing pressure fall back to the mainland, the British take the hill.

N

Charles River

Lively (Second Position)

SOMERSET

Boston Harbor

Copp's Hill

Dam

Mill Pond

Boston

North Battery

Battle for Valcour Island

The schooner was one of three British ships which were dismantled in Canada and reassembled on Lake Champlain. The gundalow, below the schooner, was a double-ended and flatbottomed vessel armed with nine-pounder cannon.

Opposite: The British Inflexible, a fully-rigged sloop mounting eighteen twelve-pounder cannon, was manhandled from the St. Lawrence to Lake Champlain.

After Québec was reinforced, Carleton advanced on Montréal, having 11,000 men at his disposal. The American commander, John Sullivan, determined to fight at Sorel on the St. Lawrence, but all Americans eventually withdrew to Crown Point where smallpox and malaria sapped their strength and morale. Lack of food, shelter, and clothing together with verminous conditions reduced this sole shield against Carleton moving down the Lake Champlain invasion route. The British advanced to St. Johns, but Carleton realized that to sail down the lake would be dangerous because a squadron of American vessels would destroy small troop transports.

Meanwhile, Benedict Arnold was busy constructing more vessels until his flotilla included the *Royal Savage* and *Revenge* schooners, the sloops *Enterprise* and *Liberty* and the cutter *Lee*. Additionally, seven gondolas (gundalows), flat-bottomed, single-masted boats with three cannons and forty-five crewmen) the *Boston*, *New Haven*, *Providence*, *New York*, *Jersey*, *Success* and *Spitfire*, and three galleys, *Washington*, *Trumbull* and *Congress* completed his flotilla, armed with ninety cannons.

For his part, Carleton ordered that the square-rigged *Inflexible* and the schooners *Maria* and *Carleton* should be dismantled on the St. Lawrence and transported and reassembled on Champlain. His shipwrights and carpenters built a fleet and they were disassembled and dragged on rollers over twelve miles of muddy roads. This took ninety days. The British also built a seven-gun gondola, some twenty gun-boats, with twelve- or eighteen-pounder cannons in the bows, and a huge raft (radeau) armed with twenty-four-pounders and crewed by three hundred men, named the *Thunderer*. The British Captain Charles Douglas had good naval officers with him. One Midshipman, Edward Pellew, later fought the first major ship-to-ship action in 1793 against the French Revolutionary frigate *Cléopâtre*, which he defeated with the *Nymphe*.

Arnold sailed north and drilled his crews near Bay St. Ann above Cumberland Head. On 11 October 1776, Arnold saw the British fleet accompanied by five hundred boats full of soldiers sailing down the lake. Arnold's flotilla was anchored in the lee of Valcour Island and Carleton passed it before realizing where Arnold was. Beating against the wind, the British engaged in a general action at 12:30 P.M. Firing at musket range, the British fired round and grape-shot at the Americans until dark. Arnold later reported that the *Congress* received seven shots between wind and water, was hulled twelve times, and the mainmast and yard damaged. The *Washington*, lost its mast and the *New York* lost all its officers except the captain. Arnold decided to return to Crown Point to repair his flotilla and replenish shot and powder, which was three-quarters spent.

Arnold later reported that the next afternoon on 12 October, Carleton's fleet laid itself alongside the American vessels and engaged. The *Congress* confronted several ships and after its rigging and hull were shattered, Arnold ran *Congress* ashore and set her on fire. Other vessels struck to the British or were sunk. Arnold said, "…with four gondolas, with whose crews I reached Crown Point, through the woods, that evening, and very luckily escaped the savages, who waylaid the road in two hours after we passed, I reached this place (Fort Ticonderoga)."

Arnold had suffered a major defeat losing most of his vessels and command of Lake Champlain. However, the stubborn defense of the invasion route persuaded Carleton to retreat to St. Johns because winter was approaching. In this respect, Arnold had won time for Washington and when 1777 ushered in an invasion from Canada, the Americans were prepared. General Gates had time to rebuild the American northern force, strengthen Fort Ticonderoga, and assemble reinforcements.

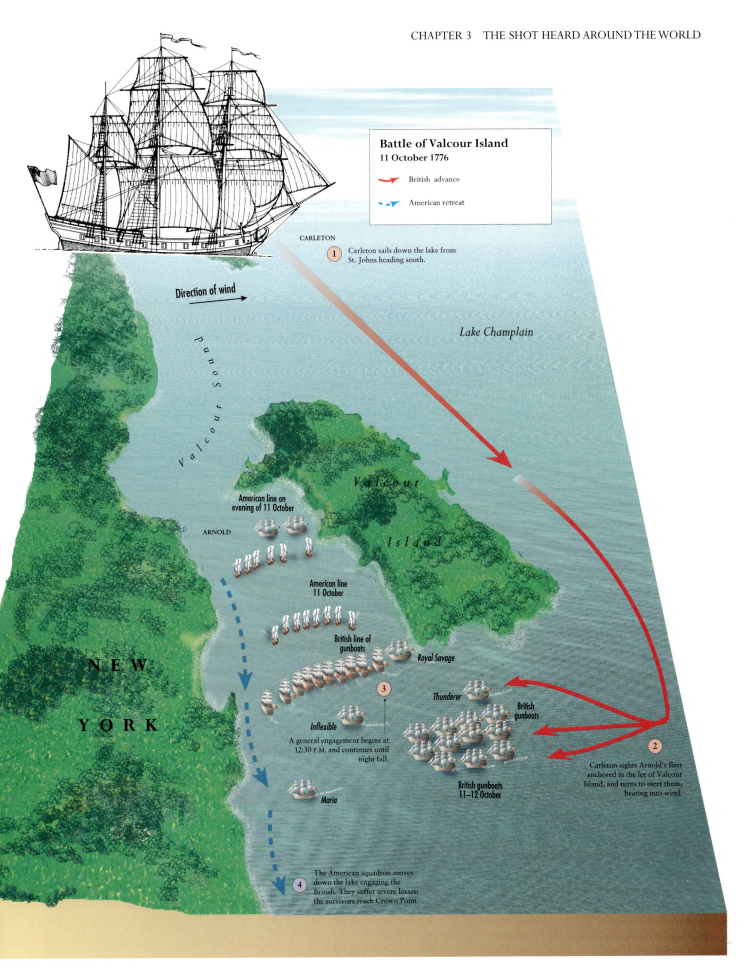

Battle of Valcour Island
11 October 1776

→ British advance

- → American retreat

CARLETON
1. Carleton sails down the lake from St. Johns heading south.

Direction of wind →

Lake Champlain

Valcour Sound

American line on evening of 11 October

ARNOLD

American line 11 October

British line of gunboats

Royal Savage

Thunderer

British gunboats

Inflexible

3. A general engagement begins at 12:30 P.M. and continues until night fall.

N E W

Y O R K

Valcour Island

British gunboats 11–12 October

Maria

2. Carleton sights Arnold's fleet anchored in the lee of Valcour Island, and turns to meet them, beating into wind.

4. The American squadron moves down the lake engaging the British. They suffer severe losses; the survivors reach Crown Point.

77

Chapter Four
Washington Assumes Command

"Rebellion, which a twelvemonth ago was really a contemptible pygmy, is now in appearance become a giant more dreadful to the minds of men than Polyphemus of old, or the Sons of Anak." American Loyalist after Burgoyne's surrender.

The campaigns of 1777–78 saw mixed blessings for the Americans. The Northern campaigns were characterized by initial reverses at Fort Ticonderoga and at the Battle of Hubbardton, but even the latter defeat showed seeds of an American military renaissance. The fall ushered in American success when Herkimer fought off an attack by Joseph Brant and Loyalists at Oriskany ultimately leading to raising the siege of Fort Stanwix. An American victory over British Brunswick troops at Bennington by New Hampshire, Vermont, and Massachusetts militia was a further encouragement, particularly enjoyable because the militia were green troops. The subsequent Saratoga campaign displayed American determination and a dogged fighting capacity that defeated Burgoyne at Freeman's Farm and Bemis Heights. The following British surrender by General Burgoyne disarmed the British after which Burgoyne's army was due to be shipped to England on parole. However, Congress repudiated the Saratoga Convention and British and German soldiers were placed into the appalling conditions of prisoner of war camps. The Saratoga campaign compensated for the defeats and reverses of the central campaign and caused the British to redeploy their troops. Ticonderoga and Crown Point were evacuated and Clinton relinquished the Hudson Highlands. After the end of both the northern and central campaigns, the British held New York City, part of Rhode Island, and Philadelphia.

The central campaign was a disappointment to Washington. Howe left New York with an invasion fleet and landed near Philadelphia. Dispersing American skirmishers at Cooch's Bridge (September 1777), Howe defeated Washington at the Brandywine, while Wayne was put to flight at Paoli. Congress fled Philadelphia leaving it open to Howe's occupation on 26 September. Washington attempted to disrupt Howe's main camp at Germantown, but an overcomplicated plan confused his officers, or they were incompetent, and he was yet again defeated. He then led his troops into a winter encampment at Valley Forge.

The condition of the American forces at Valley Forge has reached legendary proportions in the mythology of the Revolution. In reality, the stories are partially inaccurate. First, Washington chose this position owing to its defensibility and capability of defending Congress' new location at York, Pennsylvania, and the state government at Lancaster. Washington was encamped throughout the winter and his troops suffered from lack of supplies caused by poor communications: mud-ridden roads, frozen rivers, and lack of transport. Additionally, the quartermaster's section of the army was in total disarray. The troops were cold, hungry, and dressed in tattered uniforms, and many walked barefoot. Weaponry was rusting, morale was dropping, and illness took its toll. Latrines were not dug and soldiers relieved themselves anywhere, while dead livestock and horses remained unburied or unburned. Disease ran rife: typhus, smallpox, dysentery, and tuberculosis killed many. Enlistments expired and desertions were normal. The army of 11,000 which entered Valley Forge shrank rapidly. Mutinies were not unknown and the officers found it difficult to contain fractious troops. Some 2,000 men died, probably because this was the first time that so many American soldiers had been congregated in such close proximity. The weather was cold, but the winter was comparatively mild with usual snowfalls of 4 inches; only one measured 12 inches, on 11–12 January. The main reason for the death rate was the impossibility of feeding, clothing, and equipping 9,000 men for six months. Not only were communications poor, but the Quartermaster's department failed to hire transport thereby exacerbating the problems. Foraging brought in supplies and by spring the American troops were in fine fettle. Hospitals were established and medical care provided at such locations as Allentown, Bethlehem and Princeton, among others. Eventually, food and clothing were provided, together with pay, and recruitment increased the army to some 13,000 men.

Another problem facing Washington was the constant bickering among the officers. Throughout 1777, petty wrangles split the officers. Benedict Arnold and Ethan Allen quarrelled symbolizing the cleavage between New England and New York officers. St. Clair

was accused of disloyalty and major General Schuyler was targeted as a foreigner, of Dutch extraction, and distrusted by so many that Congress replaced him with Horatio Gates prior to the Saratoga campaign. Valley Forge saw such hostilities continue. Generals Gates and Conway corresponded and dreamed of the former replacing Washington as commander-in-chief. This conspiracy collapsed and Conway resigned, returning to Europe after being wounded in a duel. General Cadwallader had called him out for disloyalty to Washington and shot him in the face. This issue was possibly serious because Gates had beaten Burgoyne, but Washington was twice defeated. Congress might have promoted Gates, but Lafayette became involved and discredited Conway.

Despite the conditions at Valley Forge, patrols and skirmishes continued throughout the winter in the region between Valley Forge and Philadelphia. Several locations witnessed actions such as the bridges at Darby, Quintin's, and Hancock's, the Crooked Billet Tavern, Marple and Barren Hill amongst others. To briefly mention some of these actions, the Quintin's Bridge (18 March) engagement occurred when British Colonel Mawhood led three regular regiments, the Queen's Rangers and the Loyalist New Jersey Volunteers, on a foraging drive in south Jersey. When confronted by 300 American militia, Mawhood sprung a trap on them killing some thirty while many Americans drowned when seeking to escape across the bridge; their deaths remained uncounted. Mawhood then moved against another militia unit (400) guarding another bridge, Hancock's. When the British attacked, they found only 30 Americans who were bayonetted (21 March), some in cold blood; even one boy trying to escape up a chimney was pulled down and stabbed. The owner of the house where they slept, Loyalist Judge Hancock and his brother were also killed in the massacre. The incident enflamed local passions and exacerbated conflict between Loyalists and patriots in the region. Mawhood looted this part of New Jersey, Salem County, thereby preventing Wayne from using the area to supply Valley Forge.

Opposite: *Americans tended to believe that a committed armed citizenry would offset lack of discipline and experience. However, Washington's view was, "They are by no means such Troops, in any respect, as you are led to believe of them from the Acts which are published. I daresay the Men fight very well (if properly officered) although they are an exceedingly dirty and nasty people."(Letter to Washington's manager, Lund Washington, 20 August 1775)*

Spring witnessed further British raids, especially in Pennsylvania, between the two armies. The local militia's task involved preventing British foraging, warning Washington of impending attacks, and stopping local farmers trading with the enemy. British raids were mounted against settlements such as Bensalem, Smithfield, and Newtown, capturing wagons, livestock, and soldiers. The local militia, under Lieutenant Lacey, achieved little in defense and eventually 400 were attacked at Crooked Billet (1 May) with the Americans sustaining some 84 casualties. Lacey failed in all his tasks, the militia being an inappropriate force to prevent raids. A more mobile force of dragoons or mounted infantry might have succeeded.

A final action, before the British evacuated Philadelphia, took place after Washington sent Lafayette with a mixed force of 2,200 Continentals, militia, and Indians, toward the city to ascertain British intentions. Learning of Lafayette's proximity, Howe led 6,000 British troops to capture him. The Frenchman, located at Barren Hill, was eventually caught between two British forces. Lafayette slipped away and later conducted a brief rearguard action to keep out of trouble. The Americans had left their campground by platoons marching rapidly in columns following von Steuben's training, rather than walking in pairs in a ramshackle stroll. Barren's Hill showed that Washington had regained confidence after a hard winter, displayed renewed aggression, and signalled that his army was ready for battle again.

This action, orchestrated by Washington and Lafayette, and subsequent feats, were made possible by a variety of factors; one important development was a new system of training inculcated into the American army by Friedrich Wilhelm von Steuben. This German had arrived in Portsmouth, New Hampshire on 1 December 1777, under the auspices of Benjamin Franklin, Silas Deane, and the French Secretary for War, the comte St. Germain. Congress supported him "as a successful officer of Frederick the Great of Prussia" and he was sent to Washington to help train the Continental Army. Von Steuben found no unified set of army regulations, a crude command structure, and constant conflict between officers of different states. He realized that a total reorganization and overhaul was necessary and here he was supported by Washington who realized that defense by the citizen in arms, the militia, was an impossible myth and that America required a number of core, well-trained regiments with long service enlistments, which could meet the enemy on equal terms. Hence, training in infantry line musketry, battlefield drill and maneuvers, and bayonet fighting were essential. Additionally, Washington recognized that the Quartermaster Department required reorganization, centralization, and a coordinated support and supply system.

Von Steuben formed pilot or model platoons and put them through basic training with the aid of an interpreter. Not only did he train infantrymen, but he involved noncommissioned officers, and officers too. He realized that American soldiers fought because they wanted to, rather than wear a conscript's uniform and suffer the harsh discipline and flogging meted out in so many European armies. He pared arms drill down to the minimum and similarly adapted field formation movements. He recognized that Americans had particular non-European fighting skills and these could be integrated into more formal military tactics. By leading and training from the front and explaining reasons for his orders, he won the respect of the soldiers and this facilitated training. His model platoons, once trained, were sent to drill the rest of the army and two drill sessions a day turned the Continentals into a thoroughly professional body, with maneuvers formulated for each military unit from platoon to regimental level.

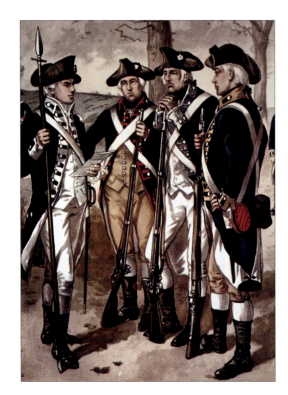

Infantry militia uniforms varied by state, but each man was required to turn up with musket, bayonet, sword or tomahawk, and munitions. Continental Line Regiments, too, possessed different colored uniforms, but were normally made from blue broadcloth, with different colored coat facings, as shown above.

His methods were enshrined in an official military manual, the *Blue Book*, which remained in service until the War of 1812. New tactics were developed from the American experience of fighting from behind field fortifications as at Breed's Hill, and also following the experience of the Saratoga campaign at Hubbardton (July 1777). Here, an American force, routed by a bayonet charge, after an initially successful fight, remained in part on the battlefield, skirmishing in a fighting withdrawal and, thereafter, took to the woods. The British found that their elite light infantry and grenadier battalions had been severely mauled, so much so that Burgoyne was wary of a rapid advance toward Albany as was his plan thereby allowing Gates' troops to congregate around the British positions. American breastworks and field fortifications constructed of logs again proved excellent cover to lay down defensive fire to break up British attacks. Ensuing Southern campaigns would see American multiple militia lines, protected by fences and natural defenses, acting as skirmish lines to disrupt British advances, before they retreated leaving the enemy to confront small well-drilled Continental soldier armies. Similarly, Oriskany (6 August 1777) witnessed a stubborn resistance, organized by Herkimer, and an adaption of tactics on the battleground showed not just fortitude and flexibility but a recipe for victory. The general fire and verve which Americans could display, and observed by von Steuben, was also seen at the Battle of Bennington (16 August 1777).

Von Steuben's value and genius lay in his understanding of how Americans fought best. No Prussian drill was introduced at Valley Forge but a mixture of European and American techniques adopted to suit Revolutionary warfare. His undoubted professionalism at winter quarters was essential to the achievement of American independence, and his training was implemented in a short time period.

As a result of the victory at Saratoga, France recognized the independence of the United States and on 6 February 1778, two Franco-American treaties were signed: the first involved friendship and trade, while the second introduced an alliance that would be effective when war broke out between Britain and France on 17 June 1778. On 19 June 1778, Washington left Valley Forge, while Howe resigned from commanding the British forces, with Clinton taking his place. The British left Philadelphia on 18 June and Washington's hardened army pursued by a more northern route while awaiting an opportunity to pounce. When the two armies clashed at Monmouth, von Steuben's training paid off and the Americans adopted his linear formations and

fought the British to a standstill in the European fashion. A second benefit stemming from Valley Forge was that the Quartermaster department was reformed and, Washington knew, that thereafter, despite occasional shortages, his army would be supplied.

The fortunes of 1777–78 were diverse but, ultimately, America gained an ally and a skillful, flexible fighting organization which allowed quick and complex maneuvering. Finally, Monmouth signalled to the French that the United States was a valuable ally and friend in the French onslaught on the British Empire.

The first artillery unit was raised in Rhode Island, but it took the genius of Henry Knox, the man who moved cannons from Ticonderoga to Boston in thick snow, to make the Continental artillery equal to the British.

Battle of Long Island and Harlem Heights

After Britain evacuated Boston in March 1776 and during the aftermath of the American retreat from Canada, General Sir William Howe decided to occupy New York City, while placing his forces under the protection of the British fleet commanded by his brother, Admiral Richard Howe. This commenced a campaign designed to cut off New England from the remainder of the colonies. Meanwhile, Washington, in anticipation, started to fortify New York and Brooklyn. Since independence was declared on 4 July 1776, Washington and the Americans had a country to defend not grievances to redress.

The ever-cautious General Sir William Howe who, with his brother, commanded the British forces in the New York area.

During June and July, British forces landed on Staten Island. Comprising some 32,000 men, including 9,000 Hessian mercenaries, Howe's army had the benefit of a fleet that could seel up the Hudson River and outflank the American army by isolating New York from the rest of Manhattan Island. The Americans constructed field fortifications across Brooklyn Heights and placed batteries on lower Manhattan and Governor's Island. Washington was placed in an invidious position. Initially commanding 19,000 men, this force expanded to 28,000 by August 1777, but this army was insufficient to defend New York against all possible landings on Long Island and Manhattan Island. Consequently, while seeking to protect such an important city, Washington divided his forces into five commands. Three guarded the crossings from Brooklyn to south Manhattan, one was placed at Fort Washington in north Manhattan, and the final force was disposed on Long Island, eventually being commanded by Israel Putnam, a man totally unsuited to direct complicated maneuvers. Putnam was soon faced by Howe and 15,000 men who had landed at Gravesend Bay on Long Island on 22 August. Putnam's 13,000 men were dispersed along the Heights of Guan, a ridge defending the Brooklyn position. Several passes through the ridge were blocked by American soldiers. Stirling guarded the coastal pass on the Gowanus Road, Sullivan stood at Flatbush Pass and Bedford Pass. Howe feinted at Bedford and Flatbush passes and when Putnam moved the bulk of his troops there, Howe outflanked with a night march on 22 August, thrusting through the undefended Jamaica Pass. Meanwhile, the remaining force (5,000 men), under General Grant, marched on Gowanus Pass. Howe's advance eventually trapped Stirling's forces, and they were forced to surrender.

New York

East River

Washington left New York for Brooklyn, took control of the situation, and withdrew American troops into the Brooklyn fortifications, having lost two hundred dead and one thousand captured against the British casualties of four hundred. Despite the possibility of being cut off by the British navy, Washington reinforced Brooklyn in the knowledge that without it, New York was lost. Fearing American defensive strength as at Bunker Hill, Howe approached the Brooklyn position cautiously and opened up siege trenches to zig-zag toward the American defenses. Washington finally appreciated his exposed position and withdrew his defeated forces with most of its artillery on to Manhattan taking advantage of thick fog cover. However, Washington was still at the mercy of the British fleet which could prevent any escape from Manhattan. This nearly happened when 4,000 British troops landed on the island at Kip's Bay thereby threatening to prevent American forces in New York, under Putnam, from retreating towards Washington's main forces at Harlem Heights. Accordingly, Putnam fled north leaving his artillery behind.

The Heights were a good defensive position and when Hessian and British light infantry advanced (16 September), American troops hidden in a gully rose, poured gunfire into them, causing the enemy to retreat under pursuit. This skirmish boosted American morale because American troops had ultimately fought in an open field and seen the enemy run. Some 270 British casualties resulted while American losses were about 135. The impact on Howe was considerable; his advances became even more slow and cautious.

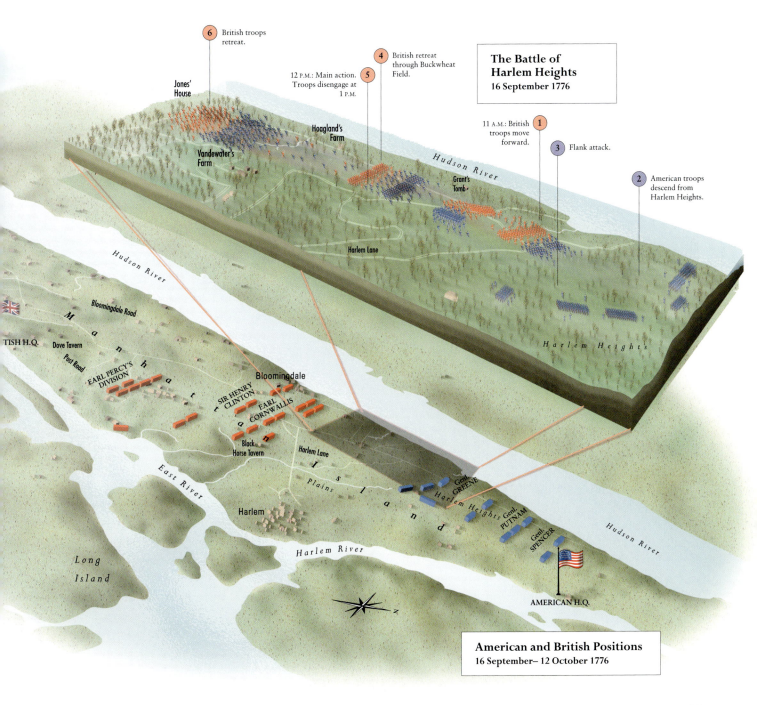

6 British troops retreat.

Jones' House

12 P.M.: Main action. Troops disengage at 1 P.M. 5

4 British retreat through Buckwheat Field.

The Battle of Harlem Heights
16 September 1776

Hoagland's Farm

Vandewater's Farm

11 A.M.: British troops move forward. 1

3 Flank attack.

2 American troops descend from Harlem Heights.

Hudson River

Grant's Tomb

Harlem Lane

Harlem Heights

Hudson River

Bloomingdale Road

TISH H.Q.   Dove Tavern

Post Road

EARL PERCY'S DIVISION

M a n h a t t a n   I s l a n d

Bloomingdale

SIR HENRY CLINTON

EARL CORNWALLIS

Black Horse Tavern

Harlem Lane

Plains

Harlem

East River

Genl. GREENE

Harlem Heights   Genl. PUTNAM

Genl. SPENCER

Harlem River

Hudson River

AMERICAN H.Q.

Long Island

N

American and British Positions
16 September– 12 October 1776

Battle of White Plains

The American success at Harlem Heights caused Howe to reflect upon measures to trap Washington on Manhattan Island. A number of amphibious landings were made on mainland New York. The first comprised 4,000 men landing at Throg's Neck, but this area was assiduously defended by a number of Pennsylvania riflemen and the redcoats were re-embarked and landed at Pell's Point. The British force advanced to be confronted at Eastchester by Colonel Glover's force of 750 men. Despite Glover's ultimate retreat, casualties were inflicted on Howe's troops. Elsewhere, at Marmoneck, a Delaware regiment damaged a Loyalist regiment led by Colonel Rogers.

Although Howe's moves were slow and tentative, they did threaten to keep Washington contained on Manhattan Island at Fort Washington. The American leader left approximately 2,800 men under Colonel Magaw at the fort, hoping that he might hamper British moves to cross the Hudson. Opposite Magaw, Greene held Fort Lee with 3,500 men, while on 22 October Washington marched to near White Plains. The Americans fortified Chatterton Hill on the west bank of the Bronx River. On 28 October, Howe's force attacked the hill on the Americans' right flank. The position was eventually carried after Hessian troops advanced through a burning field. American resistance, led by General Alexander McDougall, had been strong despite low morale owing to defeats and militia desertions. Maryland, Delaware and New York Continentals were forced off the hill as they retreated while still fighting. The Delaware rearguard fought dourly and held off British attacks. The American army survived because of stubbornness, foolish British leadership in not ordering a general attack, and accurate American artillery fire. Thereafter, Howe decided not to attack Washington's main position until reinforcements arrived. On 31 October, heavy rain ruined much British gunpowder preventing another attack. Anyway, Washington had retreated and crossed the Hudson to the mainland.

Howe, having faced such obstinate fighting, advanced on Fort Washington. This position was untenable with its water supply being the Hudson River, 240 feet below rocky cliffs, and observed by the British navy. Heavy British howitzer fire was partially impeded by a little dog biting out burning shell fuses, but the dog was eventually fragmented in an explosion. Fort Washington was forced to capitulate and Magaw was captured along with his 2,800 Americans, a truly great disaster. Then, in an unparalleled burst of energy, Howe sent Cornwallis over the Hudson at Closter in an advance on Fort Lee, where he found evidence of a hasty evacuation.

Meanwhile, Washington had divided his forces further. Lee was left at Castle Hill on the Croton River to counter any move north by Howe, while the remainder marched to Peekskill. The Hudson was crossed at Haverstraw and Washington moved to Hackensack in New Jersey where he met Greene's force from Fort Lee. At the same time, General Lee and some 4,000 men were captured or dispersed after he marched toward Morristown. Cornwallis was ordered to pursue Washington toward Newark; the Americans reached the town first arriving on 22 November.

The year 1776 had proved a disappointing year for Washington. New York had been captured, several thousand men taken, and some 2,000 men returned home after their enlistments expired in December. Washington had constantly broken a basic military dictum: never divide your forces while facing the enemy. Now, Cornwallis was at his heels reaching Newark as Washington left. Eventually, Washington crossed the Delaware River at Trenton, while destroying all river craft to prevent Cornwallis from crossing.

Elsewhere, a British force captured Newport, Rhode Island with its magnificent harbor while Sir Guy Carleton advanced southward, his part in the plan to isolate New England.

Despite losing on Long Island and needing to retreat, these experiences strengthened and trained the American troops and stiffened their resolve.

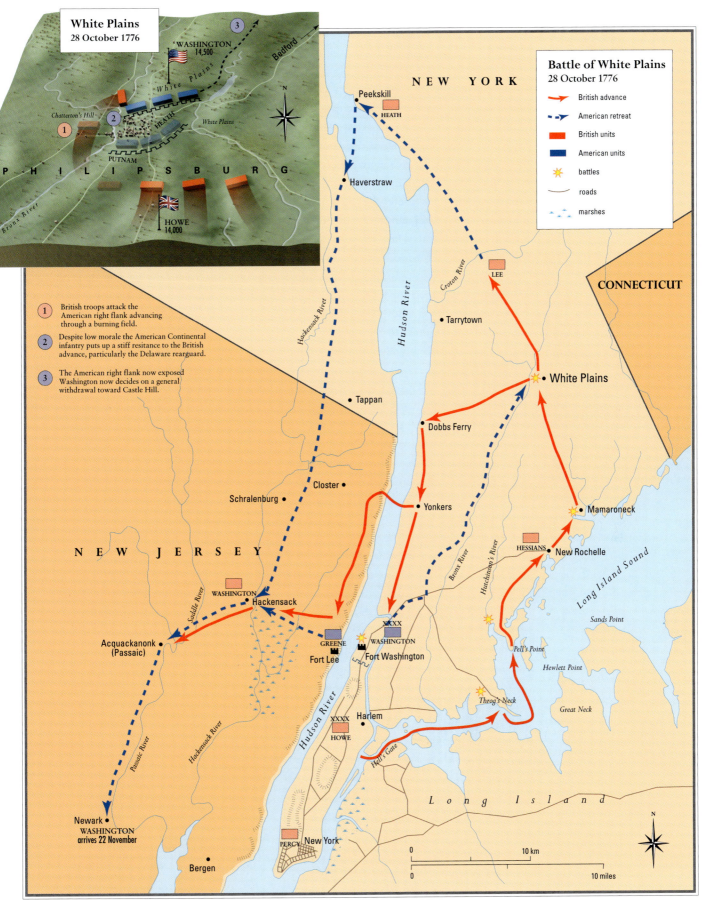

White Plains
28 October 1776

WASHINGTON
14,500

White Plains

Bedford

Chatterton's Hill

① ②

HEATH

PUTNAM

PHILIPSBURG

Bronx River

HOWE
14,000

N

Battle of White Plains
28 October 1776

→ British advance

- - ▸ American retreat

■ British units

■ American units

✦ battles

— roads

marshes

① British troops attack the American right flank advancing through a burning field.

② Despite low morale the American Continental infantry puts up a stiff resitance to the British advance, particularly the Delaware rearguard.

③ The American right flank now exposed Washington now decides on a general withdrawal toward Castle Hill.

N E W   Y O R K

• Peekskill
HEATH

• Haverstraw

Hackensack River

Hudson River

Croton River

LEE

CONNECTICUT

• Tarrytown

• Tappan

• Dobbs Ferry

✦ • White Plains

• Closter

• Schralenburg

• Yonkers

✦ • Mamaroneck

HESSIANS • New Rochelle

Hutchinson's River

N E W   J E R S E Y

Saddle River

WASHINGTON
• Hackensack

Acquackanonk
(Passaic)

GREENE
Fort Lee

XXXX
WASHINGTON
Fort Washington

Bronx River

Long Island Sound

Sands Point

✦ Pell's Point

Hewlett Point

Throg's Neck

Great Neck

Passaic River

Hackensack River

XXXX
Harlem
HOWE

Hudson River

Hell's Gate

L o n g   I s l a n d

• Newark
WASHINGTON
arrives 22 November

PERCY New York

• Bergen

N

0   10 km

0   10 miles

Battle of Trenton

While Washington retreated across New Jersey, Howe pursued at a languorous pace. He established a series of outposts, generally populated by Hessians. When the Americans crossed the Delaware, Howe returned to New York to enjoy comfortable winter quarters and to forget the war while Cornwallis decided to take leave in England. British troops robbed and raped and treated the citizens of New Jersey and Pennsylvania deplorably thereby diminishing the forces of potential Loyalism. Property was damaged and food requisitioned and such treatment helped Washington secure militia help for his embattled Continentals.

Washington decided on a military campaign. He had been reinforced by a regiment of German immigrants and 1,000 Pennsylvania Associators. Furthermore, Sullivan had managed to extract 2,000 of Lee's men who had crossed into New Jersey. So, before enlistments ran out on 31 December, Washington decided to attack Trenton in winter, this being the end point of Howe's Hessian outposts. Trenton also posed the threat of being a start point of a Spring campaign against Pennsylvania. The Hessian commander at Trenton was Colonel Johann Gottlieb Rall, an extremely arrogant officer who considered that American "clowns" could not be threatening. Consequently, he disregarded Washington's series of raids in the region. American sniping killed and wounded several Hessians and kept them awake and nervous. Rall saw no danger and parked his artillery by his headquarters instead of placing it in defensive positions.

Washington constructed a complex plan. Lieutenant Colonel Cadwalader was to cross the Delaware near Bristol with 1,900 men and tackle the Hessian garrison at Bordentown in a diversionary attack. General Ewing was to ferry 700 men across to Trenton and take the bridge over the Assunpink River to prevent any Hessians escaping. Washington would lead the main force of 2,000 men across the river at McKonkey's Ferry, nine miles north of Trenton. However, complicated plans often go awry. Ewing decided the Delaware was too dangerous and returned to quarters.

Cadwalader got his troops across the river but not his artillery. Loath to fight without cannon, he returned his force across the Delaware to their encampment.

Washington was more audacious on this Christmas night (1776). Aided by Marblehead boatmen, his men and artillery were ferried through the ice-floes to the enemy bank. The Americans were divided into two columns; one commanded by Greene advanced down the Pennington Road while Sullivan commanded the other, which marched on the right flank down the river road. Successful co-ordination brought both columns to the outskirts of Trenton just before 8 A.M.

Legend has the Hessians drunk and sleeping off Christmas celebrations, but in reality Rall had pickets on the main roads which spotted the American advance. Rall formed up his 1,400 men, but the Americans had the advantage of greater numbers and well-sited cannons. Colonel Knox pointed his artillery down King Street and

American artillery at Trenton quickly silenced Rall's four cannons and then were positioned to fire down Queen Street where Forrest's six guns soon cleared away the Germans thereby allowing Lieutenant James Monroe to capture three Hessian artillery pieces.

Queen Street and together with flanking fire from forces commanded by General Mercer broke a bayonet charge along King Street. Rall felt compelled to retreat into an orchard outside the town. The Hessians, seeing their commander dying, and realizing they were encircled, surrendered. Elsewhere, Lieutenant James Monroe, while being badly wounded in the shoulder, captured the Hessian artillery. The Americans suffered four killed and eight wounded. Nearly one thousand Hessians were captured, twenty-two were killed, and five hundred fled over the Assunpink to Bordentown. Courageous leadership and boldness in a two-column attack had broken the Hessians and encouraged further aggressive American operations. Four days after the attack, Washington and the Continentals occupied Trenton.

① Washington orders Cadwalader with 1,900 men to cross the Delaware and attack the British force at Bordentown; unknown to Washington this deployment fails.

② Ewing is instructed to cross the Delaware and hold the bridge south of Trenton; due to the condition of the Delaware River, Ewing does not carry out this order.

③ Washington, unaware that his two southern movements have not been carried out, crosses the Delaware with great difficulty. In severe weather conditions he urges his men on and approaches Trenton in two columns.

④ Pickets warn Colonel Rall of the American approach, he hastily organizes his command, but the Americans now hold the initiative. After a brief struggle along King and Queen streets the Hessians are driven back. Colonel Rall falls mortally wounded, and the bulk of his command surrenders while some 500 men escape across the bridge toward Bordentown.

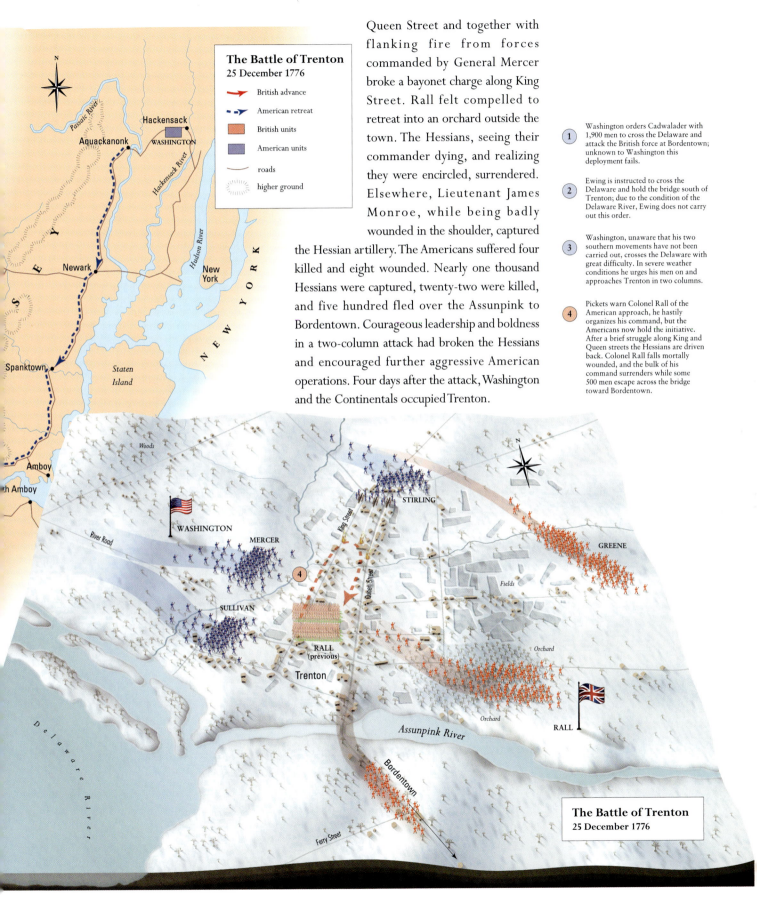

The Battle of Trenton
25 December 1776

British advance
American retreat
British units
American units
roads
higher ground

The Battle of Trenton
25 December 1776

Battle of Princeton

Washington's occupation of Trenton was made possible by the fright caused by his recent victory. General von Donop at Bordentown abandoned the Delaware line and withdrew his troops to Allentown, while the Americans posted pickets at Five Mile Creek bridge on the Post Road to Princeton. However, Cornwallis' leave was cancelled and he was given 8,000 men to crush Washington and, maybe, the rebellion.

Cornwallis' plans placed 1,200 men at Princeton under Lieutenant-Colonel Harwood, while General Leslie was posted at Maidenhead (with 1,200 men). The British commander then advanced on Trenton with 5,500 troops, and, after brushing aside skirmishers at Shabbakonk Creek, entered Trenton on 1 January 1777. He faced American entrenchments near Assunpink Creek and, when Hessians tried to force its bridge, obstinate resistance drove the British force into a night encampment.

Washington kindled fires and ordered 400 soldiers to keep them burning and to make camp noises. His forces then decamped in a night march to Sandtown with General Mercer commanding an advance guard of 200 men. Advancing along the Quaker Road to Princeton, Washington detached Mercer with 350 men to block the Post Road to Trenton and prevent British troops escaping after any attack on Princeton. Unknown to Washington and Mercer, Mawhood was marching to Trenton with 800 men to join Cornwallis. Mercer's blocking brigade was observed while moving through the woods separating the Quaker and Post roads. A British assault followed and, after initial successful American resistance, a bayonet charge broke Mercer's men who fled; the Americans were mainly armed with rifles and could not adequately defend themselves. A Pennsylvania militia unit seeking to support Mercer suffered similarly while Mercer was killed. A Continental brigade finally held the line and when Washington assumed command with other American units advancing towards the action, the British broke out of a potential encirclement with another bayonet charge, although the Americans did capture some British prisoners.

Washington regrouped his forces and marched on Princeton to settle matters with the remnants of Mawhood's forces. Some of them escaped to New Brunswick, but others blockaded themselves inside a college hall. One eyewitness watched a cannon planted before its door. Two or three discharges elicited a white flag at a window. This witness, a Sergeant R, had had his pack shot from his back during combat but replaced his losses at the expense of a British officer, which was soon stolen from him. American losses during these engagements were light: twenty-three killed and twenty wounded. British losses comprised twenty-eight dead, fifty-eight wounded, and 323 captured.

Washington wanted to march on New Brunswick while rolling up the Hessian outposts, but his men were tired and worn out by so much winter combat. He decided to make winter quarters at Morristown where his numbers fell after enlistments ran out. The presence of smallpox killed many.

Washington had achieved remarkable success; his positions outflanked Cornwallis' garrisons and communications, and British forces were withdrawn from central and western New Jersey. Furthermore, an assault on Philadelphia had been prevented. Howe was now forced into a defensive position and he realized that American units were capable of defeating British troops in small-scale actions. Also, Howe had to disperse many troops in outposts to hold down the countryside making him vulnerable to raids. American resilience was proven and Washington's victories boosted the morale of the army and Congress. Washington had also created a new army after his failure around New York, and it seemed that despite casualties, disease, desertions, and enlistments ending, Washington could always build another army.

The British 17th Regiment lost 101 men killed, wounded, or taken prisoner out of 246 men, but they fought so hard that they were dubbed the "Tigers," a term still used today for the mascot used on the athletic field by Princeton University students.

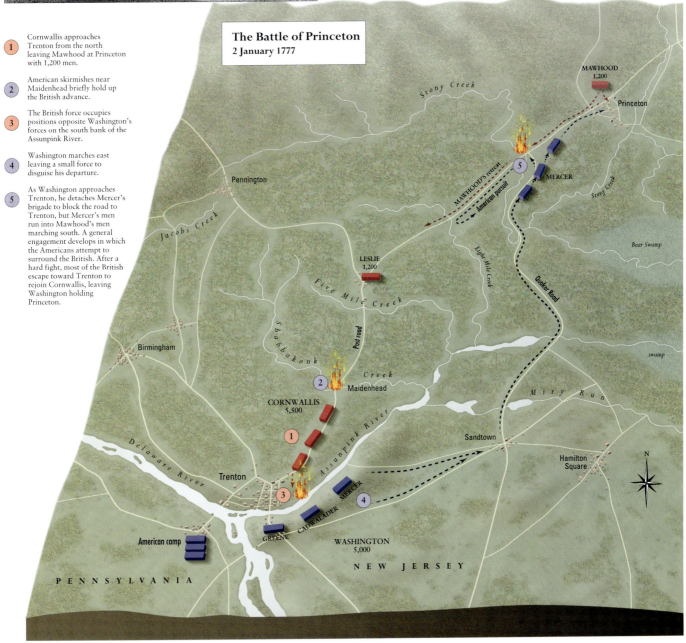

1 Cornwallis approaches Trenton from the north leaving Mawhood at Princeton with 1,200 men.

2 American skirmishes near Maidenhead briefly hold up the British advance.

3 The British force occupies positions opposite Washington's forces on the south bank of the Assunpink River.

4 Washington marches east leaving a small force to disguise his departure.

5 As Washington approaches Trenton, he detaches Mercer's brigade to block the road to Trenton, but Mercer's men run into Mawhood's men marching south. A general engagement develops in which the Americans attempt to surround the British. After a hard fight, most of the British escape toward Trenton to rejoin Cornwallis, leaving Washington holding Princeton.

The Battle of Princeton
2 January 1777

MAWHOOD
1,200

Princeton

Stony Creek

MAWHOOD'S retreat

American pursuit

MERCER

Stony Creek

Pennington

Bear Swamp

Jacobs Creek

LESLIE
1,200

Eight Mile Creek

Quaker Road

Five Mile Creek

swamp

Post road

Shabbakonk

Miry Run

Creek

Maidenhead

CORNWALLIS
5,500

Delaware River

Sandtown

Hamilton Square

Trenton

N

MERCER

CADWALADER

WASHINGTON
5,000

American camp

GREENE

N E W   J E R S E Y

P E N N S Y L V A N I A

Ticonderoga and Hubbardton

George III awarded the Order of the Bath to Burgoyne for this victory at Fort Ticonderoga, but then took back this gift because he thought Burgoyne would rest on his laurels.

In 1777, British military plans envisaged General Burgoyne advancing south from Canada via Lake Champlain to capture Fort Ticonderoga, then to Albany. Meanwhile, Lieutenant Colonel Barry St. Leger was to march from Fort Oswego down the Mohawk River Valley in combination with General Howe advancing northward from New York. Thus, New England would be isolated from its Southern and Middle Colony allies and the war shortened in England's favor. This complicated plan, conceived by Burgoyne and approved by Lord George Germain, was never coordinated. Burgoyne was ordered to meet Howe at Albany, but Howe's operations up the Hudson were left to his discretion with dire consequences for England.

Burgoyne gathered his army at Cumberland Point on Lake Champlain. Poorly designed and ill-trained for fighting over harsh terrain, the force comprised nearly eight thousand men: three British brigades, and three Hessian brigades under Major-General Baron von Riedesel. Several hundred Indians and Canadians also joined. Encumbered by a huge baggage train, 138 artillery pieces and numerous women, including Baroness von Riedesel and her three children, this military force crawled towards Fort Ticonderoga.

The fort had been garrisoned by a small British force since it had been seized from the French during the Seven Years' War. In May 1775, Benedict Arnold and Ethan Allen with his Green Mountain Boys captured it in a surprise attack, and, in 1777, Ticonderoga was commanded by General Arthur St. Clair with 2,500 men. The British advanced down the western bank of Lake Champlain, the Germans on the east. Early July witnessed the British forces reaching the fort. Burgoyne realized that Mount Defiance overlooked the American fortification and saw it was undefended. Accordingly, General Phillips was placed in charge of cutting a road up the mountain and emplacing cannons and howitzers to enfilade the fort. St. Clair's men noticed activity on the crest of the mountain and guessed the British intent. Consequently, at night, on 5 July, St. Clair abandoned Ticonderoga and crossed Lake Champlain on a pontoon bridge to an American-occupied position on Mount Independence, which had held Riedesel's soldiers at Eagle Creek. The main American force

marched towards Hubbardton in Vermont, while four hundred sailed down the lake to Skenesboro.

When Burgoyne learned about the American escape, he dispatched light infantry and grenadiers under General Fraser to catch them. These 750 men caught the American rearguard under Colonel Seth Warner north of Hubbardton. The New Hampshire regiment, commanded by Colonel Nathan Hale, was overrun while taking breakfast. The remaining two American regiments took to the woods, built breastworks and field fortifications from logs and laid down defensive fire. Although British officers of the day considered American troops to be inadequate in the open, they showed a great respect for their forest-fighting techniques, which turned every tree into a bastion while they constantly sniped with muskets. One Hessian officer remarked how American troops sometimes loaded their weapons with several small and large bullets, which caused terrible wounds.

Fraser outflanked Warner cutting off his escape route to Castleton. When Warner saw Riedesel's Hessians arriving, he risked defeat so his men were ordered to disperse into the forests and meet at Manchester. Several American units eventually met at Fort Edward on the Hudson. Those Americans who had escaped from Ticonderoga by boat were caught by British gunboats at Skenesboro where equipment, artillery, and some prisoners were taken.

Burgoyne left a garrison at Fort Ticonderoga and advanced towards Saratoga but failed to take the easy route by Lake George to meet the wagon road to the Hudson. Instead, in total folly, he advanced over Wood Creek through woodlands towards Fort Ann after which the British had to cut a road through difficult ravined terrain and thick forest.

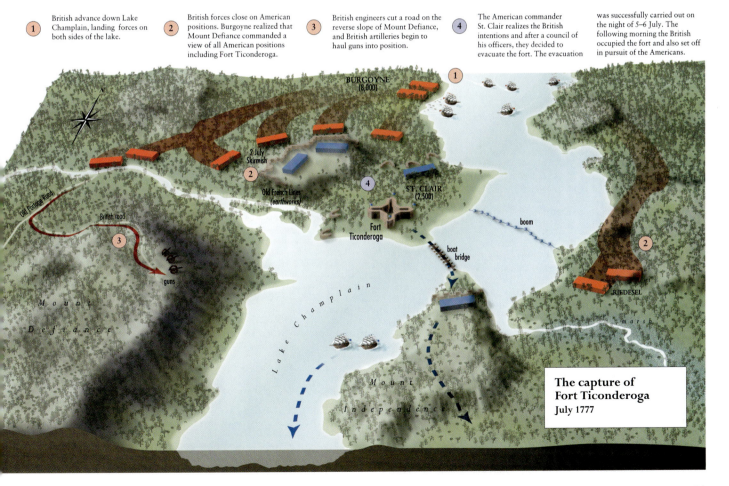

1 British advance down Lake Champlain, landing forces on both sides of the lake.

2 British forces close on American positions. Burgoyne realized that Mount Defiance commanded a view of all American positions including Fort Ticonderoga.

3 British engineers cut a road on the reverse slope of Mount Defiance, and British artilleries begin to haul guns into position.

4 The American commander St. Clair realizes the British intentions and after a council of his officers, they decided to evacuate the fort. The evacuation was successfully carried out on the night of 5–6 July. The following morning the British occupied the fort and also set off in pursuit of the Americans.

The capture of Fort Ticonderoga
July 1777

Oriskany and Fort Stanwix

**Oriskany and
Fort Stanwix**
August 1777

⚜ battle site

🏰 American fort

➤ American advance

➤ British advance

◼ American force

◼ British force

⋯ elevated ground

marshes

forest areas

Colonel Barry St. Leger with 800 British troops, Sir John Johnson with Canadian Loyalists and Joseph Brant with 800 Indians were to pour down the Mohawk Valley to meet Burgoyne and Howe at Albany. St. Leger landed at Oswego on 25 July with his mixed force and advanced on Fort Stanwix via Oneida Lake and Wood Creek. The fort guarded the portage between the creek and the Mohawk River. The British commander thought that Stanwix was unmanned and was disconcerted to find it occupied by Colonel Peter Gansevoort with 750 Continentals. The Americans refused to surrender and after St. Leger's artillery failed to breach the walls the British forces laid siege to the fort.

Colonel Nicolas Herkimer, commander of the Tryon County militia, learned of St. Leger's position and gathered his men at Fort Dayton and advanced towards Fort Stanwix. Many of St. Leger's troops had returned to Wood Creek to

construct a cleared route back to Lake Oneida, when news of Herkimer's approach reached the British. Accordingly, Joseph Brant and some 400 Indians and Tories were dispatched to ambush Herkimer at Battle Brook, six miles from Stanwix. Brant assaulted the 800 colonial militia in a narrow ravine. The action was intense and raged for hours. Herkimer suffered heavy casualties after marching into the trap, despite the use of Oneida scouts. Attacked from all

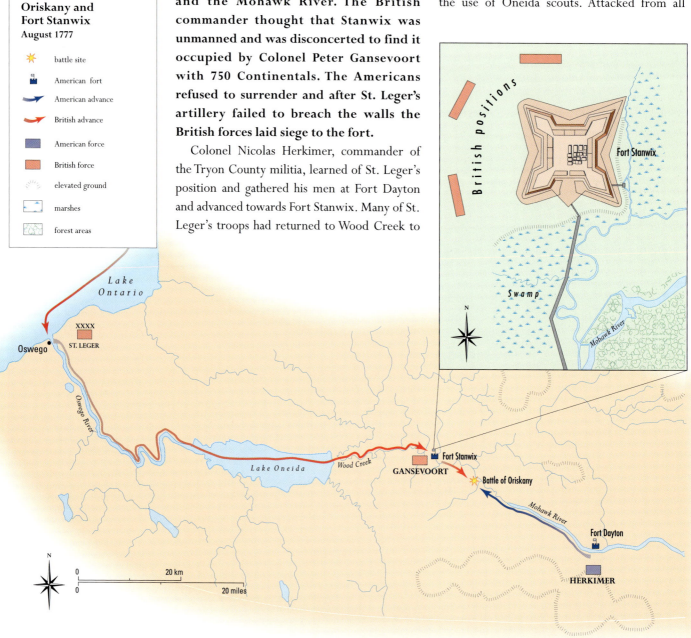

sides, the Americans formed a circle and vigorously defended themselves. Brant was reinforced by British troops and Herkimer welcomed a relief column from Stanwix. The fighting grew harsher and only slowed down at 11 A.M. because of rain. When the weather improved, the action moved in favor of the militia when Herkimer changed tactics. Normally, after a militiaman discharged his muskets, the Indians would rush forward and kill him before he reloaded. Now men fought in pairs with one man guarding the other. The British hoped to deceive and infiltrate the militia by sending in a Loyalist unit with their coats turned inside out, but this ruse was detected. Six hours of hard fighting convinced Brant to retreat thereby forcing the Loyalists to disengage. The Americans lost 150 to 200 killed and some 50 wounded while the British allies lost at least 150. Arguably, in proportion to the numbers in combat, this Battle of Oriskany was the bloodiest and hardest fought action of the Revolution.

While the battle was taking place, Gansevoort ordered a sortie, led by Lieutenant Colonel Marius Willett, into the besiegers' camp, where his troops destroyed nearly all personal possessions and camp equipment. This upset Brant's Indians who had fought so hard. Although the Americans survived the ambush, Herkimer was mortally wounded and failed to survive a leg amputation; casualties were so high that the militia column retreated, while St. Leger resumed the siege of Fort Stanwix.

The British commander was frustrated by Gansevoort's refusal to surrender and threatened a potential Indian massacre of any remaining garrison if the British managed to break in. Meanwhile, Willett left for reinforcements and met Benedict Arnold with a 900 to 1,000-man relief column. This force had been sent by General Schuyler who riskily depleted his own units facing Burgoyne at Fort Edward. St. Leger's Indian allies heard of Arnold's advance and, deceived by rumors and lies gathered from other Indians as to its strength, retreated. St. Leger was thus forced to decamp and retreat to Oswego. Burgoyne later blamed St. Leger's failure on the lack of Loyalist support, poor intelligence concerning the Stanwix garrison, and the behavior of the Indians.

1 Hearing of the American relief column under Herkimer, the British decided to send an ambush force of some 400 Indians, under Chief Joseph Brant, accompanied by a few Tories.

2 The ambush force attacked at 10 A.M. as the Americans passed through a ravine.

3 The Americans formed a defensive perimeter and put up a vigorous defense. The fight continued through rain squalls and by 11 A.M. the battle had swung in favor of the Americans. The Indian ambush force began to melt away, followed by the Tories. Both sides claimed victory; however, Herkimer's column was obliged to fall back.

The Battle of Oriskany
6 August 1777

Battle of the Brandywine

Part of the 1777 British war plan was for Howe to attack Philadelphia with the main British army while St. Leger and Burgoyne were attempting to isolate New England from the other colonies. Howe's operations were most peculiar. He waited for weeks in Spring and early Summer and engaged in pointless and unproductive maneuvers in New Jersey in an effort to tempt Washington into battle. Meanwhile, Washington was merely observing Howe while worrying about the nature of Burgoyne's northern expedition. Rather than marching directly upon Philadelphia which would have been quicker, on 22 July, Howe sailed from New York with 18,000 men in transports. It took them six weeks to reach the Chesapeake. This delay weakened his men and wasted supplies. When landed at the Head of the Elk, his

Howe ferried troops up the Elk River to the Head of the Elk, but it had taken two weeks to reach the Chesapeake, with temperatures in the 80s, with horses dying in vast numbers, and with the troops suffering from fever.

army was only forty miles nearer to Philadelphia than when he commenced his voyage.

Meanwhile, Washington sent reinforcements, led by Arnold and Morgan, to aid Schuyler against the British northern thrust. Washington's main task was to protect Philadelphia, because Congress was housed there and the city was performing the function of a capital. As Howe advanced, he was tormented by skirmishers at Elkton, Wilmington, and Cooch's Bridge between 28 August and 3 September before meeting Washington's army of 8,000 Continentals and 3,000 Pennsylvania militia at Brandywine Creek.

The subsequent battle highlighted the inadequacies of both Washington and Howe. The former left himself open to a flank attack, while Howe, never fully pressed home his advantages. Realizing that the Brandywine could be forded, Washington placed troops under Armstrong, Sullivan, and Stephen to guard Pyle's, Brinton's, and Painter's fords while Greene dug in at Chadd's Ford. Howe sent Lieutenant General von Knyphausen in a feint attack against Chadd's Ford and brought it under artillery fire. Washington was convinced that the main assault was occuring and continued to hold the banks of the Brandywine, despite contrary reports from a small American detachment under Hazen at Wister's Ford who saw a British flanking march. Howe and Cornwallis moved around the American right using Trimble's Ford to cross the West Branch of the Brandywine and Jeffrie's Ford on the East Branch. The British forces then occupied Osbourne's Hill, which overlooked the American position providing Howe with a magnificent opportunity to roll up the American divisions in detail. His hesitation allowed Sullivan, Stephen, and Stirling to swing around their troops into a defensive line at Battle Hill.

Howe attacked, some American troops under Sullivan collapsed, and Greene was ordered to reinforce Washington at Battle Hill. Marching four miles in forty-five minutes, Greene's men entered the fray and engaged in savage hand-to-hand conflict. Elsewhere, Knyphausen, seeing the reduction in American forces at Chadd's Ford, immediately assaulted the remaining part of Greene's troops there and routed them. Informed of this, Washington extracted his troops from the main battle and withdrew east to Chester. British casualties totalled some 600 while the Americans lost about 900 dead and wounded and 400 captured, but Washington retained an army in being.

Howe followed slowly clashing briefly with the Americans at Warren Tavern in the Battle of the Clouds and seized an enemy supply depot at Valley Forge. Washington suffered a further setback on 21 September when General Wayne's 1,500 men at Paoli Tavern endured a surprise and cruel night attack. Using a bayonet charge, the British killed and wounded 153 Americans, the rest fleeing. Howe and Washington sought to outmaneuver each other and the latter saw Howe countermarch his way across the Schuylkill River, which the Americans had viewed as a barrier. The British army then marched upon and occupied Philadelphia on 26 September. Congress fled to Lancaster and then New York, leaving Washington dictatorial powers.

The Battle of the Brandywine
11 September 1777

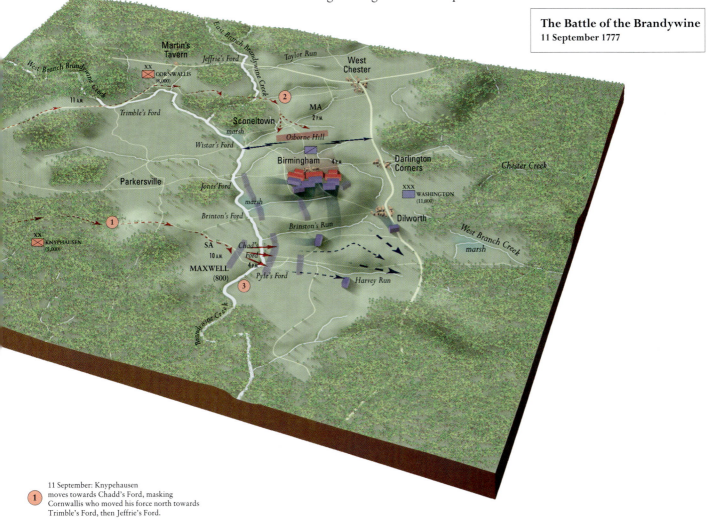

1 11 September: Knypehausen moves towards Chadd's Ford, masking Cornwallis who moved his force north towards Trimble's Ford, then Jeffrie's Ford.

2 At 2:00 P.M. Cornwallis' troops march over Osborne Hill confronted only by a small cavalry force. They brush this aside and push on to the settlement of Birmingham.

3 On hearing the clash of forces, Knypehausen launches his attack, capturing most of the American artillery. Facing increasing pressure on two fronts, Washington is obliged to withdraw.

Saratoga Campaign

General Gates (above) gained credit for the victory at Saratoga, but the groundwork for success was laid by Kosciuszko, a Polish volunteer, who selected the battleground and by the valour of Benedict Arnold and Daniel Morgan, and the militia officers who supplied him with a preponderance of manpower.

Burgoyne's troops comprised 650 Loyalists, 500 Indians, 3,000 Redcoats, 3,000 Germans, and a large artillery train. After taking Ticonderoga and leaving a garrison there, encumbered by a large baggage train and officers' families, the British struggled onward while the commander of the American northern army, General Schuyler destroyed all bridges, erected road blocks, created swamps by diverting streams, burned crops, subjected the advance to guerrilla attacks, and reduced British progress to one mile per day. One month was spent marching to Fort Edward.

Desperate for food, Burgoyne sent two detachments of Hessians, accompanied by Indian allies, to seize American stores at Bennington. Unknown to Baum, the Hessian commander of the forage column, Colonel John Stark was in the region with 1,500 men, who were added to Seth Warner's remnants from Hubbardton. Also these troops were enraged by the knowledge that Indian scouting parties had murdered and scalped Jane MacRae together with other women and children. The angry but inexperienced militia attacked Baum's force, which was dug in at the top of a hill. Stark planned a double envelopment while he assaulted the hill frontally. The Hessians held out until Baum was killed, and then they fled. Elsewhere, a relief column comprising Colonel Breymann with 600 men arrived too late to affect the situation, but a hard-fought engagement followed until Hessian ammunition ran low. Breymann retreated, but this was rapidly turned into a rout. Bennington was Burgoyne's first disaster with some 200 dead and 700 missing or captured. Stark became an immediate hero boosting American morale by the Bennington victory. Burgoyne's criticism of the Indians' behavior was so harsh that they left him.

Eventually, Burgoyne approached Saratoga but found his way blocked by General Gates who had built an entrenched position on Bemis Heights with some 7,000 men. Because Gates was receiving militia reinforcements daily, Burgoyne

found himself in a sensitive position. In New York, General Clinton failed to march north in support, a stain upon his military reputation, and St. Leger only reached Fort Stanwix placing it under siege. He soon abandoned this effort, retreating to Fort Oswego when faced by Benedict Arnold, and St. Leger lost his Indian allies after they heard exaggerated reports of Arnold's strength.

Burgoyne felt obliged to advance on Gates. Americans under Arnold and Morgan met the British center at Freeman's Farm on 19 September, where each side launched uncoordinated frontal attacks. However, unsupported by Gates, American riflemen sniped at British officers and when some Germans under Baron Riedesel outflanked the Americans, they retired leaving the British holding the battlefield but with 600 lost compared to 300 Americans. Burgoyne later wrote, "Few actions have been characterized by more obstinacy in attack or defense. The British bayonet was repeatedly tried ineffectually."

Despite falling morale, depleted supplies, and desertions, Burgoyne refused to retreat and attempted to force Gate's position on Bemis Heights. On 7 October, some 6,000 British troops attacked Gates who had over 11,000 effective soldiers. Elsewhere, General Clinton, commanding New York in Howe's absence, advanced up the Hudson with 4,000 men and captured Forts Clinton and Montgomery. He considered this sufficient support for Burgoyne. Inspired by a wounded and fearless Arnold, the British were repulsed losing 600 men and several important officers. The demoralized British retreated leaving their wounded, guns, and baggage, but, being surrounded by 20,000 converging American troops, failed to get far. On 17 October, Burgoyne surrendered agreeing that his army would no longer serve in the war. The American success at Saratoga induced France to enter the war against Britain; Spain and Holland soon followed creating a worldwide war. The Saratoga disaster caused the British to evacuate Ticonderoga and Crown Point together with the Hudson highlands.

Battle of Freeman's Farm, 19 September 1777

Battle of Bemis Heights, 7 October 1777

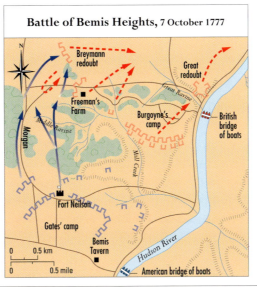

Saratoga Campaign
19 Sept. – 17 Oct. 1777

- British advance
- U.S. advance
- British withdrawal
- British fortification
- U.S. fortification
- battle (U.S. victory)

1   3 August 1777: beginning of siege by
St. Leger.
6 August 1777: Battle of Oriskany.
22 August 1777: St. Leger retreats to
Fort Oswego.

2   17 October 1777: surrounded by an
overwhelming American force Burgoyne
surrenders.

American troops emerge from dense woodland to successfully confront Burgoyne's British regulars.

Battle of Germantown

Although Washington was disappointed at the loss of Philadelphia, his troops were building their confidence and he could always refill his ranks, despite loss. Howe, on the other hand, awaited reinforcements from abroad. Additionally, once Philadelphia was captured, Howe had to stretch his resources to defend the city before mounting any new campaigns. Furthermore, Forts Mercer and Mifflin could interdict his supply route on the Delaware.

Howe's main camp lay around Germantown, five miles from Philadelphia, and it was vulnerable to attack. Washington had 13,000 men and decided to execute a complicated assault plan. Four separate columns would march at night to reach their start points simultaneously, a particularly difficult operation given the communication methods of the day. A Maryland militia column on the extreme left never arrived because its commander, General Smallwood, failed to understand his orders. The extreme right flank was covered by General Armstrong's Pennsylvania militia which advanced to the confluence of the Schuylkill River and Wissahickson Creek. Armstrong shelled Knyphausen's camp in a desultory fashion, but his troops failed to advance further. The attack was, therefore, carried out by a column on the right, led by Sullivan, accompanied by Conway and Wayne, with Stirling commanding his reserves; the left column, led by Greene, incorporated Stephen's and MacDougall's divisions.

While approaching the British camp, Washington bumped into British light infantry, which stood its ground before being routed. One British regiment shielded itself in Chew House but was savagely attacked by one of Stirling's brigades led by Maxwell. A staunch and successful defense cost the Americans dearly. Washington was unaware of his militia's failure to implement their orders and allowed Wayne to push back the British fast. Meanwhile,

Greene's column arrived to join the battle and it crashed into the rear of Wayne's men. A drunken General Stephen ordered his troops to fire and Wayne's troops replied in self-defense. The British troops seized this opportunity to counterattack and Wayne's forces were pushed back with Sullivan's to collect Maxwell at Chew House and retreat. Greene continued his forward move but was soon compelled to withdraw when his advance-guard suffered two flank attacks. The battle cost Washington some 650 dead and wounded with 483 captured; Howe reported 537 dead, but the numbers might have been more. Washington and Howe recognized that the battle was hard fought and close. More importantly, American forces had fought in the open and the Continental's spirited attacks held and forced the Redcoats to retire at one stage. The battle showed the French how Washington was alert to military opportunities and demonstrated how America could be a useful ally against the British when a Franco-British conflict began on 17 June 1778. General Stephen was court-martialed and replaced by the Marquis de Lafayette. Howe shortened his lines and sought to clear the Delaware to succor Philadelphia ready for winter. Forts Mercer and Mifflin and sundry warships blocked the river. An attack on Fort Mercer by von Donop left him dead with 400 other casualties. Eventually, British artillery

Greene stood 5 feet 10 inches tall with a squint and suffered from asthma. A damaged knee made him walk strangely, so his troops called him "the Crab."

PHILADELPHIA

HOWE
9,000

bombardments ended the brave defense of the forts, which fell or were evacuated in this river campaign.

Meanwhile, Washington prepared to spend the winter at Valley Forge where he could reorganize his troops, replace his time-served Maryland and Virginia militias, and re-equip his troops. Valley Forge would allow him to observe and mask Howe in Philadelphia and prepare for a spring campaign. Furthermore, despite just adequate generalship, the American fighting spirit kept the war alive and an army intact. Britain was also shown that capturing important cities did not win a war.

1. The British encamped in and around Germantown discount the possibility of an American attack and do not entrench their positions.

2. The Americans under Washington's command approach in four separate columns.

3. Washington with the two central columns, assuming that all his forces have arrived, orders the attack to begin.

4. British units put up stubborn resistance to the advancing Americans causing them severe losses.

5. Elements of Greene's Corps arrive on the battlefield, and in the confusion created by fog and smoke Stevens' men open fire on Wayne's troops, who initially return fire, thinking the British have somehow gotten behind them.

6. Sensing the confusion in the American ranks, the British hold their retreat and organize a counterattack, driving the Americans off the field and pursuing them for about ten miles.

Before Howe reached Germantown, British light infantry and cavalry attacked Americans at the Battle of the Clouds on 16 September 1777.

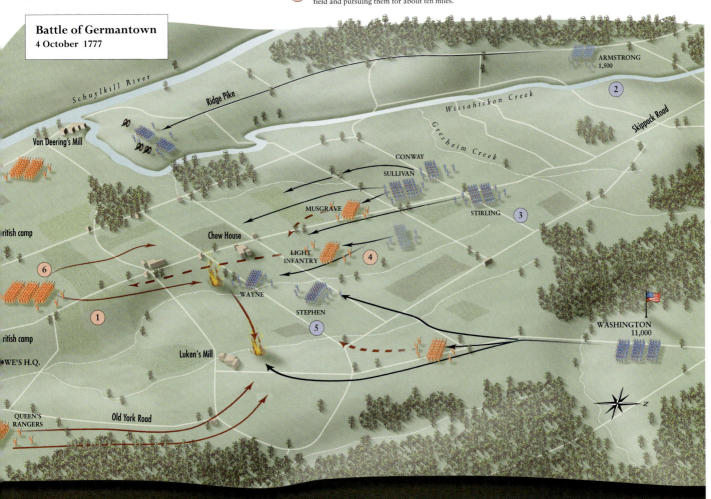

Battle of Germantown
4 October 1777

Northern Stalemate

After France entered the war, the American conflict became less important to Britain, which wished to defend its islands, protect its empire, and capture French sugar islands in the Caribbean. Fewer troops reached Howe and his successor, Clinton, and British strategies were

During the Northern Stalemate, Connecticut and Rhode Island lacked military support. They later chose to field a regiment of 138 African Americans, officered by Christopher Greene, and this unit saw action at Rhode Island, Yorktown, and Oswego.

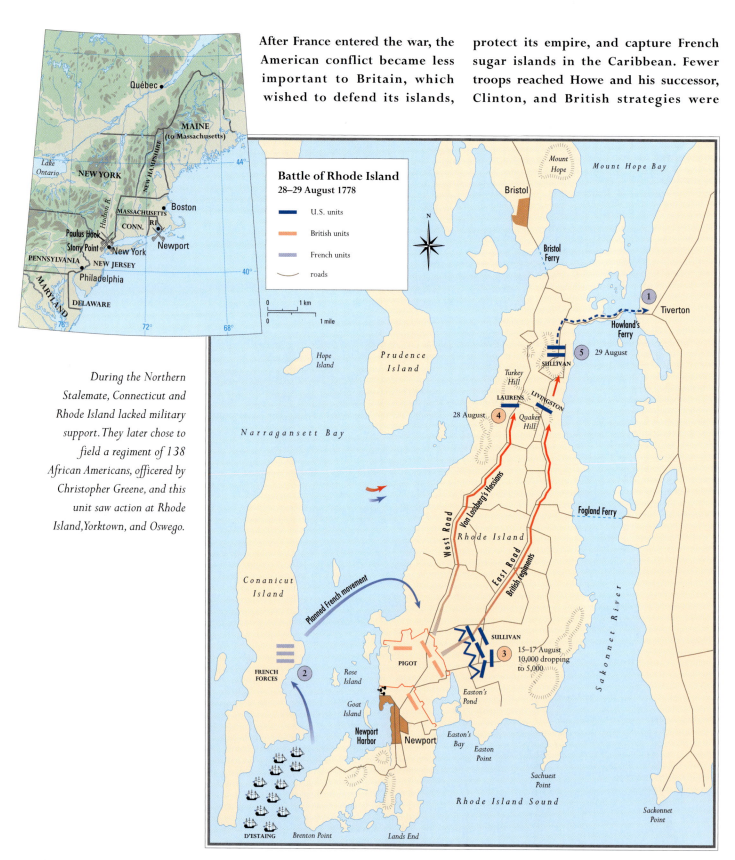

Battle of Rhode Island
28–29 August 1778

- U.S. units
- British units
- French units
- roads

compelled to change. **Amphibious raids would be made on the New England coasts, while military activity would shift south to be based in Savannah and Charleston which would also be nearer to operations in the West Indies.**

On 18 June 1778, Sir Henry Clinton marched his 13,000 troops from Philadelphia to New York. Washington observed the evacuation and pursued the British with equal forces, which had been toughened by von Steuben's training. The Americans waited for a favorable opportunity to attack. Harassed by skirmishers, especially Morgan's riflemen, Clinton was marching from Allentown to Middleton and arrived near Monmouth Courthouse. Here General Lee, returned after a prisoner exchange, attacked Cornwallis' rearguard but retreated for no sound reason. Washington stopped the retreat, and rallied Lee's forces until reinforcements could be inserted into a counterattack. A bloody fight ensued and Clinton withdrew north to Sandy Hook to replenish his supplies. The Continentals had proved themselves equal to British regulars in an engagement costing each side several hundred casualties. In July, Washington next blockaded Clinton in New York, while American forces were positioned at White Plains. Meanwhile, General Lee was courtmartialed and cashiered. From mid 1778 to 1781, the northern and middle states saw no major operations, but some fierce fighting continued.

In 1778, Loyalist and Indian guerrilla warfare was directed against Pennsylvania and New York and massacres occurred under Joseph Brant, the Johnsons and Sutters at Cherry Valley, Minnisink, and the Wyoming Valley. In 1779, Daniel Brodhead's expedition from Fort Pitt to attack Indian villages resulted in destroyed dwellings and crops, but the Indians were stirred to further raids against frontier communities. In August 1778, the French and Americans mounted a combined operation against Newport, Rhode Island. After landing French troops in Narragansett Bay, Admiral d'Estaing reembarked them and sailed his fleet to confront a

British force off the bay's entrance. Eventually, a gale damaged both fleets and the French admiral refused to reanchor in the bay lest he become trapped by the British and he sailed away. American troops, which had advanced the length of Rhode Island, retired in a fighting retreat with actions at the Battle of Rhode Island (28 August) and at Butts Hill (29 August) before leaving the island.

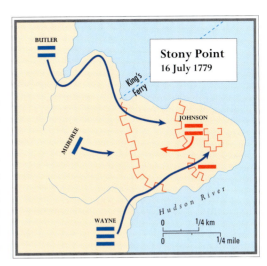

Stony Point
16 July 1779

On the lower Hudson, on 31 May 1779, the British seized the American outpost at Stony Point which guarded the ferry linking American forces in New York and New England. Washington ordered Brigadier General Wayne to lead his men in a nightime bayonet attack (16 July) through swamp and against fortifications. A thirty-minute fight witnessed 133 British casualties and the capture of 500. American losses were 95 killed and wounded. Thus, Wayne ended a potential threat to West Point, an important American fortress on the Hudson.

On 19 August, Major Henry "Lighthorse Harry" Lee asked Washington whether he might emulate Wayne by attacking Paulus Hook, a British strongpoint on the New Jersey shore of New York harbor. Given permission, Lee's troops stormed the fort inflicting fifty casualties on the British and taking 150 prisoners but only incurring five casualties. He then evacuated the point and retreated, leaving his prisoners, the magazine unexploded, and the cannon unspiked. However trivial the attack, any victory was a propaganda success in the Northern Stalemate and showed the British that any strongpoint could be surprised.

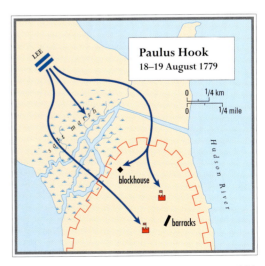

Paulus Hook
18–19 August 1779

Chapter Five
The Help of Foreign Friends

"He looks like a hero; he is very cold, speaks little, but is frank and courteous in manner; a tinge of melancholy affects his whole bearing, which is not unbecoming; on the contrary it renders him, more interesting…" Count Jean Axel de Fersen on Washington before meeting General Rochambeau, September 1780.

The outbreak of the American war gave France the chance to seek revenge for defeats suffered during the Seven Years' War. From 1776, the French supplied the colonies with surreptitious aid; for example, the first two years of the conflict witnessed America importing about 90 percent of gunpowder used, most of it from France. The June 1778 British defeat at Saratoga demonstrated American determination, and France was persuaded to enter the battle. June 1779 saw Spain gingerly joining France, chiefly activated by a desire to destroy British influence in the Gulf of Mexico and to capture Gibraltar. In 1780, the British government declared war on the Dutch Republic because that state had long traded with the colonies and had only just joined the Russian-inspired League of Armed Neutrality.

Each country possessed different war aims and these were not always synchronized with American ambitions. The French Foreign Minister Vergennes considered that the British economy and navy depended on the American trade monopoly and subsidizing the American Revolution would weaken Britain and tip the European balance of power in France's favour. French policy towards the Revolution developed slowly—prolonging the war would drain Britain. Accordingly, the French government loaned £40,000 to a private company, Roderigue Hortalez & Co., which would buy government arms and munitions at below-market prices. These supplies would then be sold on credit to America against the security of future tobacco crops. Spain was persuaded to provide matching funds. Between 1775 and 1778, France refilled its naval arsenals, repaired its fleet, and prepared to engage in combat with Britain and its navy. Diplomacy during these initial Revolutionary years was tense, with Britain angry over American privateers using French ports, and with America resentful at the expulsion of an American naval squadron (1777) from a French harbor to appease Britain. The eventual Treaty of Alliance and of Amity and Commerce (1778) was generous to the United States, recognizing their independence, and giving them most-favored-nation status in trade. France renounced claims to Canada but not Newfoundland and guaranteed American liberty, sovereignty, and independence

Lafayette was fascinated by the American struggle with Great Britain and genuinely believed in the cause of freedom. After fighting for America as a general officer he returned to France and made proposals for the Declaration of the Rights of Man and Citizen.

forever. France appeared to gain little except the opportunity to undermine Britain in Europe and the world.

Spain was a reluctant partner to the anti-British coalition. However, Governor Bernardo de Galvez of Louisiana provided America with gunpowder, but the Spanish Foreign Ministry under José de Moñino y Redondo, conde de Floridablanca, was uninterested in American independence. Spain chose not to wage war until Britain refused negotiations over the status of Gibraltar, and only then did Floridablanca sign the Treaty of Aranjuez (April 1779). France agreed to continue the war until Spain acquired Gibraltar, and, possibly, other territorial objectives in Florida and Minorca. Thus, Spain's entrance into the war turned it into a European conflict with global dimensions and moved its main theater to the Caribbean. In sum, the Spanish stand was incompatible with French agreements in the Americas, but France was constrained by requiring the addition of the Spanish navy to combat Britain. Spanish views of the American situation are best judged by the Spanish failure to recognize U.S. independence until after the war had ended, and 1783 witnessed a separate peace with Britain.

The Dutch position was self-inflicted. The Dutch government allowed its merchants to ship food and naval supplies to French ports where they were trans-shipped to America aboard French craft. The role of the Dutch West Indies as a warehouse for privateers and rebel trade also offended Britain. By 1780, British privateers were allowed to attack Dutch shipping and, finally, in December 1780, British naval vessels attacked Dutch merchantmen and war was declared. By 1781, the Dutch navy, despite its smallness, was essential to America, as British and French resources were stretched, and Spain virtually left the naval war. Holland could turn the North Sea into another theater of war and could attempt to interdict the British Baltic trade. The Dutch Republic benefited from being able to concentrate its fleet, designed for shallow waters, and the British navy could ill-afford to sail inshore to seek action. The Dutch relied on

Suffren to defend the republic's interests in Ceylon and their stubborn fighting abilities meant that British and Dutch fleets ignored each other after the drawn Battle of the Dogger Bank (August 1781). Had the Spanish or French fought with the commitment and ferocity of the Dutch, then the British navy would have experienced severe, if not insurmountable, difficulties. Britain was fortunate that the Dutch fleet never joined its allies in the Caribbean or the English Channel.

The involvement of France in the American Revolution coincided with the emergence of a British southern strategy. Lord Germain, the Colonial Secretary, believed that the South was a hotbed of Loyalism and that Britain could capture and hold the South with Loyalists taking over the roles of regular troops, releasing these for formal combat duty. Britain imagined that the South could be rolled up region by region and also the area was closer to the West Indian war theater. Germain and his advisors forgot that between 1776 and 1778, the South had been bedevilled by a savage guerrilla war between Loyalists and patriots. The British capture of Savannah (December 1778) and the repulse of a Franco-American assault (October 1779) were blows against independence, an inspiration to local Loyalists, and patriots' morale was diminished. American mutinies, caused by currency depreciation and supply deficiencies, broke out at West Point (1 January 1780), Morristown (Connecticut Line, 25 May 1780), Fort Stanwix (New York Line, June 1780), Morristown (Pennsylvania Line, January 1781), Pompton (New Jersey Line, January 1781), and Morristown again (May 1781), and further disheartened the Revolutionary cause. Added to the earlier treason of Benedict Arnold (September 1780), the 1779–80 period was a time of unmitigated disaster. The British capture of Charleston (May 1780), Tarleton's massacre of Buford's 3rd Virginia Continentals at Waxhaws, South Carolina (May 1780), Gates' disaster at the Battle of Camden (August 1780), and Tarleton's defeat of Sumter's guerrilla force at Fishing Creek merely accentuated American failure.

Despite 1780 being a disastrous year in the South, the North did bring some sunlight. Convinced that Washington was losing men, that the New Jersey economy was collapsing, and that Loyalists were waiting to rise up, General von Knyphausen dispatched 6,000 men from Staten Island to raid New Jersey to pin down American troops that might otherwise confront a desired Clinton raid into Virginia. However, local militia and Washington's Life Guard commenced

delaying tactics and eventually New Jersey militia arrived with the 3rd New Jersey Regiment and they harassed the British. Joined by the Pennsylvania and Connecticut Continental Brigades, the British were held and they returned to Elizabethtown on the way back to New York. Clinton returned to this city and planned a new raid on Springfield comprising 5,000 men under von Knyphausen. This force captured Springfield, but the American militia were incensed by the death of Mrs. Caldwell, a popular reverend's wife, allegedly at British hands. The American militia inflicted several hundred casualties and the British forces retreated. These two battles ended the northern campaigns but also demonstrated the strength of the militia when sufficiently aroused and motivated.

The years 1780–81 witnessed the turn of the tide. Ferguson's Loyalists were annihilated at King's Mountain (October 1780) and Tarleton smashed at Cowpens (January 1781). Thereafter, Greene's Fabian tactics and a war of attrition against Cornwallis saw British effectives decline in number after Guilford Courthouse (March 1781), Hobkirk's Hill (April 1781), and Eutaw Springs (September 1781). Greene succeeded in reducing British outposts and pushing the British into Savannah and Charleston. The military shadowboxing of Lafayette and Cornwallis in Virginia (May–July 1781) ended with the British fortifying themselves in Yorktown and surrendering in October 1781 after a classic siege, which was planned and executed by Rochambeau.

This French Lieutenant-General was an excellent diplomat, administrator, and soldier. Solving insurmountable resource and transport problems, he sailed from Brest and arrived in Newport, Rhode Island, on 11 July 1780 after a ten-week voyage. A tense episode in Franco-American relations commenced when Rochambeau ignored Washington's exhortation to attack New York and, instead, rebuilt the health and condition of his men after the debilitating voyage, and went into winter quarters. Previously, Admiral d'Estaing had invested Savannah (Autumn 1779) with Lincoln's Continentals and militia. Severe casualties after a forewarned assault and the fear of seasonal storms caused d'Estaing to sail away. American resentment grew rapidly at d'Estaing's attitude because even earlier he had left Sullivan in the lurch during the Franco-American expedition against Newport, Rhode Island (August 1778). There, fearful of the British fleet and suffering from storm damage, d'Estaing sailed for Boston and Sullivan was forced to evacuate Rhode Island in a fighting retreat. Hence, American views of the French commitment to the cause were somewhat jaundiced. Thereafter, Rochambeau, ever the diplomat, repaired Franco-American relations and cooperated with Washington, Lafayette, and Admiral de Grasse in surrounding and investing Yorktown.

Benedict Arnold's treachery has been

mentioned and, unlike Loyalists who had not shed their allegiance to King George III, Arnold's attempt to betray West Point to the British in September 1780 made him a most infamous and notorious figure. His bravery at Québec and during the Saratoga campaign do not compensate for his later behavior. Despite outstanding qualities of leadership, he could not readily negotiate with his peers nor could he reconcile himself to civilian authority. Arnold resented being passed over for promotion. Also, when he was military governor of Philadelphia, Arnold was tactless with other authorities and tended to speculate and therefore, perhaps, abuse power. Arnold later maintained that his treachery would end the war quickly and save America from the further destruction of war. After joining the British, Arnold led raids into Virginia, burned New London, massacred defenders at Fort Griswold, and won general American hatred. In December 1781, Arnold and his wife sailed to England. He was a liability to Britain. His attempt to raise a Loyalist force during the fall of 1781 helped increase the hostility towards Loyalists, despite the differences between them. Loyalists generally wished to continue under the government of Britain. Some saw aristocratic Americans controlling colonial assemblies as more unjust than overseas rule or saw them as responsible for most colonial problems. Loyalists were often found among large landowners and these often accepted traditional deference patterns of behavior. When Cornwallis entered Georgia and the Carolinas, he found that his continued presence was essential to preserve Loyalist political control. Once the British left a region, Loyalism collapsed because its adherents never managed to establish well-organized local committees or their own militia units.

In North Carolina, Highland Scots proved especially Loyalist and 1780–81 saw a savage civil war with major battles such as Ramsour's Mill (20 June 1780). Here, some 1,300 Loyalists faced about 1,200 patriots in two different units. A confused battle resulted in some 340 combined casualties. South Carolina Loyalists played a significant part in defending those southern outposts later captured by patriot forces during 1781. Likewise, Georgia witnessed partisan warfare, incited by a British presence. Georgia militia and Tories fought at Kettle Creek. Loyalist John Boyd's 350 South Carolinians joined 250 North Carolina Loyalists under John Moore. They faced Andrew Pickens in a messy and chaotic fight during which Boyd was mortally wounded, causing the Loyalists to panic and collapse. Eventually, the Loyalists lost some 169 men; the remnants which reached British lines were formed into the North Carolina Royal Volunteers under Moore and the South Carolina Royal Volunteers. Other parties of Loyalists were attacked and contained by the guerrilla forces of Marion, Sumter, and Pickens.

The Yorktown surrender and Greene's campaigns ended the major aspects of the war. However, some land operations continued between 1781 and 1783. Washington re-invested New York (November 1781), Rochambeau returned to Rhode Island and left for France in December 1782. Elsewhere, Greene secured the South but was too weak to take Charleston. The year 1782 saw the evacuations of Wilmington (January), Savannah (July), and Charleston (December) with the troops being concentrated at New York. They sailed for Britain on 4 December 1783. Further west, an Indian and Loyalist raid into Kentucky led by Caldwell and Simon Girty burned Bryan's Station and then those forces retreated. Pursued by 182 mounted militiamen, against the advice of Daniel Boone, the Americans were ambushed at Blue Licks. Seventy-seven militia were killed, including Boone's 21-year-old son, Israel. Such Indian conflicts continued until the Battle of the Thames in 1813, but Blue Licks (19 August 1782) is considered to be the last battle in the Revolutionary War.

Opposite: *When approaching the enemy, fleets formed a line of battle with each vessel a set distance from the next. This tactic could be used when fleets were sailing in parallel or approaching from opposite directions. When sailing in parallel, guns could be brought to bear for a long time period with ships supporting each other. Sailing in line was, however, a hindrance to initiative and only a very brave commander would violate Fighting Instructions and break formation to attack the enemy's line.*

Savannah and Charleston

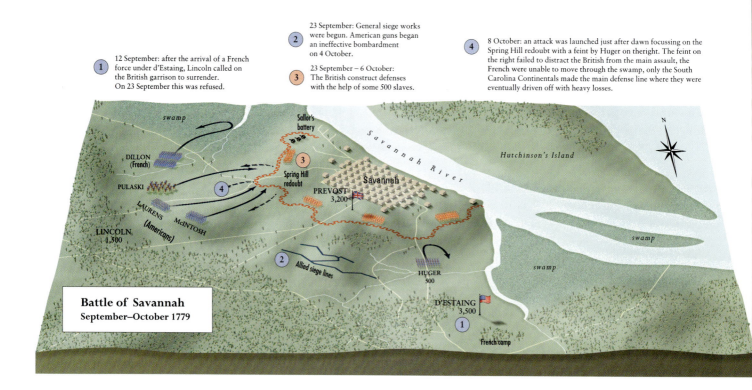

1 12 September: after the arrival of a French force under d'Estaing, Lincoln called on the British garrison to surrender. On 23 September this was refused.

2 23 September: General siege works were begun. American guns began an ineffective bombardment on 4 October.

3 23 September – 6 October: The British construct defenses with the help of some 500 slaves.

4 8 October: an attack was launched just after dawn focussing on the Spring Hill redoubt with a feint by Huger on theright. The feint on the right failed to distract the British from the main assault, the French were unable to move through the swamp, only the South Carolina Continentals made the main defense line where they were eventually driven off with heavy losses.

Battle of Savannah
September–October 1779

The French and Spanish declarations of war against England stretched British resources because troops were needed for operations in Florida and the West Indies. Clinton was induced to part with 5,000 soldiers who were sent to St. Lucia, and another 3,000 men who were dispatched to St. Augustine in Florida. However, this latter force, under Lieutenant Colonel Campbell landed at Savannah instead and defeated 1,000 American militia under General Robert Howe (29 December 1778). The British presence fanned Loyalist hopes, especially when Major General Augustine Prevost arrived from Florida and after Campbell seized Augusta, Georgia. Despite Moultrie repelling a British attack at Port Royal and Andrew Pickens' militia defeating a Loyalist brigade at Kettle Creek (14 February 1779), an American attempt to retake Augusta failed.

Prevost decided to capture Charleston, but Washington sent General Lincoln south with a force of Continentals and Prevost felt compelled to retreat and he regained Savannah after a successfully defended rearguard action at Stono Ferry (19 June). Savannah was now invested by Lincoln and troops landed by French Admiral d'Estaing (12 September). On 8 October, French and American troops attacked Savannah, but Prevost was forewarned and repulsed the allies who lost 828 killed and wounded. To Lincoln's annoyance, d'Estaing refused to continue the siege, embarked his troops, and made sail, while Lincoln returned to Charleston. The Savannah campaign persuaded the British that the Southern states would be a fruitful area to occupy because they believed that the population was heavily Loyalist; Germain agreed and sponsored future Southern operations. The Americans, however, knew differently but French behavior at Savannah as at Newport also taught them that the French were writing their own war script and American confidence in them dropped.

Despite failed attempts at taking Charleston in 1776 and 1779, Clinton was determined to take the city. British troops were withdrawn from Rhode Island, and after General von

Knyphausen was placed in command with 15,000 men at New York, Clinton sailed (26 December) to Charleston with 8,500 troops and a fleet of transports and warships. Dispersed and damaged by gales, Clinton's force finally landed thirty miles south of Charleston on 11 February 1780. Elsewhere, one ship containing 200 Hessians landed in Cornwall, England, blown there by the fierce winds. Clinton marched to James Island and seized Fort Johnson (6 March), and, after receiving reinforcements from New York, he crossed the Ashley River and commenced constructing siege lines in late March. British warships forced the passage past Fort Moultrie (Sullivan) and anchored in Charleston harbor. Despite forty cannons, probably all twenty-four-pounders, the fort only caused forty casualties and the loss of one foremast, apart from balls passing through a ship but doing no real damage. This was a poor showing compared with 1776 when two British ships went aground and a third set on fire.

The only possible way for Lincoln to retreat was up the Cooper River, which was defended by 500 cavalry under Huger at Monck's Corner. Tarleton's Loyalist Legion surprised this force capturing one hundred men and fifty wagon-loads of arms, ammunition, and clothes; he then guarded the north bank against escapees from Charleston. On 6 May, Fort Moultrie surrendered and Clinton asked Lincoln to surrender. A refusal engendered an artillery duel. American General Moultrie reported: "...it was a glorious sight, to see them (shells) like meteors crossing each other, and bursting in the air; it appeared as if the stars were tumbling down." On 12 May, Lincoln capitulated, surrendering 5,400 men, militia and Continentals, and weaponry, the worst American disaster of the war.

Sergeant Jasper replaces the flag over Fort Moultrie, previously shot away under heavy bombardment by the Royal Navy.

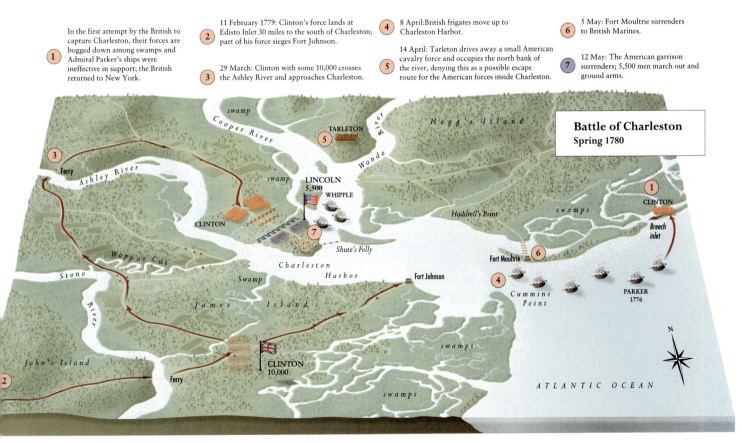

Battle of Camden

The fall of Charleston convinced General Clinton that South Carolina was in British hands and Loyalist Americans would help consolidate control. However, guerrilla bands led by Francis Marion, Thomas Sumter, and Andrew Pickens waged a hit-and-run campaign against small British outposts and the Carolinas fell into civil war after Clinton returned to New York.

A major British weapon was Lieutenant Colonel Tarleton's green-coated Legion of dragoons and light-infantry. They carried out many raids destroying American supplies, wagons, and men in "no quarter" warfare. His force caught 350 Virginia Continentals at Waxhaws in May 1780 and sabred all but one hundred. This butchery roused the countryside and bitter skirmishing continued all summer with partisans fighting Loyalists and British regulars. Actions took place at Ramseur's Mill (20 June), Williamson's Plantation (12 July), McDowell's Camp (15 July), Rocky Mount (1 August), and Hanging Rock (6 August). This last, hard-fought battle involved 800 Carolinian militia and 500 Loyalists who lost 200 men.

Meanwhile, Brigadier General Johann de Kalb collected 1,400 Continentals from Delaware and Maryland at Cox's Mill, North Carolina. Congress placed General Gates in overall command and he decided to attack the British 1,300-man garrison commanded by Lord Rawdon at Camden. Rather than marching along a safe route via Salisbury and Charlotte, Gates advanced across barren, Loyalist country without adequate provisions. Rawdon had been informed of Gates' movements and was reinforced by some 900 men, sent by Cornwallis from Charleston.

The American force witnessed desertions from the militia. Gates' men suffered from intense heat and sickness after eating green corn and unripe fruit. On arriving slightly north of Camden, Gates foolishly gave Thomas Sumter 400 men to attack a supply column moving towards the garrison. Cornwallis decided to advance towards Gates in a pre-emptive attack and the two forces collided with each other in the night. Each side pulled back and regrouped. Cornwallis commanded some 2,000 men, over half being Loyalist militia, and Gates led some 3,000 men.

Gates mistakenly placed his Virginia and North Carolina militia on the left opposite a British regular regiment. He obviously remembered militia valour during the Saratoga campaign. All the Continentals were placed on the right. When the British infantry advanced on the militia in the morning (16 August), panic ensued with the militia tossing aside loaded muskets and equipment and running. The American position was now exposed as the Redcoats wheeled into de Kalb's Continentals. These troops fought fiercely, stood firm, and were nearly annihilated. Baron de Kalb suffered eleven wounds and died three days later. This "most disgraceful defeat of the war" ruined Gates' reputation and he was replaced by General Nathanael Greene. Over 800 American dead and wounded and 1,000 prisoners gave Cornwallis a brilliant victory, which defended Camden, removed all Continentals from South Carolina, and laid North Carolina open for invasion. Tarleton's cavalry, after his attack on de Kalb, pursued American troops and met Sumter's force at Fishing Creek on 18 August killing 150 and taking 300 prisoners. Meanwhile, Gates had fled to Hillsborough after riding 180 miles in three and a half days.

On 8 September, Cornwallis left Camden

and marched towards Charlotte while being opposed by patriot guerrilla bands led by Davidson, Graham, and Davie, which attacked foraging parties, captured scouts, and cut off messengers. Cornwallis next invaded North Carolina sending a detachment to seize the port of Wilmington as a supply base and a force of Loyalist militia was placed to protect his left flank from attacks launched out of the mountains. Here, frontiersmen were assaulting Loyalist posts such as Thicketty Fort, Fair Forest Creek, and Musgrove's Mill.

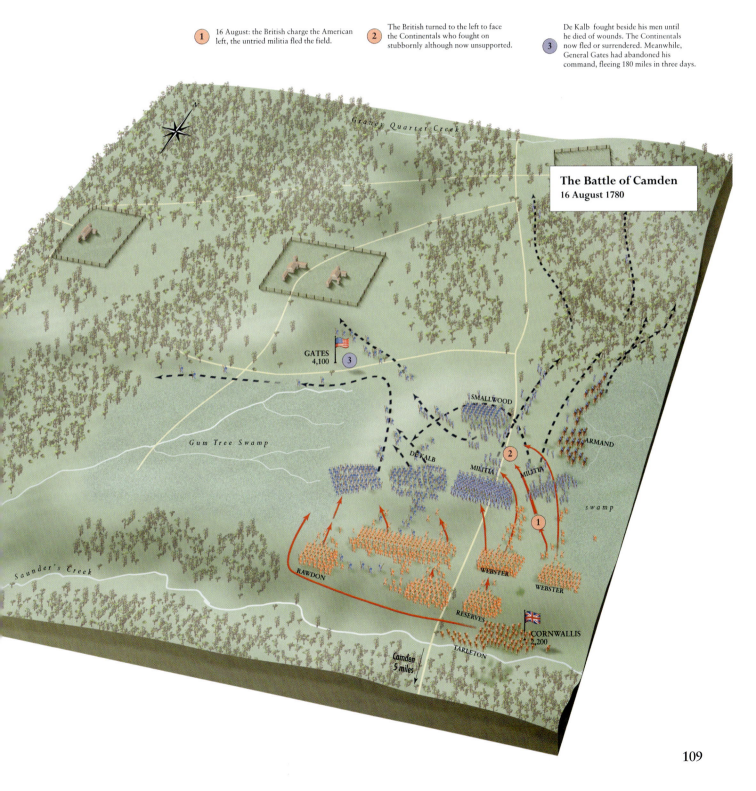

① 16 August: the British charge the American left, the untried militia fled the field.

② The British turned to the left to face the Continentals who fought on stubbornly although now unsupported.

③ De Kalb fought beside his men until he died of wounds. The Continentals now fled or surrendered. Meanwhile, General Gates had abandoned his command, fleeing 180 miles in three days.

The Battle of Camden
16 August 1780

Battle of King's Mountain

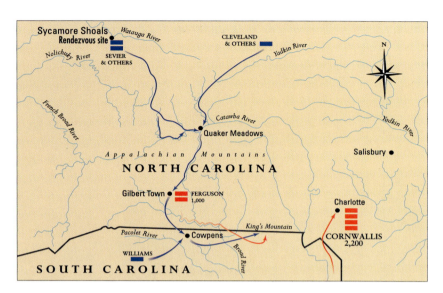

Cornwallis realized that the seizure and occupation of North Carolina could only be achieved by combatting American guerrilla bands and destroying any remaining Continental forces in the South. American soldiers were actually gathering in South Carolina and frontiersmen from over the mountains, commanded by Isaac Shelby, Elijah Clarke, and Charles McDowell, had conducted raids ending in that at Musgrove's Mill. Accordingly, Major Patrick Ferguson and his Loyalist force was to screen the British left flank and hopefully destroy patriot bands.

Ferguson was a firm believer in Loyalist militia and drilled and trained his men into a highly disciplined unit, which pursued the patriot frontier force to Gilbert Town. He issued a challenge that if these mountain men did not disperse, he would cross the mountains, hang their leaders, and burn their villages. Shelby and John Sevier, with other frontier leaders, agreed to a rendezvous at Sycamore Shoals on the Watauga River. Sevier and Shelby had 480 men drawn from what is now Tennessee and they were joined by William Campbell with 400 Virginians together with 350 from Wilkes and Surry Counties, North Carolina,

under Benjamin Cleaveland and Joseph Winston. Because of interpersonal North Carolinian rivalry, the Virginian, Campbell was given command. The force made its way over the mountains, collecting another 1,000 men from both Carolinas.

Ferguson withdrew towards Cornwallis at Charlotte and encamped on King's Mountain, a spur of the Blue Ridge Mountains. This hill rose some 60 feet above the surrounding terrain and comprised a plateau about 600 yards long and 70 to 120 yards wide. The camp was protected by steep, rocky, wooded sides making the mountain a veritable mini-fortress.

Campbell's men separated into various columns, intending to fight Ferguson from a variety of directions. The assault was to be conducted using wilderness battle techniques by using the trees as cover. This policy favored Campbell's men as they crept up the hillsides to attack the Loyalist red-coated militia from cover. An irregular but destructive fire frustrated Ferguson who launched bayonet charges against the Americans driving Campbell's personal column down the hill. A South Carolina Loyalist officer, Captain Alexander Chesney, later reported: "In this manner, the engagement was maintained for near an hour, the mountaineers flying when there was danger of being charged with the bayonet, and returning again as soon as the British detachment had faced about to repel another of their parties."

Ferguson ran from one danger point to another directing his troops by whistle signals. Attacked from eight different directions, Ferguson was surrounded, and eventually shot down by several musket balls. His second in command, Captain De Peyster, recognized his hopeless situation, and raised a white flag to surrender. However, some patriots continued to slaughter men who had dropped their weapons and raised their arms. Ferguson's force was destroyed with 157 dead, 163 wounded, and 698 captured. The mountain men suffered 28 killed and 64 wounded. This remarkable event was unusual in that all participants were Americans. Additionally, Cornwallis' timetable was disrupted and he decided to overwinter at Winnsborough, South Carolina, rather than attempt to continue any invasion of North Carolina. Campbell's victory encouraged rebellion in South Carolina and disheartened Loyalists. The British retreat was harassed by Davidson, Davie, and General Daniel Morgan. The victory proved that the Carolinians had the spirit to defend their states and provided the encouragement to appoint Greene to command the South. A more somber postscript was the trial of Loyalist officers for treason. Several were hanged and the grisly business only ended when rumors suggested that Tarleton was approaching on a rescue mission.

The American militia were normally expert marksmen and were often backwoodsmen experienced in Indian fighting. Some, known as minutemen, because they guaranteed to take up arms at a moment's notice, fought the Redcoats on the Lexington-Boston road.

1 7 October:
The Americans divided into small groups and advanced through thick woodland to surround Ferguson's force on King's Mountain.

2 Loyalist counterattack drove back Campbell's force several times; each time, the frontiersmen returned and opened fire on the loyalists.

3 Ferguson moved around encouraging his men until he was struck down and killed. After the loss of their commander, the loyalists lost heart and surrendered.

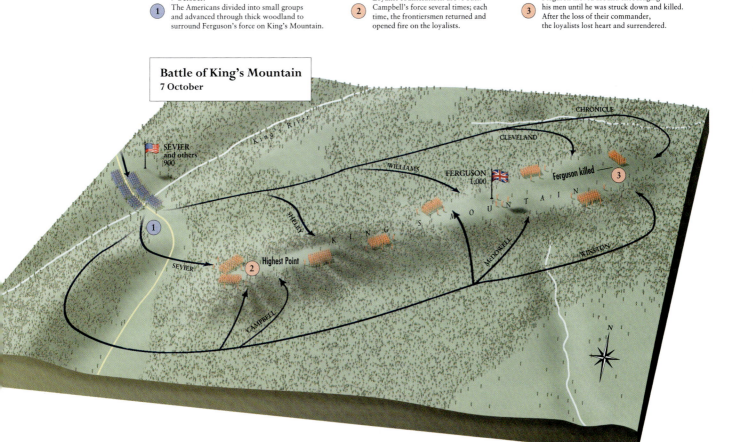

Battle of King's Mountain
7 October

Battle of Cowpens

When Nathanael Greene, a veteran of Trenton and Monmouth, assumed command of the southern forces at Charlotte, he found 1,482 men (949 Continentals), all poorly clothed and equipped. However, he was fortunate in his subordinates: Daniel Morgan, William Washington, "Light Horse Harry" Lee, and Thaddeus Kosciuszko. Kosciuszko, a Polish engineering officer, had surveyed the country widely and found that the army could be fed by crops along the Pee Dee River in South Carolina. After Greene had been reinforced by Washington, his forces grew to 3,000 men, while Cornwallis now possessed approximately 4,000 well-equipped and trained regulars.

Heavily outnumbered, Greene decided to adopt Fabian tactics and whittle down British numbers. He decided on aggression and split his forces: Greene went with General Huger and 1,100 men to Cheraw Hill, which placed him closer to Charleston than Cornwallis was. He intended to seek action in the eastern part of the Carolinas and threaten Lord Rawdon at Camden. He sent the rest under Morgan, with Washington's dragoons, to the Pacolet River in North Carolina. Greene's forces were 140 miles apart. Cornwallis responded by dispatching Tarleton with 1,100 men against Morgan while General Leslie was to observe and contain the American concentration at Cheraw Hill. Cornwallis followed Tarleton with his remaining troops.

Morgan established a position at Hannah's Cowpens with the Broad River at his back;

Banastre Tarleton, who had captured General Lee at Basking Ridge, was a vain, fairly unscrupulous but successful cavalry leader. He was well-known for a brutal streak; he butchered his enemies and broke in horses by lashing them with whips containing chunks of iron.

retreat would be impossible because the river could not be forded there. The militia would have to stand and fight. The American troops were disposed on a slope in three lines with a hill on the right and a fence to the left. The first rank was a militia skirmish line; the second comprised Andrew Pickens' Carolina and Georgia militia (with orders to fire three volleys and withdraw); and the third was formed of Maryland, Delaware, and Virginia Continentals and some experienced Virginia militia, under Howard. Washington's 120 dragoons were a reserve hidden by the crest of the hill.

Tarleton reached the Cowpens at 7 A.M. on 17 January 1781. His infantry advanced with dragoons on the flanks. The American skirmish line troubled Tarleton's Legion and the three militia volleys took a heavy toll, but when Pickens' force withdrew, Tarleton ordered his right-flank dragoon unit to attack, but they were charged in turn by Washington's dragoons and dispersed. Meanwhile, Tarleton pushed the Continentals hard, but when they appeared likely to break, Howard's Virginian militia launched a bayonet charge on the Legion, which were breaking ranks like an advancing mob. Simultaneously, Washington's regrouped dragoons attacked one flank and Pickens' reformed militia assaulted the other. This double envelopment, an American Cannae, cracked Tarleton's forces. They broke and fled and a final dragoon charge by Tarleton was driven off.

The victory was complete and devastating. Tarleton lost 100 killed and 700 captured, 200 of them being wounded. Taken, too, were 800 muskets, 100 horses, 35 wagons, and 2 cannons. Only 270 Legionnaires returned to Cornwallis who had now lost two important Loyalist forces at Cowpens and King's Mountain. Tarleton had lost his reputation and Greene had displayed qualities of a brilliant tactician. The

Americans lost twelve killed and sixty wounded.

Cornwallis pursued Morgan who retreated ninety miles to the Catawba River. Greene and Morgan reunited and retreated into southern Virginia, chased by the British who had destroyed their baggage to increase mobility and turn the entire force into light infantry. The Americans achieved safety after they had won the race to the Dan River and crossed it by boat leaving Cornwallis on the opposite bank 230 miles from supplies. Downcast, Cornwallis withdrew to Hillsborough.

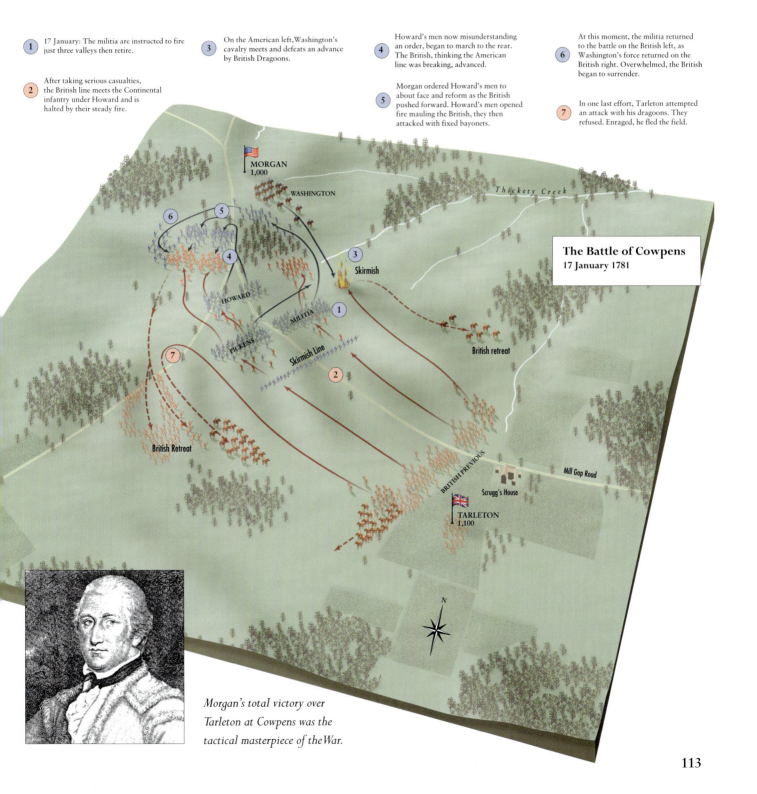

1 17 January: The militia are instructed to fire just three valleys then retire.

2 After taking serious casualties, the British line meets the Continental infantry under Howard and is halted by their steady fire.

3 On the American left, Washington's cavalry meets and defeats an advance by British Dragoons.

4 Howard's men now misunderstanding an order, began to march to the rear. The British, thinking the American line was breaking, advanced.

5 Morgan ordered Howard's men to about face and reform as the British pushed forward. Howard's men opened fire mauling the British, they then attacked with fixed bayonets.

6 At this moment, the militia returned to the battle on the British left, as Washington's force returned on the British right. Overwhelmed, the British began to surrender.

7 In one last effort, Tarleton attempted an attack with his dragoons. They refused. Enraged, he fled the field.

The Battle of Cowpens
17 January 1781

MORGAN
1,000

WASHINGTON

Thickety Creek

Skirmish

British retreat

HOWARD

MILITIA

PICKENS

Skirmish Line

British Retreat

Mill Gap Road

BRITISH PREVIOUS

Scrugg's House

TARLETON
1,100

N

Morgan's total victory over Tarleton at Cowpens was the tactical masterpiece of the War.

Guilford Courthouse

Opposite: The 1st Maryland and Kirkwood's Virginians fought the British Guards, Fusiliers, and Highlanders at close quarters and inflicted heavy casualties. Cornwallis was so worried that he ordered three-pounder cannons to be fired into the struggling troops thereby killing and wounding his own men as well as the Americans. The ploy helped the British extricate themselves from the fight, and they were able to reform faster than the Americans and the latter eventually retreated in good order.

In February 1781, Greene dispatched Lee's Legion and militia across the Dan to attack Tarleton, but they ran into a group of Loyalists under Dr. John Pyle and killed ninety of the Tories. On 23 February, Greene crossed the Dan and engaged in marching and countermarching with Cornwallis, which nearly ended in a battle at Reedy Ford Creek at Weizel's Mill. Early March witnessed reinforcements arriving, comprising 1,000 militia and 550 Continentals thereby increasing Greene's force to 4,400 men and he decided that the time had arrived to seek a confrontation. On 13 March, Greene moved to Guilford Courthouse, a small clearing in the wilderness, which lay near the Hillsborough-Guilford County road.

Greene used Morgan's Cowpens battle plan while awaiting Cornwallis. The ground sloped towards the west for nearly half a mile. On the crest of the slope, Greene placed the Delaware, Maryland, and Virginia Continentals. Some four hundred yards in front were Virginia militia led by Generals Stevens and Lawson. These soldiers were seasoned and stiffened by ex-Continentals and were regarded as steady under fire. They were placed in heavy woodland, while the first line of North Carolina militia under Butler and Eaton were stationed at the foot of the slope behind a rail fence at the edge of the wood. British troops would be forced at the outset to advance across some open, newly-plowed fields before fighting through the woods to the Courthouse. The American flanks were reinforced by riflemen and Lee and Washington's dragoons.

In early afternoon, on 15 March, the British crossed Little Horsepen Creek and advanced in formation, despite having just marched twelve miles. The Royal Welsh Fusiliers were the advance guard and received a volley from the rail fence at 150 yards. They marched through the fire until delivering their own volley at fifty

yards and then charged. The North Carolina militia broke through fear and because few had bayonets for hand-to-hand combat. Campbell's riflemen and "Light Horse Harry" Lee's Legion tried to steady them, but they were driven off the field by a Hessian regiment and were out of the battle. Close combat followed in the woods against the second American line where Steven's men offered determined resistance, but half an hour saw the British break through and storm ahead.

The British were faced by Huger's two Virginia and Williams's two Maryland Continental regiments. The First Maryland drove British Guards backwards with a close-range volley and bayonet charge, but the newly recruited Second Maryland broke and poured away into the woods after being attacked by the British Second Battalion of Guards. Disaster was prevented by a First Maryland flanking attack and by Washington's dragoons. Bitter fighting took place in heavy woodland where the British could not use bayonet charges and they were suffering severely. The British then commenced a cannonade to extricate their troops and both sides suffered from this fire. Greene saw gaps opening in his line and broke off the engagement, abandoned his guns, and retreated up Reedy Fork Road.

Cornwallis held the field, but his losses were reported as 93 dead, 413 wounded, and 26 missing as opposed to 79 Americans dead and 185 wounded. Cornwallis' victory cost him a quarter of his force and many officers. Victories like this would destroy his army. The British commenced a withdrawal to Wilmington while Greene reorganized his troops. British treatment of Americans on this retreat was harsh with much burning and plundering. However, several British garrisons remained isolated in the Carolinas. Next, Greene turned his attention to these outposts and started operations against them. He was helped by the guerrilla bands of Sumter, Marion, and Pickens.

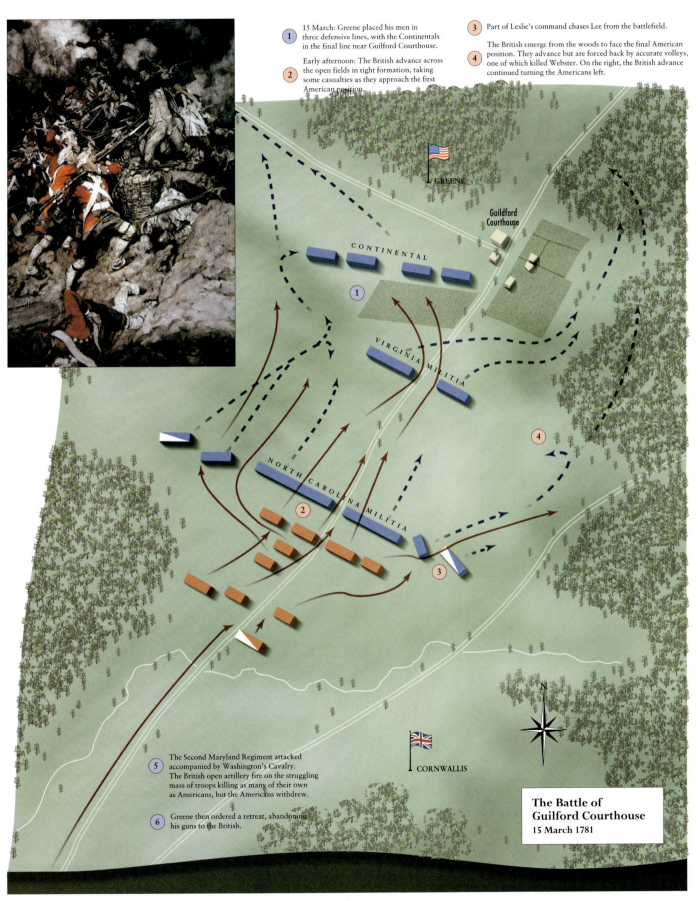

1　15 March: Greene placed his men in three defensive lines, with the Continentals in the final line near Guilford Courthouse.

2　Early afternoon: The British advance across the open fields in tight formation, taking some casualties as they approach the first American position.

3　Part of Leslie's command chases Lee from the battlefield.

4　The British emerge from the woods to face the final American position. They advance but are forced back by accurate volleys, one of which killed Webster. On the right, the British advance continued turning the Americans left.

GREENE

Guildford Courthouse

CONTINENTAL

VIRGINIA MILITIA

NORTH CAROLINA MILITIA

N

CORNWALLIS

5　The Second Maryland Regiment attacked accompanied by Washington's Cavalry. The British open artillery fire on the struggling mass of troops killing as many of their own as Americans, but the Americans withdrew.

6　Greene then ordered a retreat, abandoning his guns to the British.

The Battle of Guilford Courthouse
15 March 1781

Battle of Hobkirk's Hill

After Guilford Courthouse, Greene's forces decreased as militia enlistments expired. Lord Rawdon remained at Camden and had some 8,000 men scattered in outposts in South Carolina and Georgia. Cornwallis considered that Rawdon could mop up Greene's troops while he moved to Virginia, which he now saw as the key area to acquire to secure British victory. Cornwallis failed to recognize that Rawdon's forces were not only widely dispersed but were mainly Loyalists. The largest concentration was 900 men at Camden with Rawdon. Greene determined to excise these outposts and eradicate British occupation.

On 23 April 1781, Fort Watson fell to Lee's Legion and Francis Marion, while Greene advanced on Camden. Expected reinforcements from Sumter failed to materialize; nevertheless, Greene stationed his troops on Hobkirk's Hill, a mile and a half from Camden. American forces numbered some 1,200 Continentals, 250 militia, and 80 dragoons under Washington. The hill was a long narrow sandy ridge and Rawdon decided to attack this position. He gathered all available troops, doctors and convalescents, anyone who could carry a musket, and advanced on a narrow front to avoid detection. His troops struck the American picket line at about 10 A.M., disturbing Americans who were washing at a spring or cooking. However, the pickets bought time with furious fighting and Greene was able to place his Continentals in line.

Greene decided to launch a counterattack with a front overlapping Rawdon's. The British rapidly extended their line and caused great confusion in the First Maryland regiment by gunning down its right-hand company commander, Captain William Beaty. This company failed to advance further, thereby breaking the regimental line. Colonel John Gunby ordered the regiment to retire and reform. This endeavor failed because his force was hammered by the British and the retreating contagion spread to the Second Maryland regiment. This maneuver exposed the flanks of several other units and Greene was forced to order a withdrawal to avoid suffering heavy casualties. Ironically, he marched to the old Camden battlefield while Rawdon returned to his fortifications at Camden. The Americans lost 25 killed, 108 wounded, and 136 missing. Rawdon sustained 258 casualties of which 28 were killed. Although technically a British victory, Greene's forces remained intact and Rawdon evacuated Camden on 10 May retiring to Charleston, despite having received reinforcements on 7 May. Hobkirk's Hill signaled a British withdrawal from the South Carolina interior. Marion, Pickens, Lee, and Sumter campaigned against the remaining British forts and captured Orangeburg (10 May); Fort Motte (11 May); and Fort Watson, Fort Grunby, and Augusta (5 June). Only Fort Ninety-Six held out against Greene.

This thorn in Greene's side was placed under formal siege with batteries, trenches, mines, and sallies during the night in which Kosciuszko received a bayonet wound. The garrison suffered from lack of water, which slaves smuggled in camouflaged by night. A Loyalist rode under fire through the pickets to Rawdon requesting a relief force. The brave British defense caused Greene to raise the siege on 19 June. He also failed because Rawdon used three new regiments from Britain to relieve the post on 21 June. Soldiers died on the relief march because of the South Carolina heat. Any pursuit of Greene was impossible, and Rawdon evacuated the fortress. By August,

British forces could be found in Savannah and Charleston having gained nothing after an eighteen-month campaign. Rawdon fell ill and sailed for England leaving his command under Lieutenant Colonel Stewart. Rawdon was captured at sea by a French ship of the line.

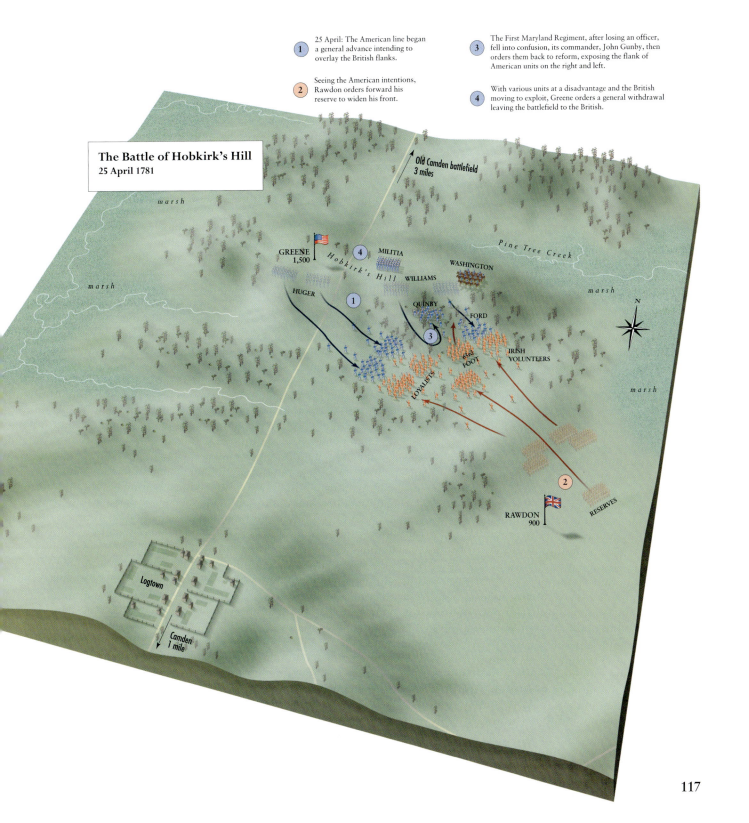

1 25 April: The American line began a general advance intending to overlay the British flanks.

2 Seeing the American intentions, Rawdon orders forward his reserve to widen his front.

3 The First Maryland Regiment, after losing an officer, fell into confusion, its commander, John Gunby, then orders them back to reform, exposing the flank of American units on the right and left.

4 With various units at a disadvantage and the British moving to exploit, Greene orders a general withdrawal leaving the battlefield to the British.

The Battle of Hobkirk's Hill
25 April 1781

Eutaw Springs

After Rawdon left, Stewart made camp at Eutaw Springs on the south bank of the Santee, fifty miles from Charleston. Meanwhile, Greene moved his troops into the High Hills of the Santee on the Wateree River south of Camden to

The Battle of Eutaw Springs was particularly bitter and bloody because deserters on both sides fought with utter desperation; capture meant death by hanging by either Greene or Stewart.

escape the heat and enervating climate. The Americans enjoyed six weeks of rest and then, on 22 August, Greene marched his 2,400 men, half of them Continentals, up the north bank of the Wateree, before crossing it at Camden. Pickens' militia joined him, and Greene advanced towards Eutaw. Stewart moved his entire force to the Springs to meet a provision convoy from Charleston. On his march, Greene incorporated South Carolina troops under Colonel Henderson, passed the Congaree River, and met Marion's militia brigade on 7 September, seven miles from Eutaw.

Stewart's force comprised some 2,000 men including the 63rd, 64th, and Buffs regiments. Greene advanced in secrecy and silence; Loyalist supporters had declined so much in numbers that Stewart received no word of the approach. Eventually, British troops, foraging for food, bumped into the American militia and were forced back to camp. However, the disturbance gave Stewart time to organize his troops with the Buffs on the right, Cruger's rescued Fort Ninety-Six troops in the center,

and the other regulars on the left.

Greene followed his normal policy of placing the militia under Pickens, Malmady, and Marion in the front line with the Continentals behind. The militia poured fire into the green troops of the Buffs, causing them to give way, but British bayonet charges restored the situation. The militia fought well, firing seventeen volleys before moving backward when Greene ordered forward General Sumner with three brigades of North Carolina Continentals. They rebuilt the American line but in turn succumbed to a British bayonet attack. Meanwhile, William Washington, who had attempted to pass his cavalry through the disordered Buffs, was wounded and captured. Greene met the advancing British regulars with his Maryland and Virginia troops and stemmed the tide and drove back the British to their camp. The Americans saw all the supplies and equipment left for the taking and commenced looting. Hungry and thirsty and after three hours of combat in extreme heat, the Americans found rum. Some British troops under Major Marjoribanks, who had been left untouched on the extreme right flank, moved his men behind a brick mansion in the camp and ambushed the looters, pushing them from the camp. The American army was now so disorganized and short of ammunition that Greene ordered a retreat in order to regroup; two cannons were left behind. Although technically beaten, Greene's force remained intact to fight again. However, he lost 138 dead, 375 wounded, and 41 missing, while Stewart lost 85 killed, 351 wounded, and 257 missing. Thus, Eutaw Springs was yet one more British Pyrrhic victory with the British losing irreplaceable troops. Stewart moved to Monck's Corner to care for his wounded, while Greene returned to the High Hills of the Santee. Eventually, Stewart sought sanctuary in Charleston, some fifty-five miles away. From that time, British and American armies in the South never met in battle, but the civil war continued until 1782. Although Greene had never won a battle, he managed to force back the British time and time again in a successful strategy. Eutaw Springs compelled the British and Loyalist allies to remain locked up in Charleston masked by Greene's army which was insufficient in size to besiege Charleston.

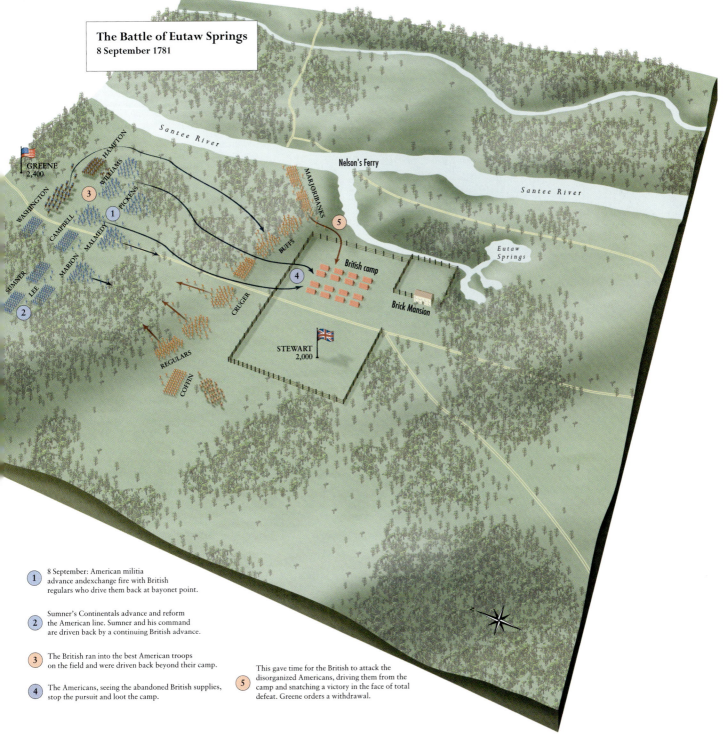

The Battle of Eutaw Springs
8 September 1781

1 8 September: American militia advance and exchange fire with British regulars who drive them back at bayonet point.

2 Sumner's Continentals advance and reform the American line. Sumner and his command are driven back by a continuing British advance.

3 The British ran into the best American troops on the field and were driven back beyond their camp.

4 The Americans, seeing the abandoned British supplies, stop the pursuit and loot the camp.

5 This gave time for the British to attack the disorganized Americans, driving them from the camp and snatching a victory in the face of total defeat. Greene orders a withdrawal.

Siege of Yorktown

Once Clinton had decided that Virginia was the key to victory in America, he ordered the American traitor, Benedict Arnold, to Hampton Roads to destroy stores, to rally Loyalists, and to prevent Greene from being reinforced. Arnold joined up with his new superior, Major General Phillips, and they proceded to destroy war materials and then linked up with Cornwallis who had marched from North Carolina. To counter their depredations, Washington sent Lafayette to a devastated Richmond. His 3,350 men were reinforced by Wayne and 1,000 Pennsylvania Continentals followed by Campbell's 600 riflemen, but his numbers were inferior to those of Cornwallis.

armies in New York and Virginia could be cut and American and French troops linked and focused on one British army, then victory was possible.

A message was sent to Admiral de Grasse in the West Indies; he sailed to Yorktown, disembarked 3,000 troops thereby reinforcing Lafayette (30 August). A British fleet led by Admiral Graves arrived off Chesapeake Bay from New York. The subsequent naval Battle of the Capes (5–9 September) forced Graves away after more French ships arrived from Newport bringing siege artillery with them. The local French command of the sea meant that Cornwallis was doomed. Meanwhile, on 21 August, Washington and Rochambeau marched south with some troops being carried by sea and arrived at Williamsburg between 14 and 26 September.

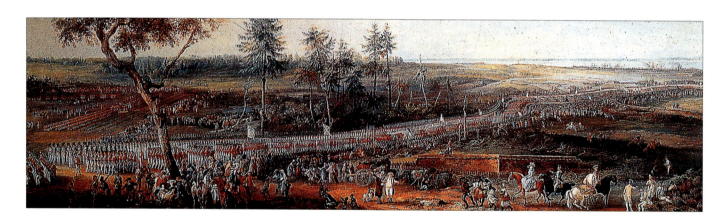

The surrendering British stared at the French as if the French had been victorious, so Lafayette ordered American bands to play "Yankee Doodle" to attract British attention to the fact that the ragged and dirty American army had also beaten them.

The British pursued Lafayette and much indecisive maneuvering ensued from May to July 1781. Clinton finally ordered Cornwallis to return 3,000 troops to New York because Clinton was convinced that an impending meeting of Washington's New York army and Rochambeau's 4,000 French troops in Newport would be aimed at New York. Cornwallis obligingly marched towards Portsmouth and at Jamestown Ford (6 July) nearly destroyed a 500-man force led by Wayne who hoped to harass the British rearguard. When Clinton rescinded his orders, Cornwallis concentrated his forces at Yorktown on 4 August. Lafayette moved his army to West Point to observe and mask the British. Meanwhile, Rochambeau and Washington concluded that if the sea communications between the British

The investment of Yorktown by Washington with 9,000 Americans and 7,800 well-equipped French regulars who together faced Cornwallis' 8,000 troops took place on 28 September 1781. The British prepared their defenses to receive fire from the new French Gribeauval artillery with its great accuracy, mobility, and punch. Washington also sent a force under de Choissey to Gloucester Point to observe Tarleton's 700 men there. Cornwallis believed that he would be relieved and preferred to give up his outer fortifications than fight. The allies advanced parallel trenches and during this process, on 14 October, two redoubts were successfully stormed by Franco-American forces and the American second parallel was extended to take in these points. The British counterattacked (16 August) under General Abercromby who took a few prisoners and spiked six guns, but this action was ineffective. Cornwallis was faced with the destruction of his fortifications, smallpox, and casualties. A plan to evacuate some troops to Gloucester Point came to nought when his boats were scattered in a storm. Surrounded, outgunned, and short of food and ammunition, Cornwallis surrendered his 8,000 men and 240 guns on 19 October 1781. Five days later, Clinton arrived at the Chesapeake with 7,000 reinforcements, but the presence of de Grasse's fleet sent him back to New York. Meanwhile, Cornwallis and his troops marched out of Yorktown to the tune of "The World Turned Upside Down" to be interned in the Virginian interior. Washington then returned his army to observe Clinton in New York.

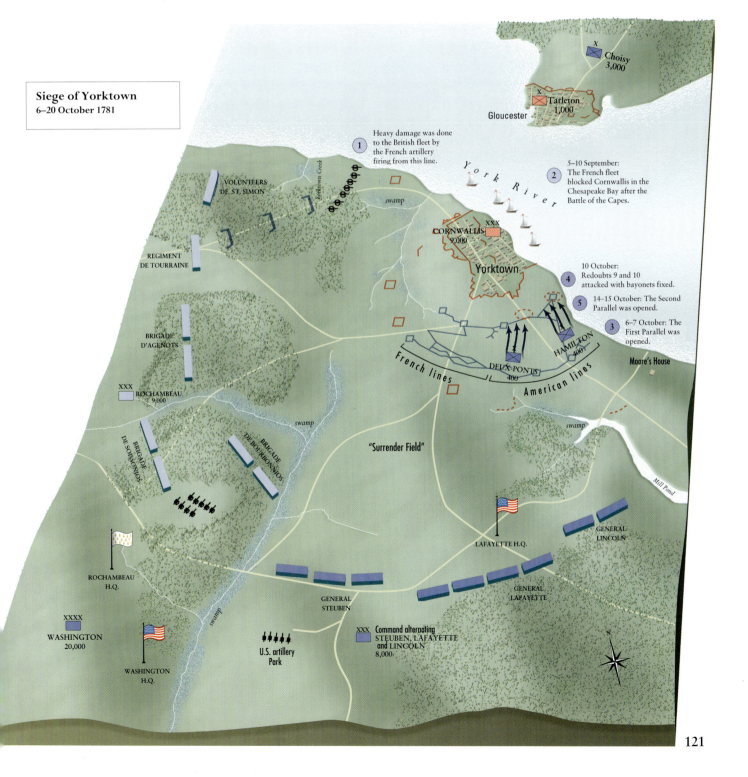

Siege of Yorktown
6–20 October 1781

1 Heavy damage was done to the British fleet by the French artillery firing from this line.

2 5–10 September: The French fleet blocked Cornwallis in the Chesapeake Bay after the Battle of the Capes.

4 10 October: Redoubts 9 and 10 attacked with bayonets fixed.

5 14–15 October: The Second Parallel was opened.

3 6–7 October: The First Parallel was opened.

CHOISY 3,000

TARLETON 1,000

Gloucester

York River

CORNWALLIS 9,000

Yorktown

Moore's House

HAMILTON 400

DEUX-PONTS 400

French lines

American lines

VOLUNTEERS DE ST. SIMON

REGIMENT DE TOURRAINE

BRIGADE D'AGENOTS

ROCHAMBEAU 9,000

BRIGADE DE SOISSONOIS

BRIGADE DE BOURBONNIOS

"Surrender Field"

Mill Pond

LAFAYETTE H.Q.

GENERAL LINCOLN

GENERAL LAFAYETTE

ROCHAMBEAU H.Q.

WASHINGTON 20,000

WASHINGTON H.Q.

U.S. artillery Park

GENERAL STEUBEN

Command alternating STEUBEN, LAFAYETTE and LINCOLN 8,000

Chapter Six
War at Sea

"In any operation and under all circumstances a decisive naval superiority is to be considered as a fundamental principle, and the basis upon which every hope of success must ultimately depend." Washington to Lafayette.

"Black Dick" Howe pursued war more efficiently than most British naval commanders. He became First Lord of the Admiralty at the end of the American war. In 1794, he won the Glorious First of June against the French and helped settle the 1787 Spithead Mutiny during the French Revolutionary Wars.

The war at sea changed its characteristics during the Revolution. In the early stages, when the conflict was purely Anglo-American, the British held the mastery of the seas in that the Royal Navy's line of battle remained unchallenged. However, American state navies and privateers could provide a severe challenge to trade and stretch British resources. In 1778, the British edge deteriorated after the French entered the fray. Despite the French navy being smaller than the British, its admirals, such as de Grasse and Suffren, posed intense threats to Britain. In 1779, Spain joined France and the total naval balance, in numbers but not necessarily quality, was overturned. Britain's position was further

weakened when Holland joined France and Spain in 1781. However, although outnumbered after 1778, Britain seldom lost local naval superiority except before Yorktown, a crucial situation benefiting Washington and Rochambeau in their march to Yorktown and their reinforcement of Lafayette in surrounding Cornwallis. Elsewhere, Britain, either through plan or accident, managed to defeat small enemy squadrons piecemeal: at Ushant, Cape St. Vincent, the Dogger Bank, and Ushant again. Only at the end of the war were British logistics stretched to breaking point, but they managed to continue to finance the huge global struggle because of a superior taxation and credit system. France slipped into financial collapse and revolution in 1789, partially as a result of the enormous costs of the Seven Years' War and the American Revolution.

When war commenced, as usual, the British navy had been neglected, since 1763, thereby preventing the mounting of an effective blockade of the American coast. The navy was brought out of peacetime mothballs and plans were laid for its augmentation. The navy required large numbers of small vessels, especially frigates, to probe the vast American coastline. As a result, Britain was largely denuded of small ships in home waters. A further burden on the fleets in American waters lay in supporting the British army ashore. Consequently, the navy could never interdict enough blockade runners, indulge in enough amphibious operations, or exert its influence inland. An idea of the British naval building program can be seen in the following numbers of vessels, remembering that captured enemy ships were often brought into the British navy. In 1775, Britain possessed 131 ships of the line, increasing to 174 in 1783; not all ships would be on active service. Fourth rates (56 guns) downward numbered 139, eventually reaching 304 at the war's end. Of these, the largest increases took place in 44-gun frigates (4–28), 32-gun frigates (35–59), 28-gun frigates (24–33), and sloops, 18-guns or fewer (38–85). However, as stated, not all vessels were in active service. Hence, the British 174 ships of the line could be reduced to 94 in 1783.

Ironically, the French navy was in good condition after losing half of its fleet during the Seven Years' War. A new fleet was constructed or rebuilt and entered the Revolutionary War in fine condition. However, constant losses and difficulties in replacement weakened the French. Despite French advantages in ship design, the general quality of seamanship was inferior to the British. The French developed three deck ships to increase firepower and upgraded their frigates' broadsides compelling other nations to copy them. The Spanish fleet was well-designed and possessed numerous warships, but they were generally under-gunned and under-crewed. The fleet's only virtue lay in bolstering and unifying with French fleets or causing the British to blockade even more European ports. The Dutch fleet was even less formidable, but it fought stubbornly and stretched the British further. The following table compares the size of the various fleets (active) over time, but the figures include only two categories for simplicity: 70 guns and over and fewer than 70 guns.

Naval statistics

		1778	1779	1780	1781	1782
Britain	(>70)	35	50	59	57	55
	(<70)	29	40	42	37	39
France	(>70)	28	38	44	44	47
	(<70)	24	25	25	26	26
Spain	(>70)	—	50	40	45	43
	(<70)	—	8	8	9	—
Dutch	(>70)	—	—	?	1	1
	(<70)	—	—	11	13	18

The American Continental Navy barely existed and played no real part in the war aside from the occasional small ship action. However, three 74-gun ships and five 36-gun frigates were laid down and the ships converted to large frigates after the war. The most well-known victory was that of John Paul Jones in the *Bonhomme Richard* against the far superior HMS *Serapis*. To counter this success was the fiasco at Penobscot Bay, now Maine, then Massachusetts. U.S. Commodore Saltonstall sailed three Continental ships plus forty Massachusetts Navy and private ships with 1,000 militia to drive away from the Bay a two regiment British occupation force. Vacillation and conflict between the Commodore and the militia leader, Lovell, achieved little. One American attack by 250 men was dispersed by 55 Redcoats firing one volley. American failure to try a naval attack against the three British ships there was further thwarted by a British naval relief force, which destroyed all American vessels or forced them to run aground and be burned. The ineptitude in not coordinating the amphibious force showed the difficulty of joint command and lack of planning. Saltonstall was court-martialed, found guilty, and dismissed from the service.

Any attempt to categorize ships of the period is difficult. Designations according to the number and weight of guns were largely meaningless by 1775. Generally, the workhorse of all fleets was the 74-gun of the line, with twenty-eight 32-pounders, thirty 24-pounders, and sixteen 9-pounders. The standard frigate (32 guns) possessed twenty-six 12-pounders and six 6-pounders. Sloops (corvettes in France) could be armed with twenty-two or twenty 9-pounders, but sometimes as few as fourteen 6-pounders. Other vessels existed such as brig-sloops, brigantines, brigs, cutters, and schooners; in America, a schooner would be a full-fledged ship, whereas in Britain it would be scarcely larger than a yacht and would be used as a postal vessel or the eye of a fleet. A novel British invention was the carronade operated on a slide rather than with wheels. Short-ranged (300–400 yards), some fired 56-pound shot filled with grape, which were devastating at close range, especially if fired through a ship's stern into a close-packed gun deck. Guns were used in a variety of ways. The British preferred close ship action where they fired into the hull seeking to dismount guns or to kill as many of the enemy as possible. Hull shots would cause splinter wounds which could kill, or the wounds might become infected with gangrene. The French tended to fire chain and bar-shot and langrage (case shot containing irregular pieces of iron) into the rigging hoping to damage yards and cordage, thus rendering an enemy vulnerable to have the bow or stern crossed with shot tearing the

"Every officer in our navy should know by heart the deeds of John Paul Jones. . . . should feel in each fiber of his being an eager desire to emulate the energy, the professional capacity, the indomitable determination and dauntless sole of John Paul Jones. . . ."
Theodore Roosevelt, April 1906.

length of the vessel; the threat of such a maneuver could also occasion surrender. Grape shot was used by either side to destroy enemy boarding parties or to clear part of an enemy deck prior to boarding.

Many historians have passed comment on the way British and French admirals commanded their fleets. According to regular British Fighting Instructions, fleets should sail in line of battle and approach the enemy sailing parallel or similarly from an approaching opposite position. This tactic would result in a slogging match and the fleet possessing the heavier broadsides or crews who could fire three broadsides to two would have an advantage. A development of this basic plan would be to outsail the enemy until the fleet could cross the bows of the enemy line and subject the vanguard to the firepower of the entire fleet crossing the T. Such operations might cripple a few ships, but normally such battles were indecisive and merely resulted in sustainable and reparable damage and some casualties. To stray from these formal naval pas-de-deux was deemed dangerous and few captains would dare break the rules to create opportunities out of tactical rigidity. The alternative approach would be to dash into the enemy fleet thereby striving to place one's fleet on both sides of the enemy. This maneuver could successfully double firepower on a portion of the enemy line and ensure partial success. A final approach adopted by Rodney at the Saintes was to break the enemy line with columns, double individual enemy ships, and fragment the opposition.

Designed by David Bushnell, the Turtle *submarine launched an attack on HMS* Eagle *but failed to fix explosives to its stern. He exploded a device containing gunpowder and Howe's captains, in grave alarm, cut their cables to avoid any repeated danger.*

In the three actions off Martinique in 1780, Rodney (17 April) sought to charge the French center, but through French action, an inconclusive line battle was fought. The second action on 15 May led to each fleet passing the other on an opposite tack with only the British vanguard fighting the French rear. The third battle (19 May) was fought at long range with Rodney losing one ship sunk. The British and French fleets returned to Barbados and Martinique, respectively, to repair and reprovision before the next bout. At the Isles des Saintes, Rodney was able to pierce the French line and a limited victory resulted.

Naval power was to prove the decisive factor in the Revolution when de Grasse seized local naval superiority allowing the Americans and French to invest and capture Yorktown. How was this possible? First, the British navy was trained to defeat the enemy in a decisive battle while blockading enemy squadrons in port. Neither of these tactics suited an American enemy that had no navy. Instead, the British had to fight a guerrilla war on land and one at sea against privateers. When fleet action proved impossible, small ships could be used to seize or rescue slaves from Americans, raid ship-building yards, destroy coastal property, or engage in amphibious operations. However, raiding often turned a local population against the British making an action counterproductive. On the outbreak of war, Admiral Graves on the American station raided the colonies to gain stores and supplies, causing immense hostility. Blockading and supporting British-held coastal cities followed to no great effect. When three European nations aided America, Britain was stretched to protect possessions in Ireland, the Channel, the Caribbean, Africa, and India. The breadth of the empire and the length of the American coastline displayed the limitations of the British navy. Even Rodney's victory over de Grasse failed to change the military situation of the American war. The importance of the navy was demonstrated in 1779 when the French attacked Jersey in the British Channel Islands. This force was repulsed but in 1781, 2,000 French troops landed and captured St. Helier. They were only pushed out when young Major Peirson rallied the 95th Foot and died while gaining victory.

The same year witnessed a more successful amphibious operation with Benedict Arnold's raid on Virginia from December 1780 to January 1781. Arnold had accumulated a flotilla with 1,800 men in the Chesapeake and landed at Jamestown with 1,200 on 1 January. Destroying a gun foundry and other property, Arnold returned to Westover and raided a plantation. After engaging local militia, he looted Cobham and Smithfield and then sought winter quarters at Portsmouth.

The Americans were incensed at the traitor's success and raised 3,700 militia to confront him together with a small French squadron sent from Newport, Rhode Island. These failed to dislodge Arnold, and a further militia and Continental advance in March 1781 was thwarted by British General Phillips reinforcing Arnold with 2,000 troops. Arnold proved how defenseless the Chesapeake Tidewater region was and his raid suggests the British navy should have mounted more search-and-burn operations in the area to destroy the Virginian economy. Arnold was replaced in command by Phillips and the two burned tobacco at Petersburg and vessels of the Virginia State Navy. However, ultimately, the only way to secure Virginia was for Cornwallis to defeat Lafayette's forces and this he singularly failed to achieve. He demonstrated that well-executed amphibious raids could be successful, but victory could only be enjoyed by the destruction of major regular forces.

The British navy failed in America for several other reasons. The Americas became a sideshow when the French threatened the British Empire as a whole. Also, factionalism and vendettas hindered operations, especially when Lord of the Admiralty Sandwich preferred safe rather than aggressive admirals. Finally, lack of resources and a coherent strategy bedevilled the British war at sea in American waters.

During the battle with the Serapis, Jones' carpenter reported that the ship was nearly sinking. The gunner heard this and ran aft to haul down the flag, but seeing that the staff was destroyed, he shouted "Quarter for God's sake, quarter." Jones consequently smashed in the gunner's skull with the butt end of a pistol.

Privateers and Pinpricks

Here, a privateer accepts the surrender of a British vessel as was common. For example, in 1780, the General Nash *seized two armed ships, one with goods valued at £10,800, the other with sugar, rum, and fruits from St. Kitts.*

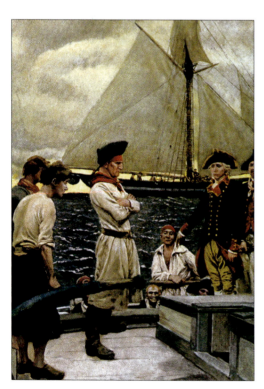

On 30 October 1775, Congress established a naval committee, which, by January 1776, bought eight ships and ordered the construction of thirteen new frigates. The separate states also built state navies and issued letters of marque, as did Congress, for privateering. The colonists had traditionally privateered during the inter-colonial wars capturing French and Spanish vessels. This experience proved invaluable in acquiring knowledge of creeks and small bays in the West Indies, which were infested by American ships.

Privateers provided two benefits for America during the Revolution. First, they imported arms, weapons and gunpowder, and tropical products. The privateers attacked West Indian and British shipping except Bermudian and Bahamian vessels. Second, depredations were so extensive that British warships were withdrawn from blockading colonial ports to police the seas around Jamaica and other Caribbean islands. Once gaps appeared in the blockade, even more privateers could slip through to transport supplies and seize cargos of rum, molasses, sugar, indigo, and other profitable products. Privateers were not altruistic; aiding America was patriotic, but profit and avarice played their part. By 1783, 2,000 privateers were working. Captured prizes would be condemned and sold with the owners, captain and crew all receiving a percentage according to proportions of investment and rank. Slaves crewing privateers would have their proportion of the prize money remitted to their owners.

Records show that 3,386 British vessels were captured between 1775 and 1783. Some were recaptured (495), others were ransomed (507), but 2,384 became permanent prizes. Dutch, French, and Spanish privateers and navies would also be involved in this onslaught on British maritime trade. These figures mean that over half of the 6,000 British vessels involved in overseas trade were taken, thereby placing strains on long-distance supplies, logistics, and insurance rates. The losses stimulated mercantile and commercial interests in Britain to lobby their government for peace.

American vessels would be protected in foreign ports where Congressional and some state agents would be found. Indeed, some British West Indian merchants were quite happy to be involved in disposing of prize ships and goods. Martinique, St. Domingue, and Dutch St. Eustatius were useful ports, and agents could provide privateers with information concerning British merchant or naval movements.

The Continental navy achieved little during the war maybe because some 70,000 seamen were involved in privateering. Nevertheless, 1776 witnessed Commodore Esek Hopkins sailing with six small ships, customized for war, from Philadelphia to the Bahamas. He raided New Providence and captured the governor, some gunpowder, and cannons before returning to Providence, Rhode Island. Some naval actions took place; for example, Captain Elisha Hinman *Alfred*'s capture of the HMS *Druid* in 1777. In 1780, the USS *Trumbull* fought a drawn battle with a 34-gun privateer, the *Watt*. In Spring 1781, the frigate USS *Alliance*, on returning from a trip to France, captured the sloops HMS *Atlanta* and HMS *Trepassy* and two British privateers. The last major action of the Continental navy took place when the USS *Alliance* was returning from France with $100,000 for the U.S. Treasury. It came upon two British frigates and a sloop. A French 50-gun ship appeared and one frigate and sloop guarded against its approach while American Captain Barry engaged and smashed HMS *Sybil*. The French ship failed to enter the fray because,

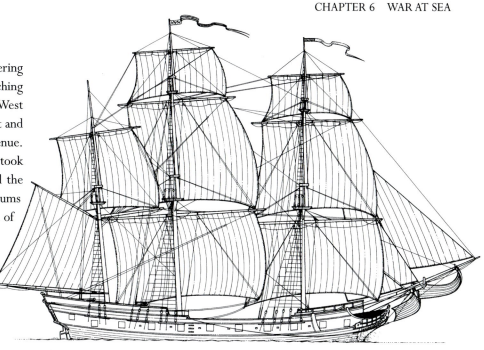

unknown to Barry, the war had ended. Privateering and minor actions were important in stretching British imperial resources and generating West Indian planter anger at the British parliament and navy for inadequate protection and loss of revenue. Connecticut alone had 250 privateers, which took some 500 British ships. The *Minerva* seized the *Hannah* with a cargo worth £80,000. Such sums were useful when Congress took 50 percent of every capture.

The Rattlesnake, *a ship-rigged sloop of war, was one of the most successful privateers, and in a single cruise against British trade in the Baltic, took prizes worth $1 million.*

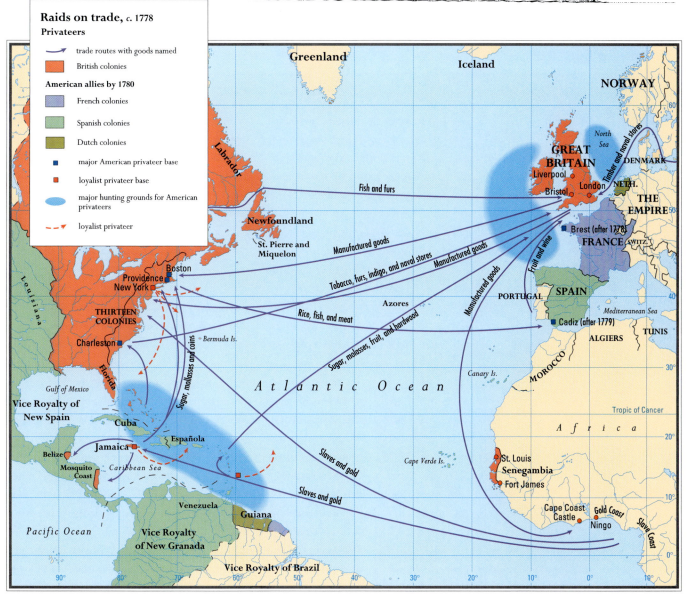

Raids on trade, *c.* 1778

Privateers

⌒→ trade routes with goods named

🟧 British colonies

American allies by 1780

🟪 French colonies

🟩 Spanish colonies

🟨 Dutch colonies

🔳 major American privateer base

🟥 loyalist privateer base

🔵 major hunting grounds for American privateers

- - ➤ loyalist privateer

127

Battle of Flamborough Head

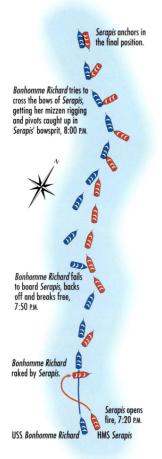

Serapis anchors in the final position.

Bonhomme Richard tries to cross the bows of Serapis, getting her mizzen rigging and pivots caught up in Serapis' bowsprit, 8:00 P.M.

N

Bonhomme Richard fails to board Serapis, backs off and breaks free, 7:50 P.M.

Bonhomme Richard raked by Serapis.

Serapis opens fire, 7:20 P.M.

USS Bonhomme Richard   HMS Serapis

Below: Battle of Flamborough Head with HMS Serapis *on the left and the American squadron on the right with the* Bonhomme Richard *on the extreme right.*

Any American claim to naval flair and aggression can best be laid at the feet of John Paul Jones. When war broke out, he was made first lieutenant of the 30-gun *Alfred* **and so distinguished himself in an action against HMS** *Glasgow* **that he was appointed commander of the** *Providence* **(1776). He captured sixteen prizes in one cruise, which took him from Bermuda to Nova Scotia; eight prizes were sent in and eight burned. Later in the year, in command of the** *Alfred,* **he brought in several more prizes.**

Jones' fame and reputation rest more on his exploits in European waters than in America. In early 1778, he transferred command to the newly built sloop, *Ranger,* and was ordered to France. Arriving with several prizes, he refitted the sloop in Brest, then, in April 1778, he sailed into the Irish Sea. Jones intended to disrupt shipping around the coasts of the Isle of Man, Cumberland, Kirkcudbright, and Wigtown, areas he knew from early days as an apprentice in Whitehaven ships and as a smuggler in the Solway Firth-Manx trade. He landed a force at Whitehaven Bay, attacked the fort and spiked its guns, and then burned some coastal shipping. Another party landed on St. Mary's Isle where the Earl of Selkirk's silver was seized (but later returned). His final action was a fight with HMS *Drake,* which he captured and sailed back to France. Disliked by his crew, Jones resigned and languished on the beach until he was appointed captain of an old French East Indiaman, the *Duc de Duras* which was renamed the *Bonhomme Richard* in honor of Benjamin Franklin.

The vessel carried forty guns with a 380-man crew, 150 French and the rest an international mix. His squadron comprised the *Alliance,* the *Pallas,* the *Cerf,* and the *Vengeance,* all sailing under the American flag. Unable to gain the confidence of his captains, the *Cerf* and *Vengeance* parted company, yet prizes such as the *Mayflower, Fortune,* and *Union* followed. Sailing into the North Sea via the Atlantic and the Orkneys, he arrived at Leith, causing alarm and dismay in Edinburgh. Forced away by a gale, Jones sighted a convoy moving southward around Flamborough Head.

The convoy was escorted by the 44-gun HMS *Serapis* (actually carrying 50 guns) and the 20-gun HMS *Countess of Scarborough.* A moon-lit battle followed after the *Alliance* chased the merchant ships. Jones engaged *Serapis,* while *Pallas* captured the *Countess of Scarborough* and then left Jones to his own devices. Jones found out that his larger cannons were of poor quality after two exploded. After an hour's combat, Jones managed to maneuver his vessel so that the *Serapis'* jib-boom locked into his rigging. The ships were tied together whereupon the *Serapis'* 18-pounders blasted the hull and lower deck of the American ship thereby driving the gun crews above; the Americans were sweeping the British quarter-deck and forecastle with musketry and grenades. One of Jones' crew in the rigging managed to toss some grenades down a British hatch and the subsequent explosion of British gunpowder dismounted guns and spread the whole length of the deck. When one American gunner learned how much seawater the *Bonhomme Richard* was taking in, he cried for quarter and Jones promptly smashed his skull with a pistol butt. Both ships were beaten, but the presence of the *Alliance* and *Pallas* forced the *Serapis* to surrender. Jones managed to sail his prize to the Dutch island of Texel leaving his own ship to sink. The action brought Jones much honor, but he held no substantial further command.

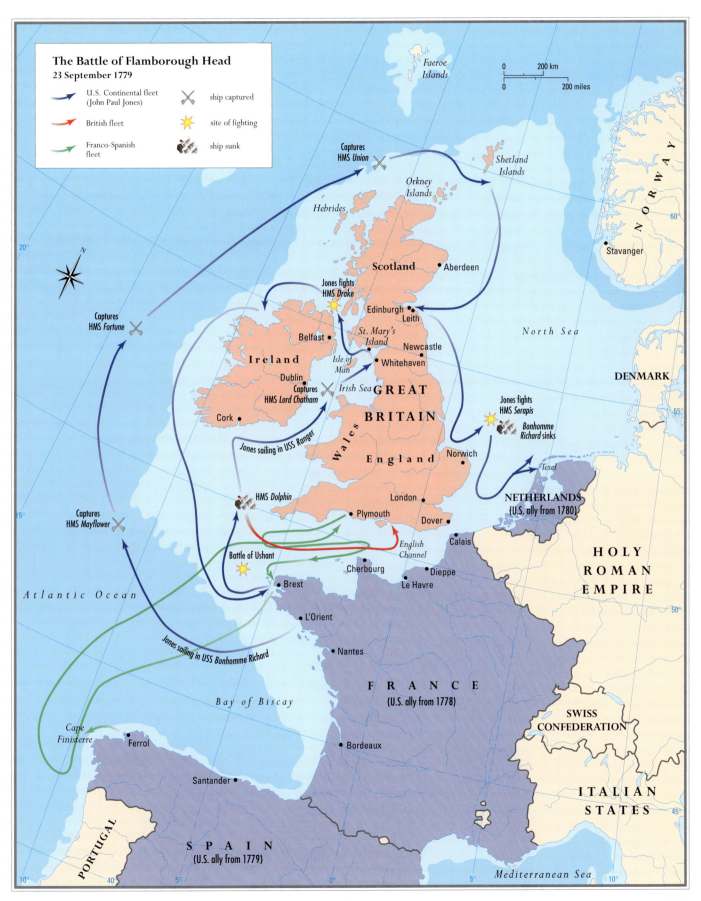

The Battle of Flamborough Head
23 September 1779

→ U.S. Continental fleet (John Paul Jones)

→ British fleet

→ Franco-Spanish fleet

⚔ ship captured

★ site of fighting

ship sunk

Captures HMS *Union*

Faeroe Islands

Shetland Islands

Orkney Islands

Hebrides

Scotland

• Aberdeen

Jones fights HMS *Drake*

Edinburgh •
Leith

North Sea

NORWAY

60°

• Stavanger

Captures HMS *Fortune*

Belfast •

St. Mary's Island

Newcastle •

Ireland

Dublin •

Isle of Man

• Whitehaven

GREAT

DENMARK

Captures HMS *Lord Chatham*

Irish Sea

BRITAIN

Jones fights HMS *Serapis*

55°

Cork •

Wales

Bonhomme Richard sinks

Jones sailing in USS *Ranger*

England

Norwich •

Captures HMS *Mayflower*

HMS *Dolphin*

London •

Texel

NETHERLANDS
(U.S. ally from 1780)

Battle of Ushant

Plymouth •

Dover •

Calais •

HOLY

Cherbourg •

English Channel

• Dieppe

ROMAN

Atlantic Ocean

• Brest

Le Havre •

EMPIRE

50°

• L'Orient

Jones sailing in USS *Bonhomme Richard*

• Nantes

F R A N C E
(U.S. ally from 1778)

Bay of Biscay

SWISS
CONFEDERATION

Cape Finisterre

• Ferrol

• Bordeaux

45°

• Santander

ITALIAN
STATES

S P A I N
(U.S. ally from 1779)

PORTUGAL

Mediterranean Sea

10°   40°   5°   0°   5°   10°

0   200 km
0   200 miles

20°

N

15°

Battle of the Chesapeake, 1781

De Grasse's victory at the Battle of the Chesapeake sealed Cornwallis' fate. The presence of the French fleet helped surround the British and also prevent succor from reaching them by sea.

The Battle of the Chesapeake (Virginia Capes, 5–9 September 1781) was the crucial naval battle of the Revolution. Despite being inconclusive, the action had important consequences. During the summer of 1781, Cornwallis campaigned in Virginia, eventually incarcerating himself and 8,000 men in Yorktown while awaiting the arrival of a rescuing British fleet in the Chesapeake.

The British navy had, until this time, enjoyed naval superiority in American waters. The major opposing fleets, the British under Rodney and the French commanded by de Grasse, were fencing in the Caribbean while smaller British and French squadrons were based at New York and Newport, Rhode Island, respectively. These had met in March off Cape Henry (First Battle of the Virginia Capes). Commodore Destouches' eight ships of the line met Admiral Arbuthnot's similarly sized force. Although crippling three British ships, Destouches returned to Newport relinquishing the command of the sea to Britain.

The situation suddenly changed when de Grasse brought his twenty-four liners to the Chesapeake on 30 August together with 3,000 military reinforcements. Simultaneously, the Rhode Island squadron under de Barras sailed to join him, while Washington and Rochambeau left New York for Yorktown. Cornwallis was now the focus of converging forces. Realizing that de Grasse had left the Caribbean, Rodney sent Rear Admiral Hood with fourteen ships to reinforce Rear Admiral Graves at New York. Hood visited the Chesapeake on route and found it empty.

Graves sailed for the bay with his nineteen liners and found de Grasse's fleet at anchor just inside Cape Henry. The British knew they needed a victory to regain naval superiority and as the French beat out of the bay, Graves had advantages of wind, tide, and formation. Had Graves any Nelsonian tendencies he would have

ordered a general chase and dashed in to the midst of the clutter of French ships. Instead, he adopted the classic line of battle, which allowed de Grasse enough time to set his own battle line into good order. The scene was set for a traditional cannonade, which began at 4 P.M. Two and a half hours of action followed, but Hood's rear division never came into action. Graves flew contradictory signals simultaneously causing confusion among his captains. The *Shrewsbury* was the first ship into action losing seventy-two dead and wounded to French gunfire. The hull and masts were so shot through that the *Shrewsbury* fell out of line. The second British ship in line was the *Intrepid* and she suffered likewise with fifty-six casualties. The *Terrible,* which entered the fray with five pumps keeping her afloat, took in over two feet of water every twenty-five minutes and later sank. The fiercest fighting occurred between the two vanguards; the French *Diadème* was entirely shattered being engaged by two or three ships; she lost 120 men with sails and rigging shot away. Eventually, sunset ended the action.

Both admirals insisted that they would re-engage, but four days after the battle, so many ships being damaged, Graves decided not to resume action. Hood sought to persuade Graves to seize the former French anchorage at Lynnhaven Bay at Cape Henry, a strategy he had once used in the West Indies, but Graves refused. The opposing fleets eventually lost touch and de Grasse returned to the Chesapeake on 11 September, and Graves limped back to New York. Cornwallis was now doomed and he surrendered on 19 October. American victory was assured by de Grasse's actions.

Naval historians have wondered why Graves failed to enter the Chesapeake; but, at that time, he did not know Cornwallis' precarious position. De Grasse, however, did; so why did he engage in a battle in which he might be defeated and place the Americans in a difficult position?

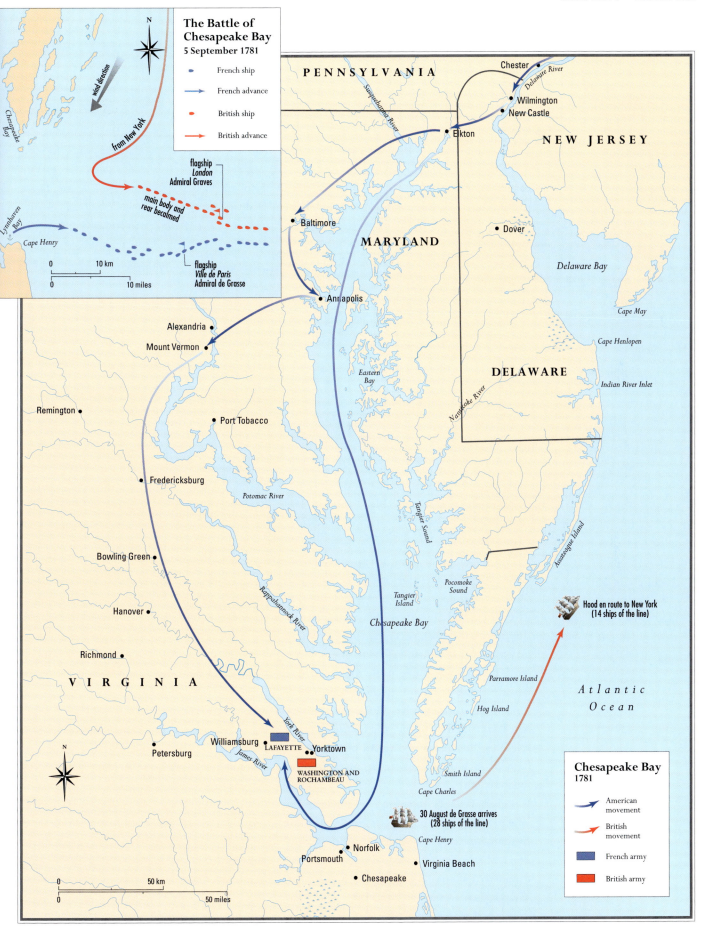

**The Battle of
Chesapeake Bay**
5 September 1781

- ●●● French ship
- → French advance
- ●●● British ship
- → British advance

wind direction

from New York

flagship
London
Admiral Graves

main body and
rear becalmed

flagship
Ville de Paris
Admiral de Grasse

Chesapeake Bay

Cape Henry

Lynnhaven Bay

0   10 km

0   10 miles

PENNSYLVANIA

Chester

Delaware River

Wilmington

New Castle

NEW JERSEY

Susquehanna River

Elkton

Baltimore

MARYLAND

Dover

Delaware Bay

Annapolis

Alexandria

Mount Vernon

*Eastern
Bay*

Cape May

Cape Henlopen

DELAWARE

Nanticoke River

Indian River Inlet

Remington

Port Tobacco

Fredericksburg

Potomac River

Rappahannock River

Bowling Green

Hanover

Tangier Sound

Assateague Island

Pocomoke
Sound

*Tangier
Island*

Chesapeake Bay

Hood en route to New York
(14 ships of the line)

Richmond

VIRGINIA

Parramore Island

*Atlantic
Ocean*

Hog Island

Petersburg

Williamsburg

LAFAYETTE

York River

Yorktown

James River

WASHINGTON AND
ROCHAMBEAU

Smith Island

Cape Charles

30 August de Grasse arrives
(28 ships of the line)

Portsmouth

Norfolk

Cape Henry

Virginia Beach

Chesapeake

0   50 km

0   50 miles

Chesapeake Bay
1781

- → American movement
- → British movement
- ■ French army
- ■ British army

Rodney's Naval Campaigns

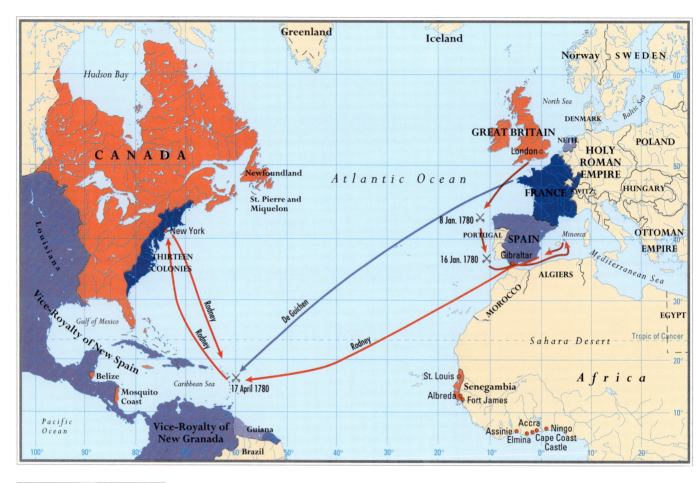

Rodney's naval campaigns, 1778–80

→ French fleet movements

→ British fleet movements

▉ allied to the Thirteen Colonies from 1778

▉ allied to the Thirteen Colonies from 1779

▉ allied to the Thirteen Colonies from 1780

▉ British possessions

✕ battle

Toward the end of 1789 Rear Admiral Rodney was appointed to the command of the Leeward Islands, which included Jamaica and the freedom to operate in American waters. He sailed to the Antilles with twenty-one ships of the line and three hundred merchant vessels. However, he was first ordered to relieve a siege of Gibraltar. On 8 January, he captured a Spanish convoy off Cape Finisterre and on 16 January 1780, he fell in with a smaller Spanish fleet of eleven liners under Admiral Juan de Langara. Rodney managed to engage nine enemy ships in a moonlight battle off Cape St. Vincent. Two escaped, one exploded, and six surrendered, including Langara's flagship, *Fénix*. Rodney then relieved Gibraltar and also Minorca and was rewarded with a Knighthood of the Bath.

Rodney reached the West Indies on 28 March and his opponent, Admiral Count Lucurbain de Guichen arrived at Martinique soon after. The two fleets met in three inconclusive actions involving lengthy cannonading. Rodney's flagship, *Sandwich*, fired 3,228 cannon balls in the first two actions. The skirmish off Martinique on 17 April might have given Rodney a victory. He claimed that his captains were chained by old fighting instructions and had disobeyed his direct orders. However, Martinique was a technical French victory because three British ships were near to sinking, but a French attack on Barbados was prevented. In sum, relationships in the British fleet were subject to the dictates of a bullying autocrat. Despite his unpleasant character, Rodney understood strategy and realized that a junction of the French West Indies fleet with the

French Newport squadron could overwhelm the British New York squadron and place the British headquarters in jeopardy. Accordingly, Rodney sailed for New York with ten ships. Having foiled a possible Franco-American land and amphibious operation against New York, he returned to the West Indies in December 1780.

On 27 January 1781, Rodney was ordered to capture the Dutch island of St. Eustatius, which was accomplished in February together with the seizure of St. Martin. The island was used as a forum for the American colonies to trade with enemy colonies. Additionally, the island's warehouses were used to store foreign goods and St. Eustatius became a market place for American patriots who could buy gunpowder and sell their exports of tobacco, cotton, timber, and indigo. Estimates suggest that rents on the warehouses totalled £1,200,000 annually and that so many goods needed transshipment that cotton and tobacco overflowed from the warehouses to the beach. Dutch Rear Admiral Count van Bylent stated that his thirteen-month stay on the island between 1778 and 1779 witnessed 3,182 sailings from the island.

Rodney was convinced that the neutral island had supplied de Guichen with rope and timber to repair his vessels after the 17 April action off Martinique. He was also angered by the number of British merchants trading with the enemy. The British declaration of war on Holland gave Rodney the opportunity to capture over a hundred merchantmen in the harbor; a twenty-one ship sugar convoy, which had just quit the island; and the island's goods valued at some £3 million. In fact, Rodney acted improperly for he confiscated everything on the island whether it belonged to friend or enemy. The impecunious Rodney was anxious to gain his sixteenth share of prize money from lawful plunder. The most valuable prizes were shipped to England in thirty-four ships with an escort of five warships. Only eight ships reached England after being attacked by a French squadron. Rodney lost some £300,000 and money left on St. Eustatius was captured by the French when they retook the island. Rodney sailed for England leaving Hood in command.

Commodore Hotham writing about Rodney, to Lord Sandwich, said, "I can no longer wish to serve in this country, where the chief in command will assume merit to himself, and aim to aggrandize his own reputation by depreciating indiscriminately the character of every officer below him."

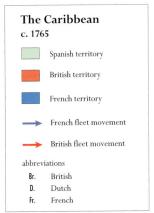

The Caribbean
c. 1765

- Spanish territory
- British territory
- French territory
- → French fleet movement
- → British fleet movement

abbreviations
Br.   British
D.   Dutch
Fr.   French

Battle of the Saintes

British naval forces were in a parlous situation in the Caribbean at the beginning of 1782. Although Britain was regaining mastery of the seas following the Battle of the Dogger Bank (August 1781) against the Dutch and the second Battle of Ushant (December 1781)

Admiral Rodney returned from England with reinforcements in late February. Stationed at St. Lucia with thirty-six ships of the line, he continued to observe enemy preparations at Fort Royal on Martinique. The British intended to prevent any French union with a Spanish fleet at San Domingo. On 8 April, the French were reported sailing from Martinique and Rodney set sail in pursuit. On 9 April, a naval skirmish took place off Dominica where Hood's vanguard was separated from the main fleet. De Grasse failed to seize this opportunity. The pursuit continued for three days with Rodney gaining all the time; the British were helped when the French were delayed after the *Zélé* collided with de Grasse's flagship, the *Ville de Paris* (104 guns). De Grasse was initially hampered by his huge military convoy, but this was sent to the port of Basse-Terre in Guadeloupe.

On 12 April, the British, with 34 ships of the line, brought de Grasse to action near Les Saintes, some small islets in the Guadeloupe-Dominica channel. Classic maneuvers followed with each fleet formed into line of battle approaching each other on opposite courses

"…The Glorieux of seventy-four guns…was so roughly handled that being shorn of all her masts, bowsprit and ensign staff but with the whole flag nailed to the stump of one of her masts breathing defiance…so became a motionless hulk."

against the French, the Caribbean was witnessing the gradual seizure of British islands by the French, such as Nevis, St. Kitts, and Montserrat. Even a brilliant maneuver by Hood at Basseterre, St. Kitts, where he seized the anchorage of the invading French and landed a relief force, failed to prevent the island from falling. A finale to this French campaign was a planned Franco-Spanish expeditionary force to attack Jamaica while supported by thirty-five ships of the line.

Phase 1

wind

Ville de Paris

Formidable

while exchanging gunfire. The wind veered during the morning and de Grasse found himself under the lee of Dominica and partially becalmed. The French line fell into disorder and gaps appeared in it. Rodney took his chance and pierced the French line with his own *Formidable*; the *Duke* and the *Bedford* did likewise, spearheading two more penetrating columns; Hood's *Bedford* actually led twelve ships through the French line. De Grasse's fleet was now broken into three sections and was in chaos. The French *Glorieux*, *César,* and *Hector* were damaged and struck. At roughly mid-day, the wind strengthened and de Grasse tried to escape towards the west. Next, the *Ardent* was taken and the *Ville de Paris* surrounded and surrendered after a vigorous fight. The French command fell to de Vaudreuil who escaped with the rest of the French fleet. Rodney gave chase but gave up in the evening. Seven French ships were taken but Hood claimed that a determined pursuit would have resulted in the capture of more enemy ships. Hood ultimately managed to take two more French liners, *Caton* and *Jason*, with a frigate, *Amiable*, and a sloop, *Cérès*, a week later when he was allowed to chase de Vaudreuil. Had Hood been allowed to pursue one day earlier, he would have caught the damaged French fleet in the Mona Passage between Puerto Rico and San Domingo. Rodney had achieved a remarkable victory and an enemy line had been broken for the first time; this maneuver was then incorporated into the British navy's Fighting Instructions. Despite the restoration of British command of the seas, the victory did not affect the outcome of the Revolution.

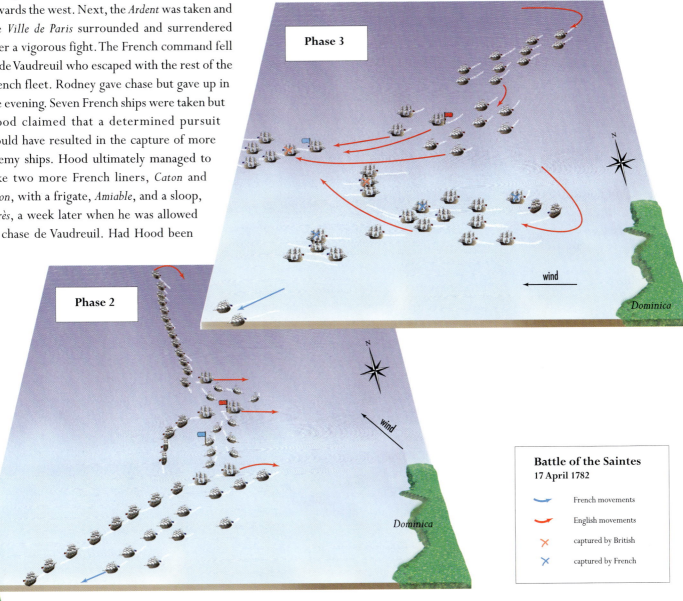

Battle of the Saintes
17 April 1782

French movements

English movements

captured by British

captured by French

Oceanic Dimensions

Saratoga altered the nature of the war for independence. When France entered the war in 1778 and Spain in 1779, Britain was placed in a difficult position. During the French and Indian War, Britain was aided by Frederick the Great keeping France occupied on land while Britain fought its battles in India, Canada, and the West Indies. The American war changed matters; Prussia was not involved and Britain was placed on the defensive.

The Caribbean became Britain's major theater of war thereby downgrading the American campaigns. Fears existed that the French would invade either Britain or Ireland; so great was the worry that Parliament encouraged the creation of an Irish volunteer force, some 40,000 strong. British activity at sea so angered Catherine the Great that she formed the League of Armed Neutrality. Furthermore, the sheer size and extent of the British Empire meant that France could choose where to attack, in the Caribbean, North America, the Mediterranean, and the Indian Ocean. The sea lanes were difficult to protect from privateers, and Spain could easily attack Gibraltar and Minorca.

The League of Armed Neutrality (1780) was a method of protecting trade. Proposed by Russia, the concept was supported by Denmark, Sweden, Prussia, Austria, and Portugal. France and Spain recognized the League and Holland would have joined but Britain declared war on the Dutch. The League demanded free passage of neutral ships from port to port and along the littoral of belligerents; freedom of carrying combatants' goods in neutral ships, except military contraband; and blockades were to be effective, not declared paper blockades.

During 1781, British resources were stretched to capacity. During this period of French naval predominance, Admiral Pierre André de Suffren was dispatched to the Indian Ocean with five ships. His tasks were to defend the possessions of France's ally, Holland, which included the Cape of Good Hope at the southern tip of Africa and Trincomalee in Ceylon. Arriving at the Portuguese Cape Verde Islands, he found British Commodore Johnstone at anchor with

five warships and 35 transports. Suffren attacked them in the neutral port of Porto Praya (16 April) and then sailed to Mauritius.

The first Indian Ocean naval engagement occurred on 17 February 1782, south of Madras. Although inconclusive, Suffren was able to land troops at Porto Novo, near France's possession at Pondicherry, recently lost to Britain. Supported by Hyder Ali of Mysore, these troops moved to Cuddalore. Four other encounters took place near Trincomalee (12 April), off Cuddalore (6 July), Trincomalee (3 September), and Cuddalore (20 April 1783). Suffren kept the British on the defensive in India and countered British superiority there. Had he received full support from his captains, he might have caused serious damage. As it was, he supported French land forces, established relations with Mysore and Hyder Ali's heir, Tippoo Sahib, and even managed to seize the strategically important harbor of Trincomalee (30 August 1782). Tippoo Sahib continued to be an enemy of Britain until he was killed in 1799 defending his capital against the British.

Nearer home, Sir Hyde Parker forced a Dutch squadron and merchant fleet to end a voyage to the Baltic at the Battle of the Dogger Bank (August 1781). This murderous action, with seven ships aside, resulted in 545 Dutch and 443 British dead and wounded. Elsewhere, Admiral Kempenfelt obtained success when he defeated de Guichen whose squadron was escorting merchants and supplies to the West Indies (December 1781); twenty transports were captured.

In the Mediterranean, the Spaniards eventually captured Minorca and laid siege to Gibraltar from 1779 to 1783. Supplied and relieved twice by sea and defended by Sir George Elliott, the British mounted a determined defense. Using red-hot shot, for the first time in history, Spanish floating batteries were destroyed. Near starvation, Gibraltar was supplied for a third time by Lord Howe in October 1782 and the Treaty of Paris finally ended the siege.

French frigates were such superb examples of naval architecture that captured vessels such as the Danae *(1759) and the* Hebe *(1782) became models for British 36- and 38-gun frigates.*

Battle of Trincomalee
3 September 1782

Phase 1
Attacking

Southwesterly wind

Phase 2
The Battle

⚓ British ships
⚓ French ships

RUSSIAN EMPIRE

COLONIES
Louisbourg
Boston
New York
Halifax

GREAT
BRITAIN NETH.
HOLY
ROMAN
EMPIRE
FRANCE
Rochefort
Toulon
PORTUGAL SPAIN
Cadiz
Gibraltar
Cartagena

Atlantic Ocean

OTTOMAN EMPIRE
Egypt
Nile
PERSIA
Arabia

Canary Is.

Cape Verde Is.
Gorée
St. Louis
Albredo
Ft. James

Sahara

Niger River

Assinie
Elmina
Accra
Cape Coast Castle

A f r i c a

Congo River

ANGOLA
Loanda

St. Helena

PORTUGUESE
EAST AFRICA

ZANZIBAR

Seychelles

Madagascar
Ste Marie
Mauritius
Bourbon
Fort-Dauphin

Delagoa Bay

Cape Town

INDIA
Hyder Ali
attacks 1780–81
but fails
Coote 1781
Madras
Bay of
Bengal
Goa
Pondicherry
captured by
British 1778–85
Porto Novo
1781
Trincomalee
captured by
Suffren in 1782
Laccadive Is.
Maldive Is.

Indian Ocean

Chagos
Archipelago

Brazil

Implications of War
1779–82

- 🟧 British territory
- 🟪 American colonies
- 🟪 allied to American colonies
- → British operations
- → French operations
- — Startegic trade route
- ⚓ British naval base
- ⚓ French naval base
- ⚓ Spanish naval base
- ● town (colored by sovereignty)

Chapter Seven
Other Battle Fronts: Native Americans' Dismay

"It is therefore His Majesty's pleasure, that you lose no time in taking such steps as may induce them (the Native Americans) to take up the hatchet against His Majesty's rebellious subjects in America..." Lord George Germain.

sought to uphold Indian interests after the Québec Act and the 1763 Treaty by protecting Indian lands from settler incursions. Furthermore, the British had developed an Indian Department with Superintendents for both northern and southern Indians. For example, John Stuart in the south

After General Anthony Wayne crushed Indian resistance by defeating Little Turtle's forces at Fallen Timbers, the American dictated peace at Fort Greenville whereby the Miami confederacy surrendered today's state of Ohio and a chunk of Indiana. The treaty was signed by some 1,100 chiefs and warriors.

The campaigns against the Indians and the penetration of the West were the culmination points of a devastating and terrible period for Native Americans, a turning point introducing even more bitter Indian-American wars, forced resettlement, ethnic cleansing, and culture loss.

Some historians see the entire period from King Philip's War onward as a coherent period of constant border warfare during which the Indians fought to preserve their hunting grounds, traditions, and values. The onset of the American War of Independence was unexpected by the Indians. Indian leaders told Spanish Governor Cruzat at St. Louis in 1784 that the conflict was the most direct blow, other than total destruction, that they had ever faced. Initially, the Indians regarded the war as a family feud, but gradually they realized that they must choose sides. The British exerted strong influence because they were a more dependable source of trade goods and they understood the Indians more fully. The British had

enjoyed good relations with the Cherokee and during warfare in 1760 was important in re-establishing peace. He managed to demarcate Anglo-Indian borders, although they were generally ignored by white settlers and unscrupulous traders.

Stuart strove to maintain sufficient supplies, trade goods, and presents to the tribes and chiefs thereby ensuring loyalty to the British. In 1775, General Gage urged Stuart to prepare the Indians for war, but he feared that an unstructured and unfocused use of Indian fighters would end in the killing and wounding of men, women, and children of all races leading to negative political outcomes. Instead, he desired combined Indian-regular British army cooperation. However, 1776 witnessed the Cherokee ignoring his pleas with attacks on the South Carolina frontier by the Lower Cherokee Towns while Overhill Cherokees raided villages along the Tennessee River near North Carolina and Virginia and isolated Kentucky settlements, while the Middle and Valley Cherokee surged into North Carolina. The Indians were not so much fighting for Britain as defending their land and attacking anyone who ignored the borders. American retaliation was swift and harsh with the burning of some thirty-six villages and food stores.

The Cherokee were forced to accept a treaty in 1777 which saw the cession of much territory. The 1777 Cherokee treaty talks with Virginia and North Carolina saw Chief Corn Tassel succinctly define the differences between Indian and white lifestyles. "I am sensible that if we give up these lands they will bring you a great deal more than hundreds of pounds. It spoils our hunting ground; but always remains good to you to raise families and stocks on, when the goods we receive of you are rotten and gone to nothing your stocks are tame and marked; but we dont know ours they are wild. Hunting is our principle way of living."

Stuart, meanwhile, had mediated a peace between warring Choctaws and Creeks. These tribes now became the target of British propaganda, after the Cherokee defeat, and many Creeks subscribed to the British cause although some refused, leading to a Creek civil war in later years.

Compared with the British, the Americans were short of supplies and tainted by being kin to backcountry settlers who they could not prevent from encroaching on Indian lands. The Americans were also unable to control their own troops and callous murders of Delaware Chief White Eyes and Shawnee Chief Cornstalk were instrumental in eradicating any attempts at neutrality or peace and the Shawnees were thrust into British arms by the crime.

White Eyes became chief of the Delaware nation in 1774. He was unusual in that he encouraged Christian Moravian teachings among his tribe and he hoped they would remain neutral in the white conflict. In 1778, Fort Pitt saw White Eyes seeking neutrality while a split in Delaware ranks, a situation developing in many Indian tribes, occurred with Chiefs Pipe and Wolf becoming pro-British. Fort Pitt negotiations led to an agreement between Americans and Indians

promising good relations and trade "until the sun shall shine no more, or the water fail to run in the Ohio." The same year witnessed White Eyes leading General Lachlan McIntosh's expedition against Detroit across tribal lands. He failed to return and Americans claimed he died of smallpox; in fact, Americans murdered him and the Delaware then supported Pipe against the Revolution. However, a small number of Delaware sought sanctuary at Fort Pitt. Pipe moved his people to the upper Sandusky River, leaving the Moravian Delaware isolated. The murder of ninety Moravian Indians at Gnadenhutten in March 1782 by American militia inflamed the Delaware. When U.S. Colonel Crawford was given the order to attack Wyandot and Delaware on the Sandusky, his force was defeated (June 1782), and Chief Pipe had Crawford tortured to death in retaliation for the Moravian massacre.

The Shawnee, Cornstalk, tried to keep his people neutral and at peace with the Americans at the outbreak of the Revolution. He managed to inform the Americans of occurrences in Indian territory but failed to prevent some young warriors from taking up the tomahawk. The Shawnees became divided over the war and some migrated in the face of an apparently relentless American expansion westward; one group joined the Creeks and others moved west to Spanish land across the Mississippi. In 1777, Cornstalk and other Shawnee were taken hostage by militia at Fort Randolph where they were murdered. Thereupon, most Shawnee joined the British, but divisions continued within the tribe because Cornstalk's Maquachakes Shawnee moved to the Delaware capital at Coshocton to preserve their neutrality. Later, the Shawnees were devastated by Bowman's and Clark's expeditions, but many fought on to resist until the Treaty of Greenville in 1795. However, the Shawnee joined Tecumseh at the Battle of the Thames (1813) during the War of 1812.

The experience of the Delaware and Shawnee displays the difficulties facing the tribes: internal dissension, disunity, and the feeling that Americans could not be trusted. Some Indians joined with the Americans and the Stockbridge Indians of Massachusetts enlisted as minutemen. These converts to Christianity — Mahicans and Housatonics — served as scouts and sustained heavy losses at the Battle of White Plains. The New York Oneidas enlisted in the American cause, which meant conflict with other tribes in the Iroquois Confederacy. Peoples such as the Micmacs, Passamaquoddies, and Penobscots of Maine and Nova Scotia supported the Americans, as did the South Carolina Catawbas. Within tribes, factionalism spread, and the cleavage within the Iroquois set Mohawks, Onondagas, Cayugas, and Senecas against Oneidas and Tuscaroras. The Cherokees entered the fray again with the older generation seeking peace with Americans and youthful warriors joining the British, viewing their behavior as an opportunity to regain their lands. Thus, the Revolution segmented Native American peoples and communities as they travelled different roads to survival.

The war witnessed Indian warriors attacking the American frontier from New York south to Georgia: Indians cooperated with British regulars and Loyalist units such as Butler's Rangers. The constant series of raids sapped the Americans of resources that were required for more regular warfare against British Redcoats in New Jersey and then the South. Americans were subjected to propaganda about Indian massacres, and these stories were built up to sometimes mythic proportions. The Cherry Valley massacre (November 1778) was indeed horrific in its slaughter of women and children, but only forty-six people were actually killed, casualties that would be acceptable in any other wartime skirmish, and this was war, albeit waged outside an American or British frame of reference. The incident psychologically weakened frontier society and many families moved eastward during this period of the Revolution that was fought in Indian country; thus, the American border was pushed towards the Atlantic — an Indian and Loyalist victory. The earlier 1778 Wyoming Valley Massacre in Pennsylvania is probably misnamed. Some 3,000 settlers had entered the Susquehanna Valley and these people from Pennsylvania, Connecticut, and New York were resented by the Iroquois who claimed the land as their own. The settlers established eight forts and blockhouses, which became a legitimate target for the British. Accordingly, Butler's Rangers, the Royal Greens, and Indians attacked the region and destroyed the forts taking some 227 scalps. Historians have debated the legend of the massacre, but few envisage this incident as a brilliantly successful Loyalist and Indian campaign. Brant and his Loyalist friends nearly wiped out the New York and Pennsylvania backcountry, which had been an important grain and cattle-growing region that supplied the Continental army. The legend was promoted by S. T. Campbell's poem (1809), "Gertrude of Wyoming," which also described the flamingos and palm trees in the valley! Pure horror there, however, lies in the report of small incidents. One American, Giles Slocum, witnessed John Russell, a Tory, talk to and then shoot and scalp his brother Henry, a patriot.

George Washington and Thomas Jefferson, Governor of Virginia June 1779 through June 1781, ordered and demanded the crushing of the Iroquois and the incineration of their settlements, crops, orchards, and food supplies until they fled hungry to Fort Niagara. The Oneidas received similar treatment from the Mohawks under Brant. Jefferson's desire for the extermination of the Shawnee saw the torch taken into Ohio country where American militia engaged in constant raids and warfare. Whatever the destruction to their homes, the Shawnee kept fighting. One report concerning Sullivan's capture of Chemung is written interestingly. Captain James Norris stated that the "Genl. gave orders for the Town to be illuminated, and accordingly we had a glorious Bonfire of upwards of 30 buildings at once…" After the Battle of Newtown, Nathan Davies stated that a party counting dead Indians "found them and skinned two of them from their hips down for boot legs; one for the Major the other for myself." The cruelty, callousness and butchery in this search and destroy mission was mirrored on the other side. Lieutenant Boyd and a scouting party were killed, but the officer was tortured to death. Lieutenant Erkuries recorded the finding of Boyd and a rifleman. "They was both stripped naked and their heads Cut off, and the flesh of Lt. Boyd's head was entirely taken off and his eyes punched out. The other mans head was not there." The end result of this mutual destruction was summed up by Major Jeremiah Fogg. "The nests are destroyed, but the birds are still on the wing."

Mary Jemison, who spent most of her life as a wife and mother, with the Seneca Indians, witnessed the losses to her village from the Battle of Oriskany (36 dead and many wounded). She used to house Brant and Butler when they passed by on campaign. She later reported the carnage wrought by Sullivan.

"A part of our corn they burnt, and threw the remainder into the river. They burnt our houses, killed what few cattle and horses they could find, destroyed our fruit trees, and left nothing but the bare soil and timber…we all returned; but what were our feelings when we found that there was not a mouthful of any kind of sustenance left, not even enough to keep a child one day from perishing with hunger."

All told, the Revolution won liberty for the Americans, albeit in a disunited country, but for the Indians it was an unmitigated disaster, whichever side they had supported. The 1783 Treaty of Paris ignored the Indians when Britain gave Indian territory to the United States leaving Native Americans to the devices and policies of the new state, which would soon grab their lands and attack their customs, values, and religions.

Native Americans had to choose how to live and sometimes seek new homes. Stockbridge Mahicans returned from serving the American cause to find their lands seized by greedy neighbors and their town no longer Indian. Some joined the Oneidas in New York and others migrated to Ohio, Wisconsin, and Oklahoma. Many Delawares moved west, some to join the multitribal confederacy outside American sovereignty, an alliance designed to resist any

more American encroachments. The Shawnee moved north and west, eventually reaching the Maumee River, while the Cherokee ceded more land and withdrew from the Chickamauaga border area to the Tennessee River. Choctaws and Chickasaws made peace with the Americans while the Creeks faced internal disarray. The Seminole section withdrew into Florida and their population increased rapidly as thousands of Creeks and other smaller tribes left the Creek Confederacy over policy disputes and found this new southern home. Cherokee Chief Rising Fawn (Keniteta) summed up the Revolution when he claimed that the British were "the ruin of my People."

Tenskwatawa, the Shawnee Prophet and Tecumseh's brother, moved his people to near Greenville, Ohio, and won support by claiming that the sun would disappear on a certain day. This magic was the result of an eclipse which the Prophet somehow knew would occur.

Joseph Brant

Joseph Brant moved between Native American and British societies, but he had strong views about the latter, "After every exertion to divest myself of prejudice, I am obliged to give my opinion in favor of my own people."

Joseph Brant was the most important Mohawk Indian participant in the Revolution. Born in 1742, he was educated at Eleazor Wheelock's Indian Charity School in Connecticut after being sent there by William Johnson, the British Indian Superintendent and lover of Brant's elder sister, Molly. The two Brants were very influential among the Indians and Joseph fought for the British against Pontiac. He persuaded four of the Six Nations in the Iroquois Confederacy to support Britain during the Revolution, but the Oneidas and Tuscaroras chose the American cause. Sir Guy Carleton, in Canada, would not countenance Indian raids against America because actions would drive all frontier settlers into the rebel camp. Instead, Indians could patrol and fight in self-defense.

In 1776, Brant was sent to England where he met King George and Lord George Germain. He complained to Germain about encroachments on Mohawk land by the population of Albany and appealed for redress. In the meantime, the Iroquois had been placed under the command of Colonel Butler, a man who recruited Indian warriors by getting them drunk. In September 1775, he led Indian Loyalists and a white regiment, Brant's Volunteers, in Colonel Barry St. Leger's unsuccessful expedition to seize Fort Stanwix. The Indians were so hungry and poorly clothed that they fought little and robbed retreating British and Loyalist troops. Brant, however, wanted the Indians to conduct military campaigns as a disciplined, elite, independent force, but Carleton's raiding tactics became the preferred British strategy.

Later, Brant led a group of Loyalists and Indians at the Battle of Oriskany and afterward burned a neutral Oneida village. This was the action that broke Iroquois unity; the Oneidas joined the patriots and attacked Mohawk villages. The mutual destruction of crops and settlements wiped out food supplies of Indians partisan to either side. Under Brant's leadership, the four Loyalist Iroquois nations imposed a reign of fear throughout the northeastern frontier, especially after Saratoga when the region ceased to be a main regular war zone. Brant played a partially misunderstood role in the Cherry Valley Massacre in which he actually tried to hold back Indians and Loyalists and managed to save many women and children, noticeably Mrs. Shankland and her five children. Brant has been blamed for the devastation of the Wyoming settlements in Pennsylvania. Here, in July 1778, John Butler's force of Loyalists and

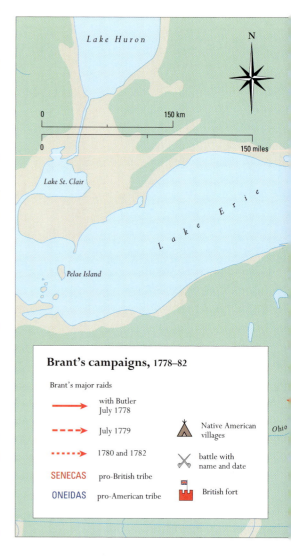

Brant's campaigns, 1778–82

Brant's major raids

→ with Butler July 1778

--→ July 1779

···→ 1780 and 1782

SENECAS pro-British tribe

ONEIDAS pro-American tribe

▲ Native American villages

⚔ battle with name and date

🏰 British fort

Indians, some being Brant's Mohawks although he was absent, attacked these new flourishing settlements on the eastern branch of the Susquehanna. Interestingly, the settlement's military commander, Zebulon Butler was John Butler's cousin. Their forces clashed and the patriots were swept aside after which the raiders roared through the eight villages in a storm of murder and destruction. Eight forts and a thousand houses were destroyed and a thousand cows seized together with sheep and pigs. Torture followed, and some inhabitants were burned to death in their own homes.

The wanton cruelty and destruction caused many settlers to move east and the barbarous nature of the civil war between patriot and Loyalist was increased. During the Revolution, Tryon County, New York, witnessed 12,000 farms abandoned and the creation of 380 widows and 2,000 fatherless children. In retaliation for the incidents, the Americans sent General John Sullivan against the Iroquois and Brant in a campaign to break Iroquois power. Brant continued his ravages and raided Minisink, New York, in 1780, where his forces caused forty-five militia casualties and later, in 1782, he planned an expedition against the American Ohio Valley villages. In reality, Brant was duped because the British never told him that they regarded Mohawk land as Crown Territory and certainly failed to consult him over the eventual cession of Indian land to America in 1783. After that date, Brant lived in Canada and engaged in missionary work for the Episcopalian Church.

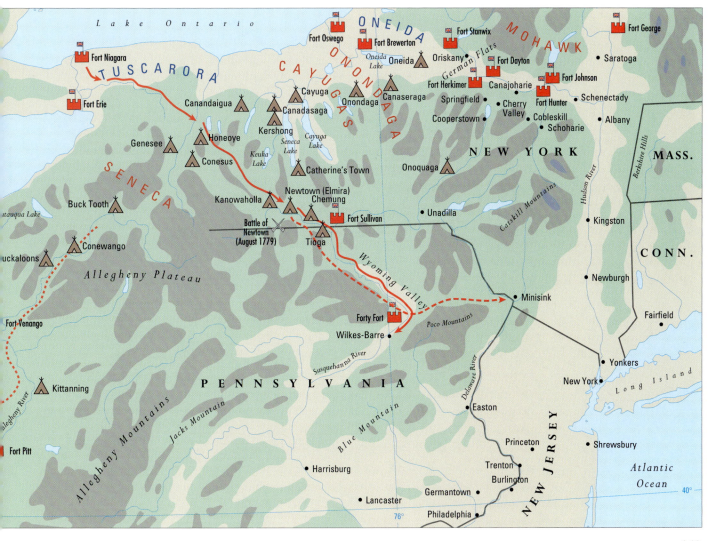

George Rogers Clark and French Possessions

In 1775, Indians became increasingly angry over the number of white settlers entering Kentucky. Consequently, Shawnees started raiding this new county of Virginia and they were further encouraged by Lieutenant Governor of Canada, Henry "Hairbuyer" Hamilton. In July 1776, a large meeting of Indians was held at Muscle Shoals to decide how to counter white settler encroachments. Delawares, Ottowas, Cherokees, and most Shawnees supported the British, but Cornstalk, a Shawnee chief, urged neutrality during the Revolutionary War. Indian raids followed and only Harrodsburg and Boonesboro were strong enough to hold out in Kentucky and Shawnees under Black Fish besieged the latter.

George Rogers Clark, a veteran of Lord Dunmore's War in 1774, organized a militia army to defend Kentucky in an aggressive fashion. He decided that he should attack the British posts (inhabited mainly by French settlers) at Kaskaskia, Cahokia, and Vincennes; this policy might prevent supplies from reaching the Indians and thereby relieve some pressure on Kentucky. Clark led 175 volunteers on a 900-mile march down the Ohio River to Fort Massac. Next, he advanced and seized Kaskaskia (4 July 1778), then Cahokia (9 July) and then a detachment took Vincennes. Clark won over the French inhabitants by promising them religious and political freedom. His fame and policies spread among the French and local Indians, such as the Kickapoos and Piankashaws. Clark's exploits also gained the respect of the Potawatami, Sac, Fox, Chippewa, Ottawa, Miami, and Winnebago peoples. Clark was thus exerting an American presence in the area, which later helped secure large territories from the Alleghenies to the Mississippi in the 1783 peace treaty.

George Rogers Clark (above left) and 180 men marched across the flooded Wabash country in February 1779 to surprise and take Vincennes where he butchered five Indians in cold blood to convince Hamilton in Fort Sackville to surrender. The Indians had been bringing white men's scalps to Hamilton to collect bounty money.

Hamilton retaliated by retaking Vincennes with 500 men in December and tried to claw back British leadership of this western region. Immediately hearing of Hamilton's success, Clark determined that he could not defend Kaskaskia and Cahokia against any large-scale British attack in Spring but might be able to seize Vincennes by a surprise assault. Accordingly, he led some 180 men on a forced mid-winter march through flood water and cold. Arriving at Vincennes, he persuaded Hamilton to surrender on 25 February 1779 after which the Lieutenant Governor was imprisoned at Williamsburg. Vincennes was renamed Fort Sackville and Clark visualized it as a staging post for the capture of Detroit.

Clark needed to consolidate his position because local relationships were becoming tense. The American garrisons on the Mississippi required supplies, but they had little hard cash to buy from the French while Continental currency was fast losing its value. Also, supplies from New Orleans were few and any attack on Detroit looked increasingly unlikely. Nevertheless, Clark posed a potential threat to Detroit and the British were compelled to concentrate their forces on defense rather than launch any campaign in the last half of 1789. Clark also noticed that his newly acquired influence among the Indians was diminishing as the Indians realized that the British, rather than the Americans, could provide trade goods for their needs.

In September 1779, Clark left Fort Sackville and moved to the expanding settlement at Louisville on the Ohio River viewing the area as a better base. Thousands of settlers were now moving into Kentucky entering via the Ohio River or crossing the Appalachians through the Cumberland Gap. Despite Clark's capture of Fort Sackville and Sullivan's success at the Battle of Newtown, their combined victories were inconclusive because the Indians continued placing pressure on New York state, the Ohio Valley, and Kentucky until the end of the war in 1783.

Clark's Operations in the West
1778–79

KICKAPOO   Native American tribes

→   Hamilton's movements

→   Clark's movements

→   Spanish movements

Lake Superior

CANADA

Lake Huron

HURON

OTTAWA

OJIBWAY

Lake Michigan

WINNEBAGO

Lake Ontario

MUNSEE

Lake Erie

Detroit

SENECA

NEW YORK

SAUK

POTAWATOMI

Fort St Joseph

MIAMI

PENNSYLVANIA

KICKAPOO

PIANKASHAW

DELAWARE

Fort Pitt

Fort Harris

Redstone Old Fort

MARYLAND

Cahokia
seized 9 July 1778

Vincennes
(Fort Sackville)
captured 25 February 1779

Baltimore

PEORIA

Kaskaskia
seized 4 July 1778

SHAWNEE

KENTUCKY

Proclamation Line of 1763

VIRGINIA

KASKASKIA

Harrodsburg   Boonsboro

Richmond

Fort Massac

Williamsburg

LOUISIANA

Nashborough
(Nashville)

TENNESSEE

NORTH CAROLINA

CHICKASAW

CHEROKEE

Charlotte

Wilmington

SOUTH CAROLINA

CREEK

Long Bay

GEORGIA

Charleston

St. Lawrence River

Appalachian Mountains

N

Sullivan's Campaigns

The Wyoming Valley massacres or campaign and similar raids in 1778 compelled Congress to order Washington to prevent these incidents from recurring. Major General John Sullivan was given the task of breaking Iroquois power, which he never fully achieved because he was unable to force a final battle against the Confederacy. Sullivan's force comprised three brigades totalling some 2,300 Continentals plus Brigadier General James Clinton's 1,000 men and 1,100 volunteers. The army was so large that the Mohawk, Cayuga, Onondaga, and Seneca warriors felt unable to confront it and withdrew, leaving their villages to be torched and their crops devastated.

Sullivan adopted a twin strategy. He would advance from Easton, Pennsylvania, up the Wyoming and Susquehanna valleys to the New York Finger Lakes. Clinton's force would leave Canajoharie near Fort Dayton and join Sullivan via the Mohawk or Susquehanna. A feint supporting attack was also made by Colonel Daniel Brodhead out of Fort Pitt into the upper Alleghenies.

Sullivan moved along poor roads and through forests and knowledge of his advance drew Loyalist Colonel Butler's Tories and Joseph Brant's Iroquois towards the main American force. The drift of Indians towards Sullivan denuded Iroquois territory of its defenses and Brodhead moved into the Alleghenies with 600 men and burned eight villages and 500 acres of crops before returning to Fort Pitt. Butler and Brant finally decided to face Sullivan near the Indian town of Chemung. They gathered 200 Redcoats, 200 Loyalists, and 600 Indians, and hid behind a brush-and-timber breastwork hoping to entice Sullivan into an ambush. However, discipline among the Indians

was lax and some were spotted by Sullivan's advance guard. Sullivan attempted to conduct an enveloping maneuver, including the use of artillery. This movement failed because the British forces deserted their positions rather than face the Continentals and artillery fire. This Battle of Newtown (29 August 1779) allowed Sullivan to march north through the Six Finger Lake region where he and his troops burned Indian villages, stripped fields of crops, and girdled fruit trees. The Iroquois homeland was wrecked and Butler and Brant could do nothing to prevent the carnage. One Indian success was

John Sullivan hoped to capture Fort Niagara, the depot that supplied marauding Indians, but instead he burned towns, granaries, and crops, and chopped down orchards. The Seneca, thereafter, called Washington, the "Town Destroyer" because he had ordered Sullivan's campaign.

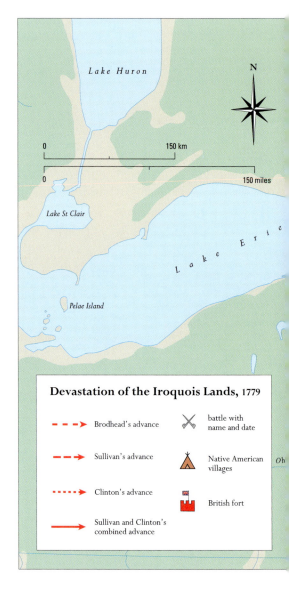

Devastation of the Iroquois Lands, 1779

- ➔ ➔ ➔ Brodhead's advance
- ➔ ➔ ➔ Sullivan's advance
- ➔ ➔ ➔ Clinton's advance
- ➔ Sullivan and Clinton's combined advance
- ✕ battle with name and date
- 🛖 Native American villages
- 🏰 British fort

an attack on an American patrol near Chenesse, the Seneca capital. Twenty-three men commanded by Captain Thomas Boyd were annihilated. Boyd was captured and tortured to death. Sullivan torched Chenesse and commenced a withdrawal to Easton, destroying remaining Iroquois villages. A Colonel Richard Butler was dispatched east of Lake Cayuga to burn more Indian townships there before ending his march at Fort Stanwix.

Overall, Sullivan burned forty Iroquois settlements and destroyed Indian food supplies, which forced the Iroquois to seek refuge and aid at Fort Niagara making them even more dependent on British resources. Indian raids continued and Sullivan's efforts might be classed as a failure. Yet, Sullivan weakened Iroquois influence and pushed American power into the western lands, south of the Great Lakes, a basis for later territorial claims. Sullivan failed to take Indian women and children hostage to be used as a lever to counter Indian raiding. However, he had further weakened the Confederacy because Oneida warriors helped him, and the Iroquois were not strong enough to mount large raids such as those at Cherry Valley, Wyoming Valley, and the German Flats. Also, civil war started to rage among the Iroquois with Oneidas and Tuscaroras being attacked by Brant. The Oneidas sought sanctuary with Americans around Schenectady and suffered the same cold and hunger as other Iroquois at Niagara.

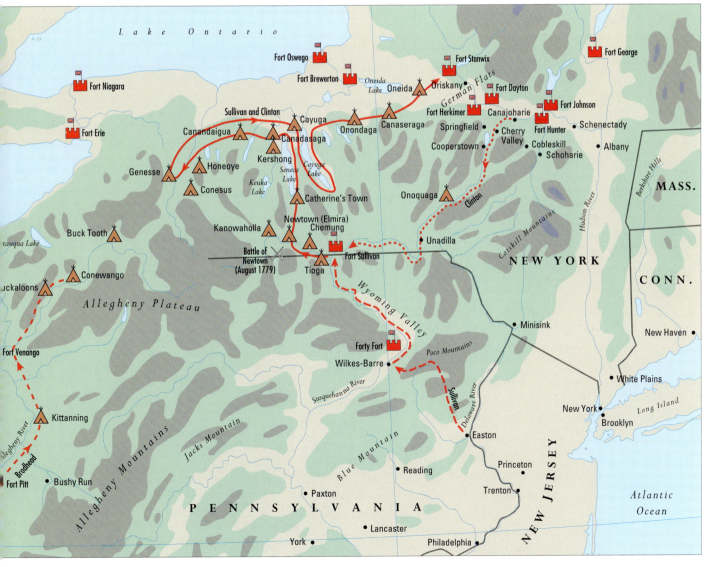

The Ohio Campaigns

In July 1779, a Continental army under Colonel John Bowman destroyed the principal Shawnee village at Chillicothe, Ohio. The enraged Indians were ready for further raids upon border settlements. In 1780, the British mounted a campaign against St. Louis and Cahokia. The force, led by Emanuel Hesse, comprised some regulars, but Great Lakes Indians constituted the main body. American garrisons in these settlements fought off the Indian onslaught and the attackers withdrew from both towns. One group traveled up the Illinois River and Clark dispatched Montgomery with a mixed American, Spanish, and French unit after them, this being one of the few occasions when Spaniards cooperated with Americans. Failing to catch Hesse's force, Montgomery destroyed a Sac and Fox village.

Elsewhere, Lieutenant Governor de Peyster at Detroit ordered Captain Bird with 250 men to assail American outposts along the Maumee–Miami Rivers. Bird eventually swelled his numbers when more Indians joined him along the way. Rather than attacking Louisville, because Clark was suspected to be there, Bird assaulted minor Kentuckian stations. Arriving at Ruddell's Station on the South Licking River, Bird sent the notorious renegade, Simon Girty, to demand its surrender. The defenders knew they stood no chance against Bird's artillery and opened the gates. Uncontrollable Indians then massacred some inhabitants before taking the rest captive. Bird next attacked Martin's Station but managed to protect the ensuing extra prisoners; the British and Indians then returned north by river.

In response, Clark mobilized 1,000 men and, taking a cannon along, he arrived at a main Shawnee village in the Little Miami Valley. The Indians fled and Clark destroyed the settlement and its crops. Clark then advanced upon Piqua town, near contemporary Springfield, Ohio. Using his cannon,

Clark defeated the Indians, but an enveloping movement was too slow to trap them. The Americans suffered sixty casualties, but Indian losses are unknown. Because raids on Kentucky slackened, it can be assumed that Clark must have inflicted a large defeat.

Kentucky was attacked again when Captain William Caldwell unsuccessfully assaulted Bryan's Station. While retreating, Caldwell was pursued by nearly 200 Kentucky militia from Harrodsburg,

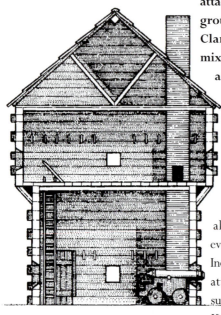

Blockhouses such as this were made to a standard pattern built of logs. The lower floor had embrasures for cannons while the upper story walls were pierced for muskets.

Boonesboro, and Lexington. These were ambushed by Simon Girty and some Indians and about 70 Americans were killed. Clark again retaliated and in November, raising another 1,000 men, marched up the Miami from Louisville destroying Indian villages and food stores. The devastation was so great that the winter of 1782 to 1783 saw a reduction in raids.

Elsewhere, in the north, the Gnaddenhutten Massacre provoked much violence. In 1782 to 1783, some Delawares who had been converted to Christianity by Moravian missionaries were removed north for safety on the orders of British Major Peyster. However, some returned to their villages to collect food. Unfortunately, they arrived in the aftermath of a Joseph Brant raid and were captured by militia commanded by Colonel David Williamson. Ninety captives (29 men, 27 women, and 34 children) were clubbed to death with a wooden mallet.

Retaliatory Delaware raids commenced and a second campaign was launched against the Indians by Crawford. His column was attacked and surrounded by Loyalists, Shawnees, and Delawares at the Sandusky River. Some 250 Americans perished; Crawford was captured, mutilated, and roasted to death taking two hours to die.

Fighting against the Delaware and their Wyandot allies continued sporadically until 1817 as part of an Indian-white conflict as the new American state expanded westward.

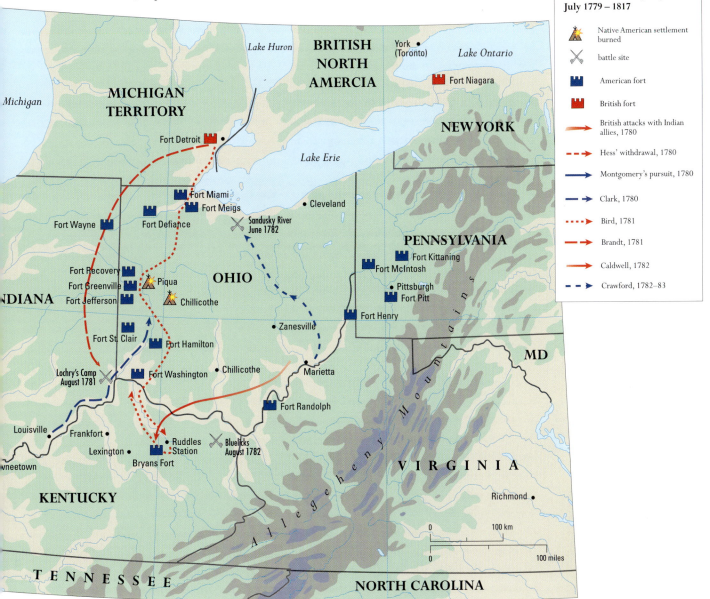

The Ohio Campaigns, July 1779 – 1817

- Native American settlement burned
- battle site
- American fort
- British fort
- British attacks with Indian allies, 1780
- Hess' withdrawal, 1780
- Montgomery's pursuit, 1780
- Clark, 1780
- Bird, 1781
- Brandt, 1781
- Caldwell, 1782
- Crawford, 1782–83

Spanish Operations in the South and West

Spain felt humiliated by the 1763 Treaty of Paris, which ended the French and Indian War. There, Spain lost Florida to Britain but gained French Louisiana. Thereafter, the Spanish monarchy developed certain policies towards Great Britain in both Europe and the Americas.

First, Spain wanted the return of Gibraltar, which had been British since 1713. Second, Spain wished to regain the Floridas and end any British influence in the lower Mississippi Valley and the Gulf of Mexico. Third, Spain wanted an end to British trading privileges in Spanish America, which were deeply resented and could be ended by war. Fourth, Spain wished to end British logging operations on the Honduran coast near Belize. Finally, Spain wanted to reduce the British Empire. Hence, Spanish assistance to the American Revolution was a desire not to win American independence but to embarrass and damage British interests. Thus, the Spanish government granted America a loan and agreed to transport military supplies via Havana and New Orleans. Meanwhile, espionage was conducted in Jamaica, the Floridas, Virginia, and Philadelphia. Spain preferred to resolve differences with Britain diplomatically, but the British refused negotiations on the status of Florida, Minorca, and Gibraltar. So Spain signed the Treaty of Aranjuez (1779) with France, the terms stating that the two would fight Britain until Spain gained Gibraltar.

The acting governor of Spanish Louisiana was Bernardo de Galvez who collected a force of Spanish regulars, Acadians, black volunteers, and Choctaws, and upon the declaration of war attacked British posts in West Florida because they were a potential threat to New Orleans. Fort Bute fell at Manchac (7 September 1779), Fort New Richmond at Baton Rouge followed (20 September), and Fort Panmure at Natchez surrendered (30 September). Spain now controlled the lower Mississippi Valley. Between February and March, Galvez campaigned in British West Florida. Landing troops from New Orleans and Havana, Galvez laid siege to Mobile, and its commander, Elias Durnford, surrendered on 14 March 1780. A relief force from Pensacola under Major General John Campbell turned back.

The Spanish commander now turned his attention to Pensacola, the capital of Florida. Using troops from Havana and Mobile, with a naval squadron from New Orleans, Galvez besieged Fort St. George near Pensacola. Lasting from March to May 1781, the siege ended when a chance shot from a Spanish cannon exploded the fort's powder magazine. General Campbell consequently capitulated. Galvez was promoted and made a count. He then became Governor of Florida and was authorized to command a Spanish army to invade Jamaica, although that invasion never took place because of the size of the British fleet in the West Indies.

Other Spanish military actions were limited to minor raids up the Mississippi Valley and action against the Honduran loggers. Galvez sent Captain Eugenio Pourré up the Mississippi from St. Louis after a British force unsuccessfully attacked the town in 1780. The Spanish troops surprised and captured the British garrison of Fort St. Joseph on Lake Michigan, near Detroit in January 1781; Pourré then returned to St. Louis. British loggers were driven from Belize and Rotan but Spanish forces led by Matias de Galvez, Bernardo's father, were unable to rid the Mosquito Coast of the British trespassers. In retaliation, the British captured Fort Omoa in Nicaragua, and invaded the area's interior. The elder Galvez drove out the British from Nicaragua but some coastal ports were occupied by the British until 1783. Elsewhere, New Providence Island was captured in the Bahamas, which were all handed to Spain in May 1782. Joint Spanish-American operations seldom took place and the Spanish government actually regarded the prospect of an independent America as a future territorial rival.

The South, 1778–81

→ Galvez movements with dates

RUSSIAN EMPIRE

Bering Strait

Alaska

Arctic Ocean

CHOCKTAWS

Fort Panmure
(Natchez)

Mississippi River

WEST
FLORIDA

Baton Rouge
Fort Bute
(Manchar)

Galvez 1779

Mobile
Fort Charlotte

New Orleans

Alabama River

CREEKS

Pensacola

Galvez 1779

Galvez from Havana 1781

Savannah

GEORGIA

Chattahoochee River

St. Mary's River

St. Marks

SEMINOLES

St. Augustus

EAST
FLORIDA

50 km

50 miles

Northwest
Territories

Arctic Circle

Greenland
to Denmark

*Vancouver
Island*

R u p e r t ' s   L a n d

(H u d s o n   B a y   C o m p a n y)

*Hudson
Bay*

Newfoundland

Québec

Montréal

Nova
Scotia

San Francisco

L o u i s i a n a

York

Detroit
Fort St Joseph

THIRTEEN COLONIES

Boston

New York

Philadelphia

Los Angeles

San Diego

Santa Fe

Tucson

El Paso

N
e
w

S
p
a
i
n

St. Louis

New Madrid

Louisville

Nashville

Williamsburg

New Bern

*Atlantic
Ocean*

Nacogdoches

Charleston

Savannah

*Pacific
Ocean*

Pensacola

New Orleans

St. Augustine

see inset above

Monterey

Gulf of Mexico

Havana

Cuba

Bahama Islands

Tropic of Cancer

Léon

Guadalajara

Mexico City

Veracruz

British
Honduras

Jamaica

Saint
Domingue

Santo
Domingo

Puerto
Rico

Mosquito
Coast

North America, c. 1780

British territory

Spanish territory

disputed Spain–Great Britain

Russian Empire

French possessions

→ Spanish attacks

400 km

400 miles

Chapter Eight
Birth of Politics

"We the People of the United States, in order to form a more perfect union, establish justice, insure domestic tranquility, provide for the common defence, promote the general welfare, and secure the blessings of liberty to ourselves and our posterity, do ordain and establish this Constitution for the United States of America." U.S. Constitution, 1787.

After Washington was inaugurated as President in 1789, he established the executive departments of state, war, and the treasury, and the first ten amendments to the Constitution, the Bill of Rights,

citizenship), the Alien Act, the Alien Enemies Act, and the Sedition Act, the last being an attempt to gag political opposition. In 1800, Adams was defeated by Jefferson who became the first president to be inaugurated in Washington, D.C. With Aaron Burr as his Vice-President, Jefferson attempted a road to harmony, to bind the wounds of internal division, and to stall his supporters' cries for an immediate purge of all past Federalist acts. Despite this appeasement, Jefferson managed to transform the bureaucracy into a republican body by the end of his tenure.

Good government was to be based upon the separation of powers with the executive, legislature, and judiciary entirely separate, unlike the political system in Great Britain. However, political gridlock would eventually materialize in later years.

were adopted by Congress and dispatched to the state legislatures. Alexander Hamilton, as Treasury Secretary, introduced policies which rekindled or kept burning the Federalist versus anti-Federalist controversy which began during the ratification debate over the Constitution. New fiscal policies such as the Funding Bill, the Assumption Bill, the establishment of the Bank of the United States, and an import tax, all generated heated discourse. Hamilton's ideas generated such differences of opinion that proto-political parties (factions, loosely aggregated interests) developed focusing around Thomas Jefferson, the leader of the Republican (later the Democrat) Party, and Hamilton and John Adams, the leaders of the Federalist Party.

Washington was succeeded by Adams as President with Jefferson as Vice-President, a recipe for stagnation and hostility, with Adams enacting repressive acts such as the Naturalization Act (requiring fourteen years of residency for

Jefferson repealed internal taxation and the whiskey excise, which had generated insurrections in western Pennsylvania and other states, eventually crushed by a variety of state militias. The 1798 Naturalization Act was voided and the residency requirement for citizenship returned to five years. The Alien and Sedition Acts expired and their victims pardoned. However, Jefferson used the Bank of the United States and retained the national debt, although he reduced its sum from $83 to $45 million by 1809 when he left office after a second term. The President also decreased the size of the armed forces because he believed that standing armies were dangerous and that a virtuous citizens' militia was sufficient for national defense. However, 1802 witnessed the foundation of the West Point Military Academy and the remobilization of some frigates to fight the Tripoli pirates on the North African coast.

A most important plank of Republican policy was the attack on the Federalist 1801 Judiciary Act.

This legislation established six new circuit courts with sixteen federal judges in new Western states. The judges were selected by Adams before he was defeated. Furthermore, another "midnight appointment" was Secretary of State, John Marshall, being created Chief Justice of the Supreme Court. He was a confirmed Federalist and held this post until 1835, thereby affecting the nature of American justice, but in a beneficial fashion. He extended the powers of the Supreme Court acquiring judicial review and also increased federal power at the expense of the states. Republicans feared any incremental move towards centralization and accordingly repealed the Judiciary Act. Additionally, the party remembered the tyrannical manner by which Federalist judges had applied the Sedition Act.

This year 1803 introduced the significant case of *Marbury* versus *Madison* into the judicial arena. Marbury was an Adams' "midnight appointment" and Secretary of State Madison refused to commission him. Marbury applied to the Supreme Court for redress and Marshall ruled that Marbury had used an unconstitutional section of the 1789 Judiciary Act to sue Madison, but the latter was also in the wrong. Marshall, therefore, had declared an act of Congress unconstitutional and hence Congressional majorities were irrelevant if they sought to implement unconstitutional policies. From this time onward, the Republicans co-existed with the judicial system, while judges learned that partisan decisions were no longer acceptable. The Supreme Court was now an equal part of government. Together with the Louisiana Purchase, the United States was consolidating itself territorially and legally and the electorate supported Jeffersonian policies by re-electing him president in 1804, based on support from northern artisans and southern farmers. Taking fifteen of the seventeen states in the electoral college, Jefferson had dropped Aaron Burr and his new running mate was Clinton of New York. Republican success displayed an increasingly coherent and unified party which had swept away the Federalists who were too elitist and old fashioned to campaign in an increasingly new and geographically wider political arena. Nevertheless, the Federalists were gradually changing with an influx of younger members who professed a new popular image and they portrayed Jefferson as a slave-owning planter, the antithesis of democracy.

Politics began to change as more people read newspapers and political debate was focused around the clam-bake, the pig-picking barbecue, and games. The increasingly populist form of political argument enhanced participation, but the Federalists divided into Younger and Older sections with no-one of the intellectual stature to confront the Virginian presidential dynasty of Jefferson, Madison, and Monroe, all of whom believed in loose federal government, neutrality, and financial economy. On 11 July 1804, Hamilton was killed in a duel with Aaron Burr and the Federalists were shorn of their leadership. The virulence of the Older Federalists is best exemplified by the actions of Senator Timothy Pickering of Massachusetts who led a group of New Englanders against the purchase of Louisiana because the acquisition would strengthen agrarian over commercial interests. In 1804, Pickering created an Essex Junta which contemplated New England and New York secession from the Union and even told the British ambassador of their notions. This disgruntled group proposed a convention to oppose and nullify federal government proposals — a contradictory view given earlier Jefferson — Hamilton conflicts. Burr, too, had strange political pretensions. After New York and New Jersey indicted Burr for murdering Hamilton, Burr sought to use the Louisiana Purchase and the U.S. army commander in the Mississippi Valley, General Wilkinson, to grab U.S. or Spanish territory for a new Southwestern state. The plot was foiled, and after an acquittal on a treason charge, Burr moved to Europe.

Adding these events together, American politics became bedevilled by an unusual situation. Federalism was weak but not dead, and John Marshall still ran the Supreme Court. Republicanism was weakened by Burr's strangeness and the parties clashed over personalities and issues. Interestingly, too, the Essex Junta showed that regional loyalties were paramount with some politicians, and this certainly undermined party loyalty.

In 1809, when Madison became the fourth President, he found that New England was back under Federalist influence, if not control, which had immense repercussions during the War of 1812. By 1814, the Madison government faced an economic blockade, near bankruptcy, and was forced to introduce internal taxes to balance the budget. New England business suffered so much that delegates from the state legislatures of Massachusetts, Connecticut, and Rhode Island plus citizens from New Hampshire and Vermont, met at Hartford, Connecticut, to reform the Constitution. Amendments were discussed such as the abolition of the 60 percent clause to eradicate the slave count and so weaken the Southern states. Also wanted was a two-thirds vote in both Congressional houses to admit new states or declare war; presidents should have a single term; and, that a new president should not be elected from the same state as his predecessor – a direct attack on Virginia. Success at the Battle of New Orleans ended this political venture and New England dreams during a period of intense nationalism after a sweeping victory over a British army. New national symbols helped integrate the American identity: the victor over both Britain and the Creeks, Andrew Jackson, became a national hero; and, the national anthem was composed. The "Star-Spangled Banner," was written by Francis Scott Key while observing the British cannonade of Baltimore, and that city's brave defense accentuated the feel-good factor among the masses.

The national assertion following the 1814 Treaty of Ghent, ending the War of 1812, witnessed Madison adopting a number of Federalist measures. Congressmen Calhoun of South Carolina and Henry Clay of Kentucky supported a protectionist economic system and the charter of the Bank of the United States had expired in 1811 so Madison and Congress refounded the Bank in 1816 to provide a bank which would provide a nationally respected institution, a reliable alternative to a multiplicity of small local banks without gold to back their notes. Madison's tariff and banking policies were pursued by his successor, Monroe (elected 1817), who ushered in the feeling of one-party politics, symbolized, perhaps, by his re-election in 1820. Monroe strove to ameliorate disunity and to promote the idea of a great American family possessing a common interest. However, the apparent disappearance of party divisions provides a misleading impression because the Republicans were riven by internal discord, the Supreme Court pursued strongly federal, nationalist decisions, and sectional interests again became obvious.

Republican presidents were chosen from a convention which had a nomination role. This party caucus was sometimes boycotted by many of the Republican Representatives. Thus, Republican Presidents did not possess a unified majority behind them. Furthermore, the Republicans never coalesced behind a "Republican" candidate for Speaker, an important position; it is the speaker who places representatives on committees and names their chairpeople. In reality, locality, region, and amiability proved more cohesive than strict, functional party loyalty. In fact, block votes of boarding-house inmates was so usual that some early Congressional directories listed Congress members by boarding house and not in alphabetical order.

The nationalism inherent in America after 1814 filtered into the Supreme Court where a series of issues increased federal power. The *McCulloch* versus *Maryland* (1819) case involved the constitutional status of the Bank of the United States. A Maryland law sought to tax a branch of the federal bank and this law was struck down. The Court said that the "implied powers" theory of the Constitution reigned and the national government was fully sovereign in its own sphere, and not the puppet of the states. Marshall also ruled that the Constitution had to survive the test of ages to come and therefore had to be adapted to changing circumstances. He supported federal supremacy as well as national economic interests, and he upheld private property rights. In *Fletcher* versus *Peck* (1819), the Supreme Court declared a Georgia law unconstitutional; the law tried to invalidate a legal contract, despite it being granted in a Yazoo corrupt land scandal. Marshall was obliged to intervene in the *Dartmouth College* versus *Woodward* (1819) case in which the New Hampshire state legislature amended the college's charter to bring it under state control. The Court decided that the charter was an inviolable contract within the terms of the Constitution. Thus, protection was granted to private endowments and also gave immunity to business corporations from state assembly interference. Another important case was *Gibbens* versus *Ogden* (1824) which involved interstate commerce. Robert Fulton ran a commercially successful steamboat (Clermont) venture on the Hudson from New York to Albany. He and his partner, Robert Livingston, were given a monopoly of the waters of New York state by a New York law. Marshall decided that such monopolies were unconstitutional because Congress had the prerogative of licensing new businesses when they crossed state lines, in this case, New York and New Jersey. The Court had ruled that "commerce" meant all types of "commercial intercourse" and within twelve months over forty steamboats were using Ogden's route. Thus, the Court removed an obstacle to trade and economic development during a time when steamboats were plying their trade on the Hudson, Ohio, and the Mississippi and its tributaries, thereby

helping the transport revolution involving the use of roads, rivers, and canals.

Sectionalism developed as the population moved westward. The Western versus Eastern states tension continued and deep-seated divisions were seen when Missouri sought admission to the Union as a slave state. Attempts were made to balance its admission by allowing the free state of Maine to enter simultaneously. This plan failed and debates continued as to how slavery should — or should not — be allowed to penetrate the Louisiana Purchase. A compromise followed with Missouri being admitted without restrictions upon slavery, while all the Purchase north of 36°30' was to prohibit slaves. Maine was allowed in in 1820 and Missouri in 1821. The Missouri Compromise held back the slavery question for twenty-five years, and was the brainchild of House Speaker Henry Clay. However, further territorial acquisitions in Texas (1845), the 1848 Mexican Cession, and the 1854 Gadsden Purchase, re-opened the vexed issue of slavery thereby laying down some foundations for such incensed sectional interests that civil war broke out. Kansas and Nebraska rejected the Missouri Compromise and opened up former native American territory to white settlement.

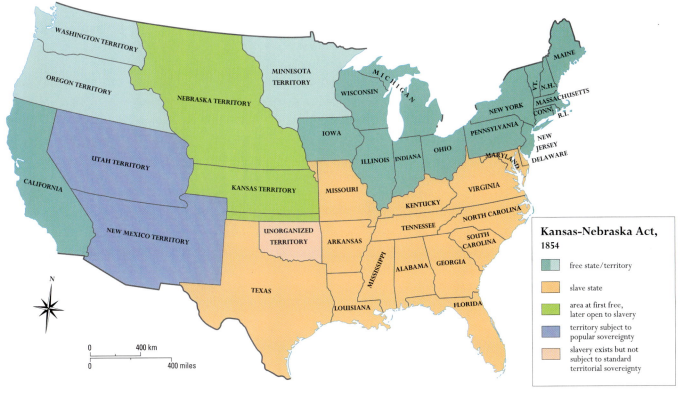

Kansas-Nebraska Act, 1854

- free state/territory
- slave state
- area at first free, later open to slavery
- territory subject to popular sovereignty
- slavery exists but not subject to standard territorial sovereignty

The Treaty of Paris

A preliminary peace treaty was signed in November 1782, and finally signed in 1783, in Paris and fighting ended as soon as the news reached the combatants. The American diplomats, John Jay, John Adams, and Benjamin Franklin, ignored Congressional instructions to be guided in negotiations by Vergennes, the French foreign minister and relied upon their own devices. A new British ministry, headed by Lord Shelburne, wanted to make peace.

The American negotiation team realized that French interests would be best served if Britain retained Canada and the area between the Great Lakes and the Ohio with Spain controlling the area south of the Ohio. Consequently, the Americans dealt with the British and the first article of the peace treaty granted American independence and gave the fledgling country the lands between the Great Lakes and the 31 degree parallel of the northern border of Spanish Florida and westward to the Mississippi River. Americans were given the right to fish in Newfoundland waters and to dry and cure their catch in uninhabited parts of Nova Scotia, Labrador, and Magdalen Island. Each country possessed the right to free navigation of the Mississippi. The United States agreed to recommend that the various state legislatures should allow Loyalists to reclaim their property. The large concessions made by the British were probably intended to encourage friendship and trade with America.

In the treaties with Spain, France, and Holland, Britain gave Tobago and settlements in Senegal to France while returning St. Lucia and Minorca and Florida to Spain. Britain regained lost West Indian islands, such as Dominica, and was granted the right of free navigation in the Indonesian islands and another trading base in

British peace propaganda of 1782, an attempt to kiss and make up while still upholding the notion of the continuation of royal control over remaining overseas possessions.

India in return for the strategic port of Trincomalee. The one group of participants in the war who were the real losers were the Indian tribes who were not consulted over the expansion of the United States into their lands. The borders with British Canada and Spanish Florida were not well defined and would lead to diplomatic difficulties in later years, Also, control of the new territories depended on the military forts at Niagara, Detroit, and Michilimackinac, and Britain refused to evacuate such posts in accordance with the Treaty unless America implemented other articles, such as compensation to Loyalists for sequestered property and the payment of debts to British merchants.

After acquiring so much extra territory, the separate states needed to resolve their western borders and the claims the states made on these lands. During and after the Revolution, all states with claims in the new territories ceded these to Congress. New states such as Transylvania, Westsylvania and the State of Franklin were not recognized by the Federal Government. The cession of the lands helped establish national loyalty and weaken parochial state loyalties.

The organization of the new lands was accomplished by the Northwest Ordinances of 1784, 1785, and 1787. The first established the national domain, while that of 1785 required that the land be surveyed by a rectangular system providing a map and plan in advance of sales to private citizens. Townships of six miles square were divided into 640-acre sections. Monies received from sales of land were to be retained, in part, for the establishment of public schools; other proceeds became revenue for the national government. When a designated area contained 20,000 people, a convention could be held, a constitution adopted, and the area would become a Territory with its own legislature and non-voting delegate in Congress. When the population of the territory equalled the free population of the smallest state (about 60,000), then it became a state of the Union.

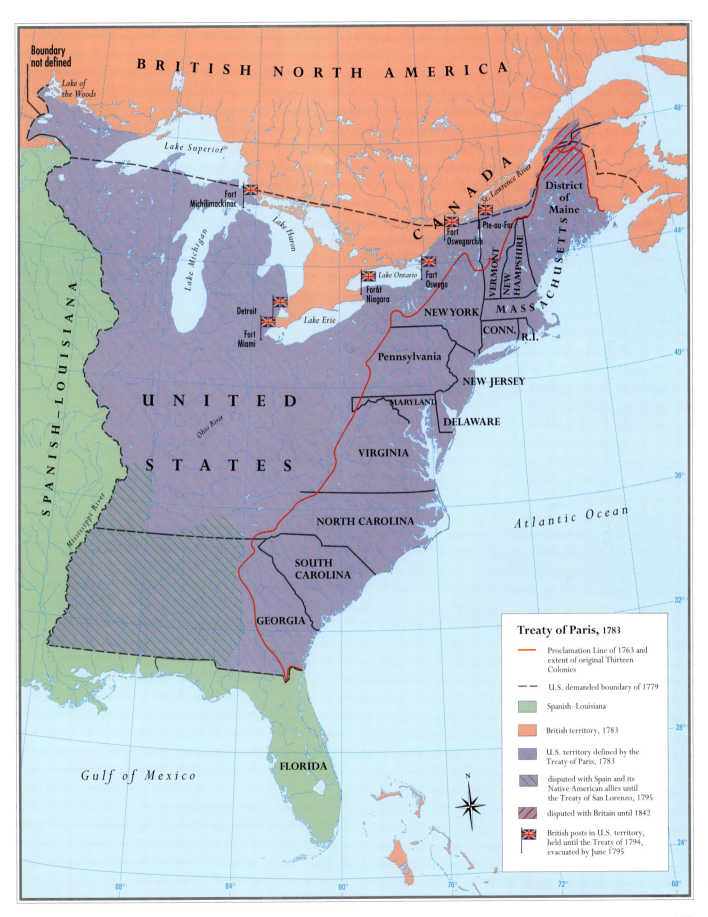

Boundary
not defined

*Lake of
the Woods*

BRITISH NORTH AMERICA

Lake Superior

Fort
Michilimackinac

Lake Michigan

Lake Huron

C A N A D A

St. Lawrence River

District
of
Maine

Fort
Oswegarchie

Pte-au-Far

Lake Ontario

Fort
Oswego

Forét
Niagara

Detroit

Fort
Miami

Lake Erie

VERMONT

NEW
HAMPSHIRE

M A S S A CHUSETTS

NEW YORK

CONN.

R.I.

Pennsylvania

U N I T E D

Ohio River

NEW JERSEY

MARYLAND

DELAWARE

S T A T E S

VIRGINIA

S P A N I S H – L O U I S I A N A

Mississippi River

NORTH CAROLINA

Atlantic Ocean

SOUTH
CAROLINA

GEORGIA

FLORIDA

Gulf of Mexico

N

Treaty of Paris, 1783

— Proclamation Line of 1763 and
extent of original Thirteen
Colonies

--- U.S. demanded boundary of 1779

Spanish–Louisiana

British territory, 1783

U.S. territory defined by the
Treaty of Paris, 1783

disputed with Spain and its
Native American allies until
the Treaty of San Lorenzo, 1795

disputed with Britain until 1842

British posts in U.S. territory,
held until the Treaty of 1794,
evacuated by June 1795

48°

44°

40°

36°

32°

28°

24°

88°   84°   80°   76°   72°   68°

Empire Loyalists

During the American Revolution, approximately 20 percent of white Americans remained loyal to King George III and were known as British Loyalists or Tories. Some Loyalists directly opposed independence and joined the British army or formed regiments of their own, such as Tarleton's Legion, comprising some 19,000 men at one time or another. Loyalists tended to be former government officials, traders with the British Empire, Anglican clergymen, former British soldiers, and many Scots in the Carolinas.

In 1777, the North Carolina Assembly demanded an oath of allegiance from its citizens, the alternative was banishment. Many strong Loyalists traveled to Britain, Canada, Florida, or the West Indies. Scots-Highlanders left in such vast numbers that the exodus has been compared with their departure from Scotland after Culloden. Many Southern Loyalists left the backcountry because their landlords were patriots. Also, in the Carolinas and

Georgia, many westerners perceived the eastern coastal elites as a pernicious aristocracy and thought British rule would protect them. Loyalists tended to be found mainly in the Carolinas, Georgia, New York, New Jersey, and Massachusetts. New York was the strongest Loyalist center, but Savannah, Charleston, Boston, and Baltimore contained strongly Loyalist elements.

Many Americans preferred to ignore the Revolution, if they could, but neutrality was often seen as enmity to America, and neutrality waned. However, after 1777, many states seized Loyalist property and used these resources to finance the war effort. In some cases, patriots used the war as an excuse to grab neighbors' property in bouts of greed.

During the peace negotiations in 1782, the position of Loyalists was discussed. The British insisted that confiscated property should be returned and an amnesty granted for all alleged Loyalist crimes during the war. Ultimately, Britain abandoned Loyalist interests and Congress agreed to recommend to states that Loyalists who had not fought could reclaim any sequestered property. Those who had fought for Britain or gone into exile had the right to repurchase confiscated property from new owners. In reality, during 1783–84, most states ignored these treaty clauses. A law in New York barred all Loyalists who had held office under British auspices, exiled themselves during the war, or joined the British from voting or holding office. Some two-thirds of the City and County of New York were disenfranchised. Men, such as Alexander Hamilton in New York and Benjamin Rush in Pennsylvania, campaigned against harsh measures, and by 1786 many 1784 laws were repealed. By 1787, most states were lifting anti-Loyalist legislation because Loyalist commercial and legal skills were needed for the new state. In 1792, New York allowed all banished Loyalists to return, but they were required to accept the state's title to their confiscated property. Manhattan property owner DeLancey lost his East Farm with its mile of waterfront, and his West Farm was divided among 175 purchasers after the Commissioner of Forfeiture sold it.

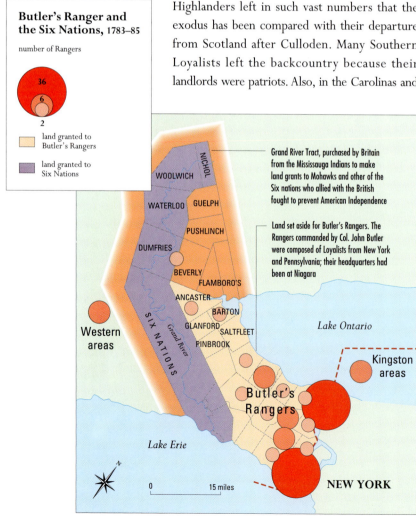

Butler's Ranger and the Six Nations, 1783–85

number of Rangers

36
6
2

land granted to Butler's Rangers

land granted to Six Nations

Grand River Tract, purchased by Britain from the Mississauga Indians to make land grants to Mohawks and other of the Six nations who allied with the British fought to prevent American Independence

Land set aside for Butler's Rangers. The Rangers commanded by Col. John Butler were composed of Loyalists from New York and Pennsylvania; their headquarters had been at Niagara

NICHOL
WOOLWICH
WATERLOO
GUELPH
PUSHLINCH
DUMFRIES
BEVERLY
FLAMBORO'S
ANCASTER
BARTON
GLANFORD
SALTFLEET
PINBROOK

SIX NATIONS

Grand River

Western areas

Lake Ontario

Kingston areas

Butler's Rangers

Lake Erie

0   15 miles

N

NEW YORK

Some 100,000 Loyalists left America and approximately 35,000 went to Canada and settled in Nova Scotia and what became New Brunswick. Another 10,000 settled in the new Upper Canada (Ontario). Other Loyalists put down roots in the other new province of Cape Breton Island. Such a large influx changed the nature of the Canadian population and made it more British than before. However, the demographic increase amongst French-Canadians meant that they were not swamped. These new Canadians, now Empire Loyalists, were instrumental in combatting American attacks on Canada during the War of 1812.

Gulf of St. Lawrence

BRITISH NORTH AMERICA 10,000

Lake Superior

Québec

Isle St. John 1,000

Cape Breton I.

Nova Scotia

Moncton

13,500

District of Maine

St. John

Montréal

Lake Michigan

Lake Huron

1,000

St. Lawrence R.

1783

20,000

Halifax

Lake Ontario

1783

NEW YORK

NEW HAMPSHIRE

Shelbourne

Lake Erie

Boston

1776

MASSACHUSETTS

CONN

R.I.

1792

To England

9000

PENNSYLVANIA

1783

Spanish–Louisiana

New York

NEW JERSEY

U N I T E D

MARYLAND

DELAWARE

S T A T E S

VIRGINIA

Norfolk

To Sierra Leone

1,200

1781

NORTH CAROLINA

1782–83

Atlantic Ocean

SOUTH CAROLINA

Charleston

GEORGIA

Savannah

1782–83

N

Mobile

1782–83

1782–83

St. Augustine

1783

1783

FLORIDA

Gulf of Mexico

Bahamas

7,000

1783

To St. Lucia 400

To Antigua 400

To Jamaica

8,000

To Jamaica

Empire Loyalists
1776–92

Spanish–Louisiana

British territory

United States, 1783

Migration routes of Loyalists, 1776–83

8,000   approximate number of Loyalist settlements

area of Loyalist settlement

Native Americans

The 1783 Treaty of Paris gave the United States title to the land east of the Mississippi despite the lack of negotiations with the Indians concerning their land. Realizing that a problem existed, Congress commenced land cession talks with northern tribes at Fort Stanwix (1784) and southern tribes at Hopewell, South Carolina (1785). The United States took the subsequent treaties as evidence that the land belonged to America and settlers were allowed in, while the Indians denied the verity of the treaties.

After the Northwest Ordinances were passed, Indians refused to accept American sovereignty and resisted incursions into their territory. Joseph Brant expressed bewilderment to Governor Haldimand in Québec especially after the Mohawks had given so much loyalty to Britain. Violent reactions followed as Native Americans defended their hunting and agricultural lands.

The Miamis were causing trouble for the Ohio Company, as were the Shawnees and Delawares. Brigadier General Harmar led 1,133 men out of Fort Washington (Cincinnati) against them and suffered 200 casualties with the militia running away. Governor St. Clair of the Northwest Territory was next authorized to pacify the Miamis and Shawnee. He advanced from Fort Washington to Fort Recovery, Ohio, with the entire regular army (600 men) and 1,500 militia plus 200 camp followers, both women and children. His force was surprised and surrounded by a large Indian force, under Little Turtle, on the Wabash (1791). The Americans suffered a crushing defeat, with 623 dead and 258 wounded, and lost 197 women and children, all scalped.

Next, General Wayne was ordered to resolve the situation. Congress authorized a larger army and Wayne advanced from Pittsburgh to Greenville and then to near what is today Toledo, Ohio. Wayne's 3,500 men caught the Miami in the Battle of Fallen Timbers using bayonet charges and a cavalry envelopment. The Indians were decisively beaten and the subsequent Treaty of Greenville (1795) was a compromise, with the United States being allowed to settle what became the state of Ohio while the northern tribes retained acknowledged rights to the northwest corner of the region. Trouble returned during 1811. Tecumseh, a Shawnee chief, exhorted Native Americans to return to old traditions and confederate against the Americans. Harrison, Governor of the Indiana Territory, defeated the Shawnee at the Battle of Tippecanoe when a major settlement, Prophetstown, was stormed. The conflict became part of the War of 1812 during which Tecumseh was killed fighting for the British at the Battle of the Thames in Ontario (1813).

In the South, the Cherokee, Choctaw, and Creek peoples supported the British during the Revolution. However, 1780 and 1781 witnessed two punitive expeditions against the Cherokee. The first, led by Lieutenant Colonel Sevier burned towns and the countryside. The Creeks ceased fighting in 1782 after the Upper Creeks were defeated by Wayne near Savannah. The same year saw the Cherokee and Chickasaws suing for peace. The power of the Cherokee was broken and vast territorial cessions were made to the United States. The Creeks signed the Treaty of Augusta (1783), which gave Georgia over 800 square miles as compensation for Creek actions during the war.

Another Creek war erupted in 1813–14 when the Creeks suffered a government's civilizing program, settler encroachment, and debts amounting to $22,000 to the Forbes Company. Internal dissension over the resolution of these problems led to a Creek civil war. Red Stick Creeks attacked Fort Mims (August 1813) and slaughtered some 250 people. Andrew Jackson, commander of the Tennessee militia, led a four-column force against the Creeks. Aided by some 500 Cherokees and some Creeks, the Red Sticks were compelled to fight at the Battle of Horseshoe Bend where about 800 Creeks were killed. The August 1814 Treaty of Fort Jackson ceded 14 million acres to the United States and destroyed Native American power on the lower Mississippi, and Indians were forced into enclaves surrounded by whites and blacks as settlers moved in.

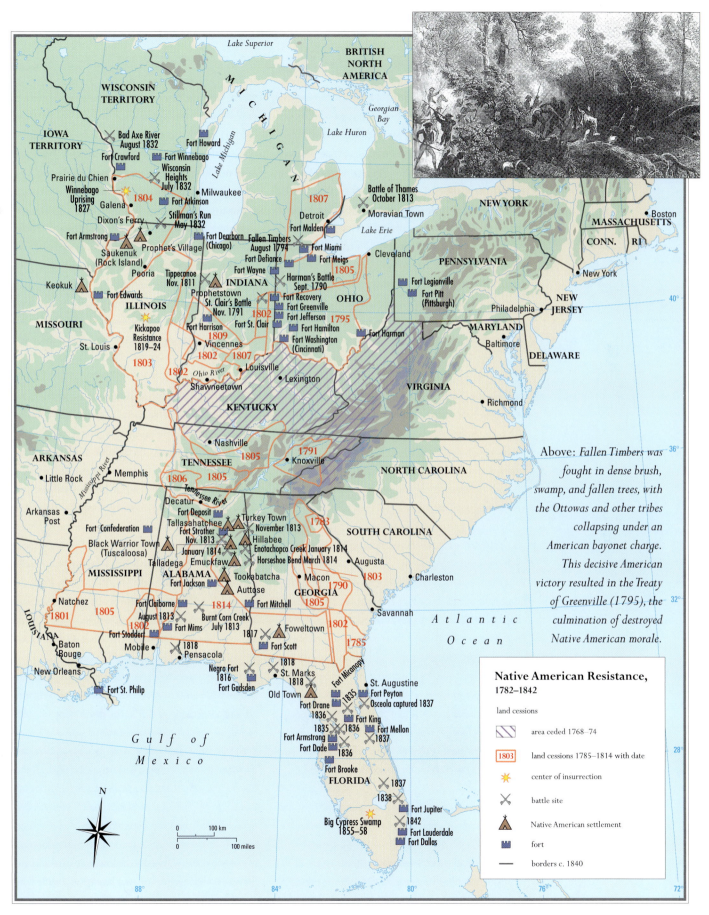

British North America

Lake Superior

MICHIGAN

Georgian Bay

Lake Huron

WISCONSIN TERRITORY

IOWA TERRITORY

Bad Axe River August 1832
Fort Crawford
Fort Howard
Fort Winnebago
Wisconsin Heights July 1832
Prairie du Chien
Winnebago Uprising 1827
Galena
1804
Milwaukee
Fort Atkinson
Dixon's Ferry
Stillman's Run May 1832
Fort Armstrong
Saukenuk (Rock Island)
Prophet's Village
Fort Dearborn (Chicago)

NEW YORK

Lake Michigan

Battle of Thames October 1813
Moravian Town
Detroit
Fort Malden
Lake Erie
Cleveland

1807

MASSACHUSETTS
CONN. RI
Boston

Keokuk
Fort Edwards
Peoria
ILLINOIS
Tippecanoe Nov. 1811
INDIANA
Prophetstown
St. Clair's Battle Nov. 1791
Fort Harrison
1809
Vincennes
1802   1807

Kickapoo Resistance 1819–24

MISSOURI

St. Louis
1803
1802
Ohio River
Louisville
Shawneetown
Lexington

KENTUCKY

Fallen Timbers August 1794
Fort Defiance
Fort Miami
Fort Meigs
Fort Wayne
Harman's Battle Sept. 1790
1805
Fort Recovery
Fort Greenville
OHIO
Fort Jefferson
1802
Fort St. Clair
Fort Hamilton
Fort Washington (Cincinnati)
1795
Fort Harman
Fort Legionville
Fort Pitt (Pittsburgh)

PENNSYLVANIA

New York
Philadelphia
NEW JERSEY
MARYLAND
Baltimore
DELAWARE

40°

VIRGINIA
Richmond

Nashville
1805
TENNESSEE
1791
Knoxville
NORTH CAROLINA

36°

ARKANSAS
Little Rock
Memphis
1806   1805
Tennessee River
Arkansas Post
Decatur
Fort Deposit
Fort Confederation
Tallasahatchee November 1813
Fort Strother Nov. 1813
Black Warrior Town (Tuscaloosa)
Hillabee
Talladega
January 1814
Emuckfaw
Enotachopco Creek January 1814
Horseshoe Bend March 1814
1783
SOUTH CAROLINA
Augusta
1803
Charleston

MISSISSIPPI
ALABAMA
Tookabatcha
Fort Jackson
Auttose
Macon
GEORGIA
1790
1805
Natchez
1805
1814
Fort Claiborne
August 1813
1802
Fort Mims
Fort Stoddert
Mobile
Fort Mitchell
Foweltown
1817
Fort Scott
1802
1785
Savannah
1801
LOUISIANA
Baton Rouge
1818
Pensacola
1818
New Orleans
Negro Fort 1816
Fort Gadsden
St. Marks
1818
Old Town
Fort Micanopy
Fort Drane
1835
St. Augustine
Fort Peyton
Osceola captured 1837
Fort St. Philip
1836
Fort King
1835   1836
Fort Mellon
Fort Armstrong
1837
Fort Dade
1836
Fort Brooke

Atlantic Ocean

32°

28°

Gulf of Mexico

N

FLORIDA
1837
1838
Fort Jupiter
Big Cypress Swamp 1855–58
1842
Fort Lauderdale
Fort Dallas

0   100 km
0   100 miles

Above: *Fallen Timbers was fought in dense brush, swamp, and fallen trees, with the Ottawas and other tribes collapsing under an American bayonet charge. This decisive American victory resulted in the Treaty of Greenville (1795), the culmination of destroyed Native American morale.*

Native American Resistance, 1782–1842

land cessions

▨ area ceded 1768–74

▭ 1803 land cessions 1785–1814 with date

✸ center of insurrection

✕ battle site

⛺ Native American settlement

🏰 fort

— borders c. 1840

88°   84°   80°   76°   72°

African Americans

American feelings against slavery are as old as the peculiar institution itself with reformers becoming extremely vociferous on the eve of the Revolution. Anti-slavery campaigners such as Anthony Benezet and Benjamin Rush supported court cases against slavery and Rush refused to practice medicine in South Carolina despite an offer of 1,000 guineas a year. By 1774, several New England and Middle colonies were prohibiting slave importation.

The Revolution itself altered African-American society. The free black population rose in numbers and the military requirements of both Americans and British offered new opportunities to African Americans. In 1775, the royal governor of Virginia, Lord Dunmore, decreed martial law and freed all slaves who were willing to fight for Britain. As for the American armed forces, as manpower shortages arose, New England states recruited black soldiers and Rhode Island established a black regiment. During the Battle for Rhode Island (August 1778), this First Regiment fought for four hours holding its ground against three British charges thereby playing an important role in Sullivan's evacuation of the island.

Britain's troop strength decreased continuously, especially when France, Spain, and Holland entered the fray. Britain adopted diverse strategies toward African Americans. Clinton and Cornwallis promised freedom of body and occupation to any African American deserting an enemy master. Slaves were seen as being an American economic resource and their seizure could only but benefit Britain. Hence, British troops stole 500 slaves in Norfolk County, Virginia, in 1779 alone. Some areas were stripped of slaves while thousands fled to British-held territory because a British victory allegedly assured freedom. Approximately 75 percent fled on foot, but many others used waterways, especially on the Georgia coast and in the Chesapeake Bay where escapees could meet British craft. In February 1777, British vessels in Chesapeake Bay took on board 300 blacks. The impact on East Florida was immense

where Governor Tomyn formed militia companies to counter any American invasion and control the sheer volume of African Americans. When the British received escaped slaves, they depleted American resources and often gained skilled craftsmen.

When the British left America, official ships evacuated African Americans, both slaves and freemen. An embarkation list dated August 1782 showed 1,568 blacks going to Jamaica from Savannah with nearly 2,000 entering St. Augustine, Florida. Private ships carried an unknown number. Many British felt an obligation that African Americans should not be returned to their former masters, providing the African Americans were healthy. When Charleston was evacuated on 14 December 1782, 5,327 African Americans accompanied the British. Half went to Jamaica, the rest to East Florida, St. Lucia, England, Nova Scotia, and New York. Some 4,000 left New York later, and many left the Floridas for Canada rather than face Spanish rule after the Treaty of Paris. Some slaves returned from St. Augustine to South Carolina with their Loyalist masters who were legally allowed to return. Many travelled to the Bahamas and the black population of Jamaica increased by 60,000 between 1775 to 1787. African-born Thomas Peter, who became a sergeant with the British, helped the Sierra Leone Company and worked with William Wilberforce. Ultimately, some 1,000 blacks survived the journey from Nova Scotia and settled at Freetown, Sierra Leone.

The Revolution commenced moves to end slavery and and started emancipation procedures. Vermont abolished slavery in 1777, as did Massachusetts, followed by Pennsylvania (1780), Rhode Island (1784), Connecticut (1784), New York (1799), and New Jersey (1804). By 1790, some 60,000 African Americans were free people; by 1800, the number had risen to 108,000. Manumissions increased as agricultural production increasingly relied on machinery and needed a smaller workforce. However, equality failed to follow emancipation and African Americans developed their own institutions and churches.

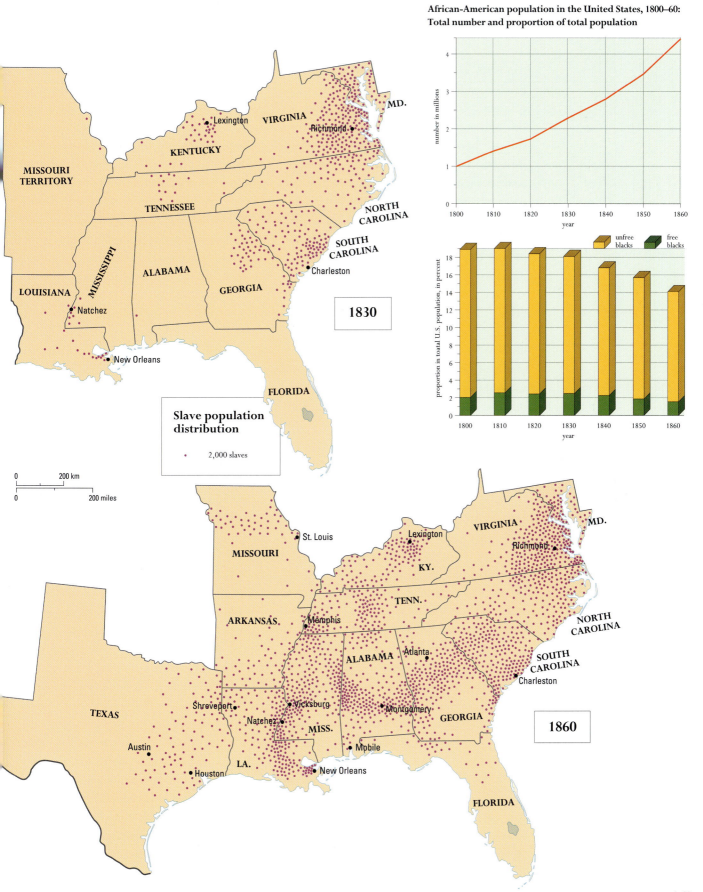

African-American population in the United States, 1800–60:
Total number and proportion of total population

number in millions

year

unfree blacks   free blacks

proportion in toatal U.S. population, in percent

year

1830

Slave population
distribution

•   2,000 slaves

MISSOURI
TERRITORY

Lexington   VIRGINIA   MD.
Richmond

KENTUCKY

TENNESSEE

NORTH
CAROLINA

SOUTH
CAROLINA

MISSISSIPPI   ALABAMA   GEORGIA

Charleston

LOUISIANA

Natchez

New Orleans

FLORIDA

0   200 km
0   200 miles

1860

St. Louis   Lexington   VIRGINIA   MD.
Richmond

MISSOURI

KY.

TENN.

ARKANSAS   Memphis

ALABAMA   Atlanta   SOUTH
CAROLINA

NORTH
CAROLINA

Charleston

TEXAS   Shreveport   Vicksburg   Montgomery   GEORGIA

Natchez

Austin   MISS.

LA.

Mobile

Houston   New Orleans

FLORIDA

Ratification of the Constitution

In 1783, America was in a perilous situation. Economic dislocations developed, partially because of the British ban on U.S. trade to the British West Indies, and a depression spread through 1784 and 1785. American politicians blamed the Articles of Confederation as being inadequate to run the country. States were experimenting with varieties of paper money, which fueled economic problems and Congress was unable to raise adequate revenue. Further difficulties occurred in Massachusetts.

The depression, combined with high property taxes, damaged impoverished and debt-ridden western farmers. The state's Supreme Court disallowed the suspension of debt collections and the legislature refused to grant relief. Consequently, farmers, led by Daniel Shays, marched on the Federal Arsenal at Springfield and state troops were used to crush the rebels. This east-west split was also found in North Carolina and Maryland, and this division informed the debate surrounding the ratification of the Constitution.

The Constitutional Convention met at Philadelphia in May 1787. Various constitutional plans were proposed and James Madison was important in establishing the principles of checks and balances and the separation of powers. Debates surrounding the style of constitution fell into two camps: the Federalist supporters of the Constitution and the anti-Federalist opponents. The anti-Federalists thought sovereignty and the protection of individual rights should reside in the separate states. They opposed a powerful, intrusive, central government. Prominent leaders of these views were Samuel Adams, Richard Henry Lee, and Patrick Henry. Generally, they were the mouthpieces of western settlers who possessed their own specific interest: cheap land, defense against the Indians, and decent roads to take their pelts and farm produce to the market place. Contrarily, coastal inhabitants feared that a cheap land policy would depress the value of their already developed land. Westerners were also angry over the political systems in some states, such as Virginia, where planter-led gerrymandering meant that western settlers were underrepresented. New England politics tended to be split between the wealthy merchant class and the small farmer who resented outside interference and felt a federal government would restrict their liberty. In the South, the east-west split was probably reinforced by a backcountry contra-tidewater division.

The Federalists felt a separation of powers was sufficient to provide good government and prevent tyranny. Also, the division of powers between states and a federal government would further ensure this protection. The Constitutional Convention, in which all states except Rhode Island were represented, prepared the Constitution, which was signed by the delegates on 17 September 1787. The document was then sent to the various states for ratification, with the proviso that the Constitution would become operative when ratified by nine states. Debate continued concerning the noninclusion of a bill of rights, with the Federalists pursuing classical republicanism and their opponents fearing that elected leaders would work for personal gain and not the good of all.

Ratification was close run. Delaware voted unanimously in favor (7 December 1787) followed by Pennsylvania (12 December, 46 to 23 votes). Next came unanimous New Jersey, Georgia, and Connecticut, with Massachusetts coming afterward in 1788. Maryland ratified on 26 April (63 to 11), South Carolina next (149 to 73), and New Hampshire followed on 21 June; the necessary nine had been achieved. Virginia voted 89 to 79 in favor, but New York opened up a lively campaign with James Madison, John Jay, and Alexander Hamilton putting forward their ideas in *The Federalist* political journal. On 26 July, New York ratified by a slim majority of three. Only North Carolina and Rhode Island held out, with the latter completing the ratification process in 1790. The United States now had a new Constitution and a new government.

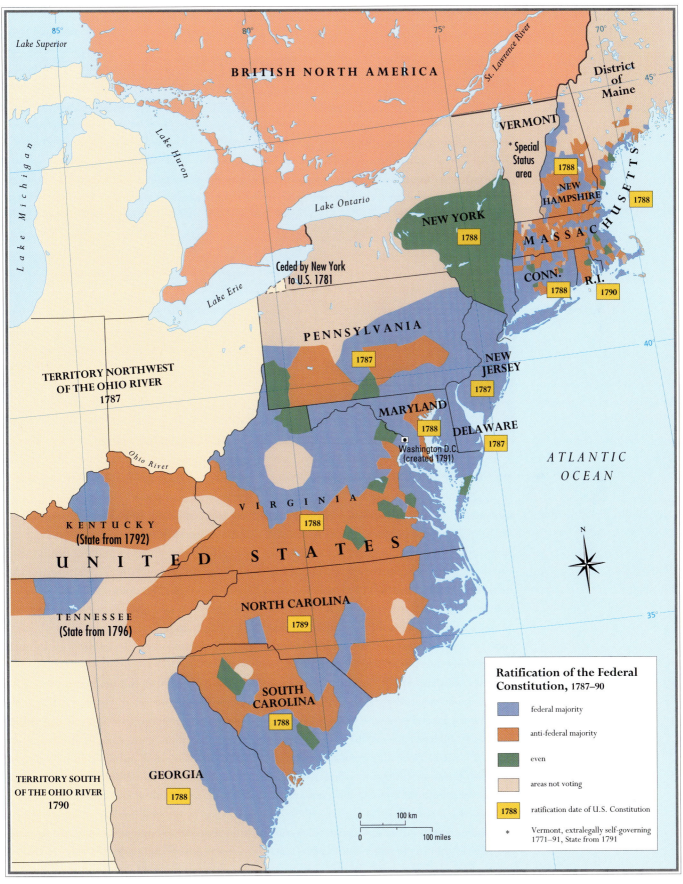

85°
Lake Superior

BRITISH NORTH AMERICA

80°

St. Lawrence River

75°

District
of
Maine

45°

Lake Michigan

Lake Huron

VERMONT

Lake Ontario

70°

* Special
Status
area

1788

NEW
HAMPSHIRE

MASSACHUSETTS

1788

NEW YORK

1788

Lake Erie

Ceded by New York
to U.S. 1781

CONN.
1788

R.I.
1790

PENNSYLVANIA

40°

1787

NEW
JERSEY
1787

TERRITORY NORTHWEST
OF THE OHIO RIVER
1787

MARYLAND
1788

DELAWARE
1787

Washington D.C.
(created 1791)

ATLANTIC
OCEAN

Ohio River

VIRGINIA
1788

KENTUCKY
(State from 1792)

U N I T E D   S T A T E S

N

TENNESSEE
(State from 1796)

NORTH CAROLINA
1789

35°

SOUTH
CAROLINA
1788

Ratification of the Federal
Constitution, 1787–90

federal majority

anti-federal majority

even

areas not voting

TERRITORY SOUTH
OF THE OHIO RIVER
1790

GEORGIA
1788

1788   ratification date of U.S. Constitution

0   100 km

0   100 miles

*   Vermont, extralegally self-governing
1771–91, State from 1791

The Constitution

The framers of the Constitutional Convention at Philadelphia concerned themselves with limiting the power of government and ensuring the liberty of citizens by separating the legislature executive and judiciary.

On 25 May 1787, fifty-five delegates, representing all states except Rhode Island, met at the Constitutional Convention in Philadelphia, George Washington presiding. The Convention was in continuous session until its task was achieved. Comprising debates and committee work, the Convention was motivated by a desire to create a functioning political and economic society based on serious philosophical ideas.

Americans were attracted to the social contract theory of John Locke, and Thomas Jefferson was certainly influenced by the notion that citizens should freely enter a contract by which they gave their freedom, independence, and sovereignty to a political center. Thus, those who rule derive authority from the consenting and governed citizenry. However, this consent was conditional in that a government which failed to achieve the goals of society was breaking the contract and therefore delegitimized itself. Together with Locke's *Two Treatises of Government* (1688), Montesquieu's *De*

l'Esprit des Lois (1748) introduced another concept: the separation of powers by which the executive, legislature, and judiciary should be separate and distinct branches of government. Although the delegates were united in purpose behind these ideas, major disputes did erupt, which were ended by compromise. The most serious disagreement was generated over the nature of the legislature. The larger states, led by Virginia, proposed a bicameral parliament elected by popular vote, which would in turn elect a Senate. The less populous states obviously favored another plan, supported by New Jersey, which would provide a unicameral legislature in which all states would have equal representation. The Connecticut Compromise solved the problem whereby all states would be equally represented in the Senate and represented in the House of Representatives according to their proportion of the population. More populous states were made happy when money bills could only originate in the House and Southern states insisted that the white population's numbers would be augmented by 60 percent of the black slave population. The less populous Southern states were mollified by the requirement of taking a census every ten years as the benchmark for apportioning representatives.

The Constitution, signed on 17 September 1787, represents a fear of government—fear of the agencies of government and those who might gain control of these institutions and misuse them. Accordingly, the Constitution contains three main lines to control any majority faction. First, the Constitution can only be amended by a two-thirds majority of both Houses of Congress and ratified by three-quarters of the state legislatures. Second, two different levels of government were created: state and national. The national, or federal, government was given specific but limited powers, those powers; not designated to the federal government remained with the states. Third, powers were subdivided and separated and further subjected to checks and balances.

Federalism, itself, dispersed power and responsibility to two tiers of government thereby preventing any accumulation of power. Each level ensured that it remained undominated by the other and the smaller states' rights were safeguarded against the national government. In the system of checks and balances, the President, the executive, has the power of veto over bills passed by Congress, but Congress can interfere with the normal functions of the executive by being the body from which legislation emanates. The President's power as Commander-in-Chief is moderated by Congress' right to declare war and raise funds for the armed forces. Also, the presidential veto can be overturned by a two-thirds majority in both Houses. The President can also be impeached with the Senate sitting as a High Court. If Congress, the President, or states act in an apparently unconstitutional manner, the Supreme Court, if a case is raised before it, can arbitrate through the process of judicial review.

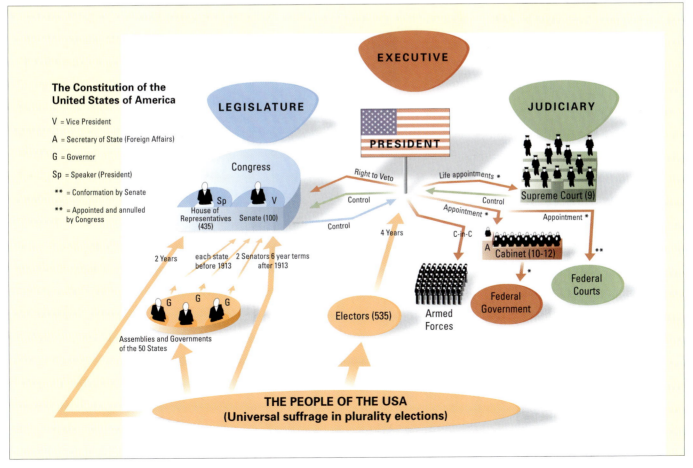

The Constitution of the United States of America

V = Vice President

A = Secretary of State (Foreign Affairs)

G = Governor

Sp = Speaker (President)

** = Conformation by Senate

** = Appointed and annulled by Congress

The Election of 1800

Although the Constitution was ratified, the anti-Federalists secured promises of amendments in return for unconditional

ratification. The first Congress possessed a strong Federalist membership and faced four immediate problems: revenue raising, the demand for a bill of rights expressed in state ratification conventions, the establishment of executive departments, and the creation of courts other than the Supreme Court.

Under President Washington, James Madison became an important member of Congress which

was persuaded to place a 5 percent tax on certain imports to raise state revenue. Madison played a significant role in enacting the first ten amendments, which established a Bill of Rights, becoming law on 15 December 1791. Three executive departments were created by Congress: State, War, and Treasury. Alexander Hamilton's fiscal policies were introduced, including the creation of the Bank of the United States. However, his policies generated differences of opinion, which stimulated the formation of political parties. In particular, Hamilton's ideas that the national government should take over state debts incurred during the Revolution proved anathema to some. States, such as Virginia, Maryland, North Carolina, and Georgia, had repaid most of their war debts. If the government assumed the responsibility for others' debts, then they would be taxed to pay such an obligation. In reality, financially viable states would pay taxes twice. Why should North Carolina subsidize South Carolina? Also, Thomas Jefferson and James Madison felt that Hamilton's policies favored wealthy merchant interests rather than farmers; they viewed agriculture as the economic backbone of future wealth and development. They complained that Hamilton supported aristocratic government and was, therefore, subverting the Revolution. They were its real heirs and they began calling themselves and their supporters Republicans. Hamilton replied by labeling his following Federalists. The growth of Democratic-Republican clubs sympathetic to the French Revolution opened up further divisions, establishing interest-group politics and the idea of an organized but loyal opposition.

Differences were reinforced by contrary views over foreign policy regarding aid to France, the Jay Treaty, and the Pinckney Treaty with Spain over Florida. Voting analyses over the lives of the first four Congresses show delegates voting by region and in cohesive groups. The Republican coalition, especially strong in the southern and middle states, comprised white planters and small farmers with a Celtic or German background; linked also, were artisans who saw themselves as independent and did not like domineering people such as bosses or Hamilton. Federalists tended to be English, dislike participatory democracy, support authority, and oppose Southern economic interests.

In the 1796 presidential elections, the Federalist John Adams became President, with Thomas Jefferson, a Republican as Vice-President because the vagaries of the electoral system. This divided partnership inaugurated a period of political inconsistency with increasing dissent leading to a Sedition Act (1798) by which Adams hoped to make political opposition a crime. Jefferson and Madison campaigned in state legislatures, inciting Republican support to oppose alleged tyrannical authority.

In the run up to the 1800 presidential election, the Federalists split into Adams versus Hamilton camps regarding the Quasi War with France. The Republicans entered the contest united behind Jefferson and Burr. They won the southern states, while the Federalists gained New England with the middle states split; but, overall, the Republican vote won. Because the Republicans voted for their candidates together, the Federalist-dominated House of Representatives had to decide between them with each state's congressmen acting in unison. Jefferson was elected President. This 1800 revolution led to Amendment Twelve whereby voting in the electoral college allowed a party ticket and separate ballots had to be cast for both President and Vice-President.

Opposite: Jefferson delighted in his Virginia mansion at Monticello and filled it with scientific artifacts and innovative gadgets, such as a polygraph, an early machine designed to duplicate letters. The President did not stand on his dignity and a visiting British minister to the United States was flabbergasted to find him wearing slippers at a diplomatic reception in 1803.

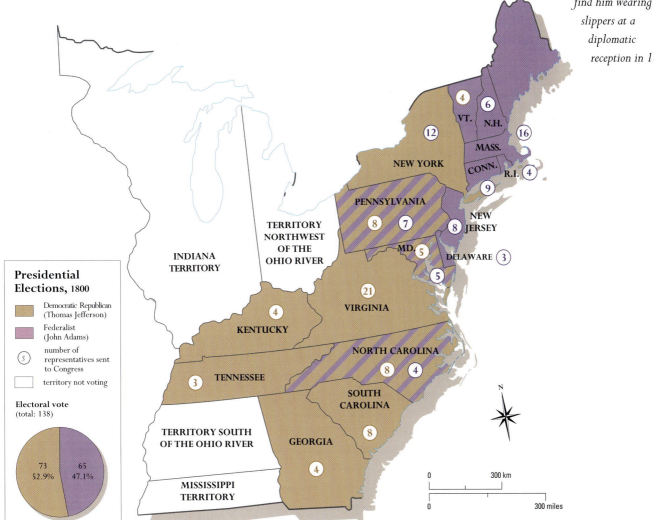

Presidential Elections, 1800

Democratic Republican (Thomas Jefferson)

Federalist (John Adams)

⑤ number of representatives sent to Congress

☐ territory not voting

Electoral vote
(total: 138)

73
52.9%

65
47.1%

People of the New Nation

The 1790 census, demanded by the Constitution, was designed to estimate representation requirements and the allotment of direct taxes among the states. The census shows the population's mix in terms of race, gender, and age, but its statistics can be criticized. Slaves were not differentiated by age or sex and they were only considered 60 percent worth of a free person. While women were included with girls, white males were divided at age sixteen when taxation and militia duties commenced.

Comprising about four million people, the population spread along the Atlantic seaboard moving inland with people moving into territories such as Kentucky, Ohio, and Tennessee. There were wide disparities between states in size and population, such as 59,000 in Delaware, 393,751 in North Carolina, and 748,000 in Virginia. The population was doubling every twenty-five years with couples having large families; therefore, much of the population was very young. However, immigrant males tended to be older and this affected the gender and age make-up in certain regions.

In 1790, the black population was 19.3 percent, but the highest concentration was in the South even though slavery had existed in the North, too. Within southern states, there could be county variations in the black population. The interior backcountry counties of North and South Carolina and Georgia were markedly different from the more coastal regions where blacks congregated on plantations. The post-war period saw an increase in the number of free blacks, and their social and economic situation improved for a short while. They had imbibed ideals of liberty and equality during the Revolution and realized strength lay in unity. This sentiment resulted in Gabriel's Rebellion in 1800, which sought to seize Virginia's capitol in a bout of political and second religious awakening. The leaders were condemned and hanged. In North Carolina, slave artisans and preachers played significant roles in conspiracies to seize planters' homes and kill their masters. These plots were uncovered and many slaves were executed in a hysterical witch-hunt. This white fear stood badly with the fact that slave labor was a vital part of the economic and social composition of the South.

The census demonstrated that the early population was extremely young, compared with recent times, and this meant that the proportion of people within the workforce was low, despite obvious childhood farm chores. The white population was fairly homogeneous with populations of 55 percent under sixteen in twenty-seven counties of the southern backcountry and two in Pennsylvania. This east-west split with younger men moving west meant that in parts of New England women outnumbered men and could not guarantee they would find a spouse. Arguably, this insecurity drove some women to Christianity during the Second Awakening and they contributed to missionary and charity work. Female organizations were established to help widows, orphans, and "fallen" women. Women's rights, education, and property were discussed, and some states modified property and inheritance laws to allow women to inherit and control property after marriage and therefore have power in local politics. Women were gaining the hallowed status of mothers of republican citizens and achieving power and influence rather than submerging themselves in male trade unions as women eventually did in Great Britain.

Frontier settlements in New York, Maine, Virginia, and Kentucky were dominated by men, while major cities such as New York, Philadelphia, and Boston had fewer males than average as in the coastal areas of South Carolina and Georgia. The accompanying maps show the complex diversity of population settlement in the United States.

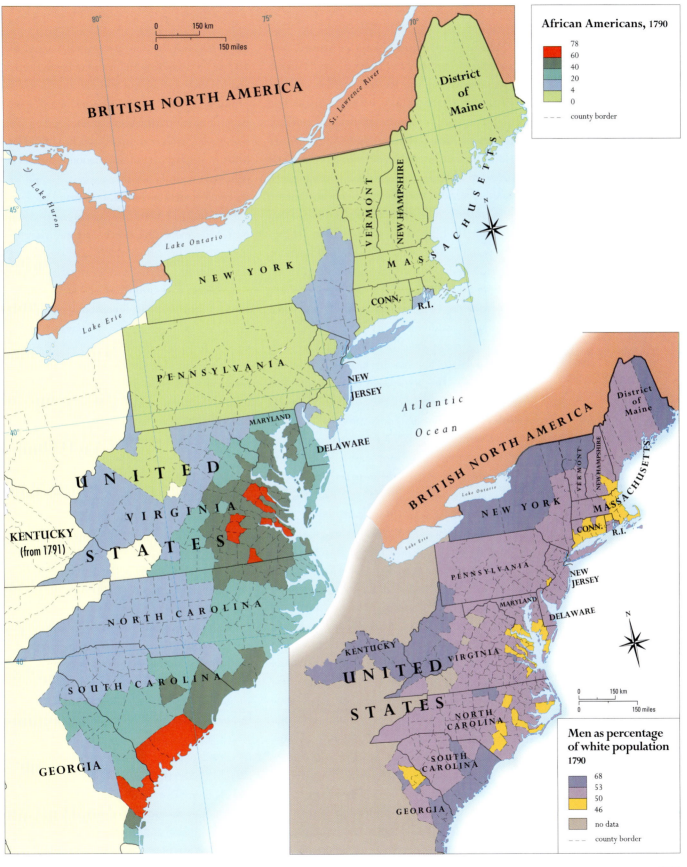

African Americans, 1790
- 78
- 60
- 40
- 20
- 4
- 0
- - - - county border

Men as percentage
of white population
1790
- 68
- 53
- 50
- 46
- no data
- - - - county border

Chapter Nine
The State Expands

"Men are born, and always continue, free and equal in respect of their rights." French Declaration of the Rights of Man and of Citizen, 1789.

The immediate aftermath of independence required a period of peace, the development of trade, an end to foreign entanglements, and negotiations to end all outstanding obstacles to peace. Some successful steps were made in these directions. The 1795 Jay Treaty reconciled immediate differences between the United States and Britain, although the border between Canada and the Louisiana Purchase (1803) required adjustment, which took place in 1818. Likewise, the Oregon country was jointly ruled by Britain and America until an equitable division was decided in 1846. Furthermore, northern Maine was disputed until 1842. Similarly, the Pinckney Treaty (1795) rationalized the borders with Florida and ensured storage rights for American goods in New Orleans, an essential policy because the Mississippi was the major arterial trade route from the continental interior to the sea.

Trade increased as America and Britain renewed their traditional commerce, with America taking the highest value of British exports, and the British Empire purchased the majority of American exports. However, the geographical expansion of the French Revolutionary Wars introduced new problems for the United States. A Quasi War broke out between America and the Directory (1795–1799) over French hostility to the Jay Treaty and this curtailed U.S. trade expansion. The growth of the French Revolutionary empire created additional difficulties for America. After Napoleon I sold Louisiana to America in 1803, the war between France and Britain, plus the latter's European allies, recommenced after the short Peace of Amiens. During the conflict, each European protagonist wanted to inherit the other's trade and the United States found itself squeezed in the middle. America had commercial links with both sides and as a neutral, became the leading food supplier and transporter to Europe and the West Indies, and also carried Caribbean products abroad. Britain attempted to prevent American free trade and maintained the right to search U.S. vessels to impress British deserters hiding among an American crew or even American mariners in an attempt to supply the Royal Navy with its insatiable demand for men. Some 6,000 to 8,000 U.S. citizens suffered such a fate, and this crime impacted upon American sovereignty. British naval captains argued that British subjects remained such even if carrying an American protection document. The U.S. Senate accused Britain of aggression and a violation of U.S. neutral rights under international law. Congress passed the Non-Importation Act, which prevented numerous British exports from entering the United States. A further incident (1807) was the attack on the USS *Chesapeake* by HMS *Leopard* after the former refused to allow a search of its decks for British deserters. Further American acts followed with the Embargo Act (1807) forbidding U.S. exports to any country as a short-term measure to avoid confrontation. New England trade suffered, which occasioned Federalist opposition to Jefferson which even debated secession. The ill-designed Embargo Act was replaced by the 1809 Non-Intercourse Act, which opened trade with all countries except France and Britain.

International arguments continued, and wartime commercial pressure on England, which suffered an 80 percent trade decrease with America, drove the government to open the seaways to American shipping. However, before the news reached the United States, President James Madison declared war on Britain alone, despite constant French depredations on American shipping. Not only were impressment, British trade Orders in Council, and a British trade monopoly cited as *casus belli* (cause of war) but also alleged British incitement of Native American hostility among the Shawnee and

Potawatomi (the former's leaders being the Prophet Tenskwatawa and his brother, Tecumseh).

America was divided over war. The West, strengthened by electoral reapportionment after the 1810 census, desired war, expansion, and the upholding of American honor, as had been already achieved by the U.S. navy against the Barbary states between 1803 and 1805 during and after the Tripoli war. The coastal areas of the states feared the diminution of U.S. trade through war. Congress voted 79 to 49 in the House of Representatives and 19 to 13 in the Senate to declare war. Despite Britain repealing its Orders in Council on 16 June 1812, the war went ahead. Maybe the desire for trade was superceded by the

shambles. Some regions, such as New England, refused to contribute troops to "Mr. Madison's War" after experiencing Federalist pressure. Some state militias refused to fight outside their own borders, while the frontier states of the South, West, and Northwest: Kentucky, Tennessee, Ohio together with the Michigan, Indiana, and Mississippi territories were extremely responsive to pleas for recruits. Accordingly, disorganized, uncoordinated, and ill-conceived attacks were mounted on Canada, the only British-ruled land which could be attacked. Victory there was considered possible because the Royal Navy could not penetrate to the Great Lakes and Britain was so locked into

The Philadelphia *surrendered to Tripolitan gunboats in 1804 after running aground. Later, Lieutenant Decatur boarded her and set the ship ablaze, escaping with only four wounded out of his boarding party of seventy.*

War Hawks urging the capture of Canada to round out U.S. territories in the north.

The conflict demonstrated American disunity and unpreparedness. West Point Academy had trained very few officers and the army relied on politicians and state militia leaders to "organize" the forces that were decentralized and in

fighting French Napoleonic armies in the Iberian peninsula that it could not afford to reinforce Canada.

America's initial strategy was to send General Hull towards Detroit, where he surrendered after confronting British troops and after Fort Dearborn was captured by mainly Potawatomi

Indians operating for Britain. The Indians were, therefore, linked to and cooperating with their British allies. Further American defeats occurred at Queenstown, near Niagara, after the New York state militia refused to cross borders, and at Lake Champlain, thereby preventing a march on Montréal; more American militia had refused to enter Canada.

This painting by H. Charles McBarron depicts the British storming an American redoubt at New Orleans, which resulted in terrible British losses, including British General Packenham.

The only joy for the Americans lay in the exploits of the big frigates: the USS *United States*, *Constitution*, *President*, and *Philadelphia*, all classed as 44 guns but actually mounting 56 guns, including eighteen 42-pounder carronades. Several single-ship actions resulted in American victory. On 19 August 1812, the *Constitution* captured the *Guerrière* (38) after dismasting her. On 12 October 1812 the *United States* met the HMS *Macedonian* (38), which suffered 104 casualties before striking. On 28 December, HMS *Java* fought the *Constitution* in a fierce four-hour battle during which the former sustained 124 dead and wounded and the latter, probably, 52. The unseaworthy *Java* was burned on 31 January 1813. The smaller USS *Wasp*, a sloop rated 18 guns, but mounting 22, captured HMS *Reindeer* on 28 June 1814. The British vessel was shot to pieces above the waterline and lost 50 percent of its crew in half an hour. Despite these resounding victories, U.S.-British naval actions only destroyed 1 percent of the British navy, while America lost 20 percent of its own ships. Between

1812 and 1814, Britain lost fifteen sloops and other small ships while fighting both America and the Napoleonic Empire, with five captured and the remainder foundering or capsizing.

In return, the Royal Navy blockaded the Delaware and Chesapeake bays, eventually extending the blockade to Florida thereby reducing U.S. trade by 90 percent. Two large British amphibious operations were mounted. The first witnessed 4,000 British troops being used against Washington and, after causing 6,000 militia to flee, the British burned many public buildings in retaliation for American incendiary activities in the Canadian capital at York, the year before. A second attack on Baltimore was repulsed by the determination of the American garrison at Fort McHenry, which endured 1,800 shells bursting in and around during a 25-hour bombardment and which repelled two British sorties.

The first assault down Lake Champlain was stopped near Plattsburgh, New York. Elsewhere, the Americans had outbuilt the British in ships on Lake Erie; U.S. Commodore Perry defeated the British at the exceptionally bloody Battle of Put-in-Bay on 10 September 1813. An American army, under Harrison, then moved into Canada in pursuit of Shawnee, Chippewa, and British forces; Harrison defeated them at the Battle of the Thames, killing Tecumseh and ending Ohio Indian unity in the process. York (Toronto) was razed and Harrison withdrew. Other British land activities commenced in 1814, aided by troops being sent from Europe following the defeat of Napoleon I. The British response saw General Packenham leading 6,000 troops against New Orleans. He was met by Andrew Jackson, fresh from victory in the Creek Wars, who established his 5,000 men, ably helped by pirate Jean Lafitte and his cannons and gunners, behind a 1,000-yard-long defensive wall. On 8 January 1815, the British advanced into a killing ground and lost 2,000 dead and wounded against Jackson's forty-five. This pointless battle occurred after the Treaty of Ghent ended the war on 24 December 1814. The victory raised the morale of the Americans and enhanced a feeling of nationalism which grew after the earlier successes at Plattsburgh and Baltimore. America was convinced that its dearly won freedom and rights, gained in 1783, had been secured by military prowess, naval miracles, and the failure of Britain; American confidence grew and Europe thought twice about adventuring into the Americas.

The war accentuated certain attitudes and characteristics of Americans in these years. An inherent desire for unity of purpose was made possible by the war. The midwestern tribes were in no condition to resist settler incursions. When the victor of New Orleans, and conqueror of the Creeks, Andrew Jackson, became President in 1829, the 1830 Indian Removal Act saw the beginning of "resettlement" ("cleansing") of Native American home territories with the Five Civilized Tribes as well as New York Indians — Delaware, Wyandot, Potawatami, Shawnee, and many others — ending up in present-day Oklahoma, Kansas, and Nebraska. Ethnic self-defense was crushed. Indians were not admitted to the full rights of citizenship because the government felt that an Indian's main allegiance lay with the tribe. Legal counsel in an 1823 federal case of *Johnston* versus *McIntosh* had argued that Indians were "of that class who are said by Jurists not to be citizens, but perpetual inhabitants, with diminutive rights…an inferior race of people, without the privileges of citizens, and under the perpetual protection and pupilage of the government." This insensitive, arrogant, and patronizing view was all too common, mirroring elite views of the British working class in the nineteenth century. The true issue of the Revolution was the rights of the white colonists before the law. People from other groups were ignored, especially the positions of Native Americans and adult black males who were often excluded from full political rights. Hence, an attitude was established and purveyed that would be challenged by other minorities, such as nineteenth-century Irish immigrants, East European Jews, and Chinese and Japanese workers in the West.

Involved in the development and expansion of

the American state was the deeply-held "credo" that white settlers had a right to all of North America. The view was prevalent in colonial land claims, which sometimes extended across the continent to the Pacific. One 1751 view by a Virginia planter, Lewis Burwell, to the British Board of Trade, said that only Americans of British

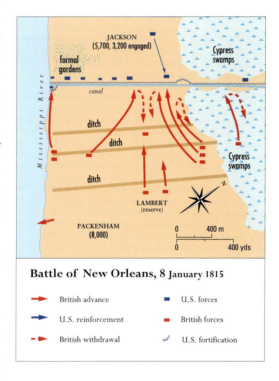

Battle of New Orleans, 8 January 1815

➡️ British advance   ▪️ U.S. forces

➡️ U.S. reinforcement   ▪️ British forces

➡️ British withdrawal   〰️ U.S. fortification

origin had rights to settled land and that remaining unsettled territories should be British colonized, and this duty, by default, fell to the United States. The concern with what lay beyond the horizon ultimately spawned Frederick Jackson Turner's 1893 paper, *The Significance of the Frontier in American History*. Turner maintained that plentiful food and cheap new land with a westward expanding frontier provided an experience which established a particular American economic development and the nature of American democracy. Historians since have argued that the land was neither free nor cheap and that the new American state expanded along numerous frontiers. During the Revolution, Americans were moving west from the former Thirteen Colonies while others moved northward from New Orleans meeting other folk journeying south on the Mississippi. Later, another frontier moved eastward from the Pacific coast.

Events during and after the War of 1812 further evolved notions developed in the Revolutionary War years. The 1814–15 New England Hartford Convention debated seceding from the Republic because of the deterioration in trade and the wartime British invasion of Maine; the politicians wished to preserve New England Federalism and the area's interests over and above the South and West. Victory at New Orleans destroyed secessionist sentiment in a bout of surging nationalism. The war had also shown the weakness of America's communications and military security. In 1815, Madison managed to triple the size of the standing army, centralize military affairs, and fortify the coast. His 1816 Tariff Act exacted import taxes on many items in an exercise of economic nationalism, supported by the Middle States against the rest. Monroe, Madison's successor, continued the insulation and isolation of America from world political issues. The Latin American colonies of Portugal and Spain acquired independence between 1808 and 1822, and the United States recognized these new countries in the latter year. Wishing to prevent France, acting on behalf of the anti-revolutionary Concert of Europe, from restoring Spanish rule in Latin America, Congress, in December 1823, heard the Monroe Doctrine, which demanded three policies. First, European nations would not colonize the Americas, a blow to Spain, as well as to Russian interests in Alaska and its chain of forts extending down the Pacific coast from New Archangel (founded 1804) to Fort Ross (1811) near San Francisco. Second, Europe must not interfere in the affairs of new American states. Third, the United States would not intervene in European affairs or in already existing European colonies in the Western Hemisphere. The Doctrine was a mere unenforceable platitude in 1823 and was only given force by the Royal Navy, because the British government assessed the Doctrine as working in its interests. Whatever the view taken, the Monroe Doctrine was an action intended to insulate America from Europe; develop trade; and build an internal expansionist, nationalist, and imperialist state.

Some 4,000 out of 18,000 Cherokee died on the journey or in stockades on the march to Oklahoma. A few hundred Cherokee were lucky to remain in the mountains of West North Carolina.

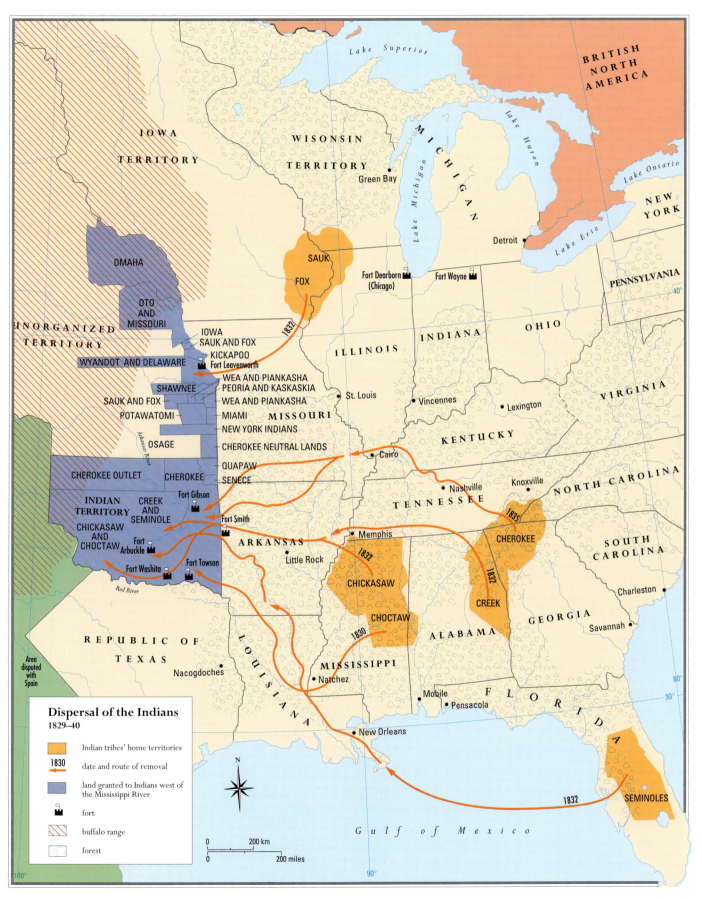

Dispersal of the Indians
1829–40

Indian tribes' home territories

1830   date and route of removal

land granted to Indians west of the Mississippi River

fort

buffalo range

forest

Foreign Policy After the War

The United States rapidly faced foreign policy problems emanating from the French Revolution of 1789 and the outbreak of war in Europe. Under the 1778 Franco-American alliance, the United States was obliged to help defend the French West Indies. Treasury-Secretary Hamilton maintained that because the treaty had been signed by the French monarchy, which no longer existed, the treaty was void and the United States should adopt neutrality. However, Anglo-American relations were becoming tense because Britain had not evacuated their forts south of the Great Lakes. Also, a British Order in Council (November 1793) refused to allow U.S. vessels to transport goods from the French West Indies to France and seized 250 U.S. ships. Chief Justice Jay was dispatched to Britain to negotiate a resolution.

Jay wanted to win the right to trade with all belligerents in the European war and win a commercial treaty, plus compensation for those slaves who left the United States when Britain evacuated in 1783. Britain agreed to vacate its Northwest posts and submit claims for compensation to arbitration for ships seized. Some American trade with the British West Indies was allowed, but compensation for slaves was lost and a change in Britain's view of neutrality did not emerge. Jay's treaty prevented war with Great Britain when the United States did not have a navy. In 1794, the United States began naval construction.

The Jay Treaty upset France and the Directory ordered French privateers to seize American ships bearing British goods. French depredations were so great that insurance rates from the U.S. coast to Jamaica rose from 6 to 40 percent. The so-called Quasi War (1798–1800) followed, fought between U.S. warships and French privateers. Captain Thomas Truxton on the USS *Constellation* (36 guns) met and captured the French frigate, *Insurgente* (40 guns), after an hour's combat off Nevis (February 1799). The captured ship was taken into the U.S. navy. In 1800, Truxton met the French *Vengeance* (52 guns) off Guadeloupe in a five-hour night duel. Despite its cannon being silenced and partially dismasted, the *Vengeance* escaped. In all, the United States took eighty-five French ships.

Regarding Spain, Thomas Pinckney went to Madrid and concluded a treaty (1795) which gave the United States free use of the Mississippi and the right to store goods in New Orleans. In return, Spain accepted the 31st parallel as the Florida boundary and would attempt to restrain Indians from Spanish territory, from attacking U.S. settlements.

Another American success occurred in North Africa. In 1801, the Sultan of Tripoli demanded protection money or his pirate fleet would seize U.S. ships and seamen in the Mediterranean. A naval squadron under Decatur blockaded Tripoli from 1803–04, burned the captured USS *Philadelphia*, and forced Tripoli to sign a peace treaty. In 1815, he coerced Tunis and Algiers to the peace table thereby making the Mediterranean safer for commerce.

The major incident in early U.S. foreign policy was the War of 1812, which inadvertently broke out over Britain's maritime policy and impressment. The land war on the Canadian border initially went in favor of the British who repelled all attacks. On the Great Lakes, U.S. Commodore Perry defeated the British at the Battle of Put-in-Bay, and after the Battle of the Thames, York (Toronto) was torched. In 1814, the British invaded Louisiana and were beaten by Andrew Jackson at New Orleans. Elsewhere, the war was characterized by successful American ship-to-ship actions, against frigates such as the *Macedonian* and *Guerrière*, while Britain blockaded the Chesapeake and burned the White House. The Treaty of Ghent (1814) ended the war and kept the status quo. A major outcome was President Madison's building of coastal forts and increasing the army's size as well as the advent of U.S. withdrawal from European affairs.

Famed for his victory over a British force at New Orleans, Andrew Jackson was involved in the war leading to the purchase of Florida, and he became America's seventh president in 1829.

The War of 1812

→ U.S. and British movements, 1812
→ U.S. and British movements, 1813
→ U.S. and British movements, 1814–15

British blockade

✕ battle

British occupied in 1814

claimed by U.S.

disputed with Britain

0   300 km
0   300 miles

BRITISH NORTH AMERICA

Lake Superior

Québec

Lower Canada

Ottawa River

Montréal

District of Maine

Lake Champlain

VERMONT

N.H.

MASSACHUSETTS

Indiana Territory

Fort Mackinac

Lake Huron

Kingston

Upper Canada

Plattsburgh

Green Bay

Lake Michigan

York (Toronto)

Lake Ontario

Oswego

Fort Niagara

Buffalo

Albany

CONN.

R.I.

ILLINOIS TERRITORY

Milwaukee

MICHIGAN TERRITORY

Battle of the Thames

NEW YORK

Detroit

Lake Erie

Erie

New York

Fort Dearborn (Chicago)

Sandusky

Cleveland

PENNSYLVANIA

Philadelphia

NEW JERSEY

Atlantic Ocean

INDIANA TERRITORY

OHIO

Dayton

Baltimore

MARYLAND

DELAWARE

Illinois River

Wabash River

Cincinnati

Ohio River

Washington

St. Louis

LOUISIANA PURCHASE 1803

Cairo

KENTUCKY

VIRGINIA

Appalachian Mountains

Norfolk

Mississippi River

TENNESSEE

NORTH CAROLINA

Huntsville

SOUTH CAROLINA

Charleston

MISSISSIPPI TERRITORY

GEORGIA

Savannah

Vicksburg

Flint River

LOUISIANA

Mobile

Pensacola

FLORIDA
to Spain

St. Augustine

New Orleans

N

Gulf of Mexico

Operations around Washington and Baltimore
19 August–17 September 1814

→ British attack
→ British withdrawal

British defeat American force and advance and seize Washington, burning many buildings, then return to their ships

12 Sept.: battle of Godly Wood

Ellicott Mills

Baltimore

Brookeville

British advance on Baltimore, strong defenses convince them to retire back to their ships

Rockville

Montgomery

12 Sept.: land
14 Sept.: re-embark
17 Sept.: depart

Maryland

Vansville

Annapolis

Tennallytown

Georgetown

Bladensburg

24 Aug.: Bridge destroyed

Alexandria

Upper Marlborough

Mt. Vernon

Secondary attack delayed by shoals. 28 Aug., capture Alexandria, then rejoin main force

Lower Marlborough

30 Aug.: re-embark for Baltimore

Benedict
19 August: British troops land

Chesapeake Bay

Virginia

N

British fleet commanded by Cochrane

0   10 km
0   10 miles

Transatlantic Revolutions

Some historians have regarded the American War of Independence as the instigator of a revolutionary movement cutting a swathe across the world at the end of the eighteenth century. The two main proponents of this view have been R.R. Palmer and J. Godechot who wrote *The Age of Democratic Revolution* and *Atlantic Revolutions,* respectively. They see a connection between the American and French revolutions lying in common hopes and political ideas, which became located in revolutions, rebellions, and political violence in Ireland, Italy, the Low Countries, Switzerland, England, the German states,

even though some people thought it did; a class struggle between the aristocracy and the middle class; and war bringing revolution and counter-revolution to various countries. Godechot considered common underlying motives and characteristics such as the growth of a new commercial middle class demanding political power commensurate with their wealth and a demographic explosion generating subsistence problems and unemployment in Europe. Whatever the use of evidence—Tom Paine's role in America, Britain, and France; the activities of Lafayette and his French soldiers allegedly taking revolutionary ideas to France; or similarities between the Declaration of Independence and the French Declaration of the Rights of Man and of Citizens—several criticisms can be leveled at Palmer and Godechot for not concentrating on distinguishing national characteristics and events. Also, if Godechot's Atlantic community existed, why were Spain and Portugal ignored?

Nevertheless, there are some possible links between America and elsewhere. France was undoubtedly damaged by the cost of helping America, thereby hastening economic collapse. Also, America acted as a catalyst, crystalizing ideas and trends already existing in France through the Enlightenment, such as the terms—nation, constitution, citizen, and rights. America demonstrated how debates about abstract political and philosophical concepts could be transformed into reality, that a social contract was possible, an oppressor could be defeated, and that the political consensus widened. Returning French troops were not noticeable revolutionaries in 1789. A few officers had roles

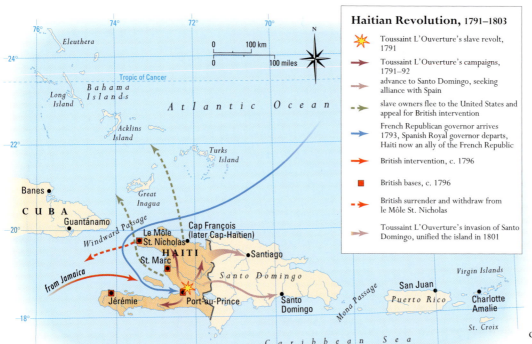

Haitian Revolution, 1791–1803

- ✶ Toussaint L'Ouverture's slave revolt, 1791
- → Toussaint L'Ouverture's campaigns, 1791–92
- → advance to Santo Domingo, seeking alliance with Spain
- ⇢ slave owners flee to the United States and appeal for British intervention
- → French Republican governor arrives 1793, Spanish Royal governor departs, Haiti now an ally of the French Republic
- → British intervention, c. 1796
- ■ British bases, c. 1796
- ⇢ British surrender and withdraw from le Môle St. Nicholas
- → Toussaint L'Ouverture's invasion of Santo Domingo, unified the island in 1801

Hungary, and Poland. Despite national differences, all were deemed to be seeking a more democratic society and form of government.

Palmer saw revolutionary common denominators lying in the idea of self-determination and individualism; the notion of a central revolutionary body, which failed to exist in the French Revolution with Lafayette becoming a member of the National Assembly and he advocated a moderate constitutional monarchy.

More importantly, the American Revolution gave the French Caribbean island, Saint Domingue, the experience of free trade whereby mainly Massachusetts and Philadelphia shipping traded with the island. By 1790, 10 percent of U.S. exports reached Saint Domingue. Growing wealth accentuated differences between French merchants and the free mulatto lower middle class. Hence, the American Revolution provided some pre-conditions for the Haitian Revolution when Toussaint L'Ouverture, a former slave, drove out the French in 1801. His lieutenant and successor, Jean Jacques Dessalines, ironically assumed the status of Emperor of Haiti. Elsewhere in the Caribbean, British-controlled islands were

left more to their own devices during the Revolution and local assemblies claimed equality with the British Parliament and often manifested a republican spirit.

In Latin America, owners of plantation economies where slavery existed, regarded the Haitian experience as a dangerous example and the Spanish and Portuguese governments liberalized their relationships with local politicians throughout their empires. However, when Napoleon conquered the Iberian peninsula, events conspired to isolate Latin America from its colonial masters and local municipal councils, and juntas became autonomous. Thus, leaders such as Simon Bolivar, San Martin, and Augustin de Iturbide obtained independence from Spain, while Brazil proclaimed independence from Portugal under Pedro, a member of the Portuguese royal house.

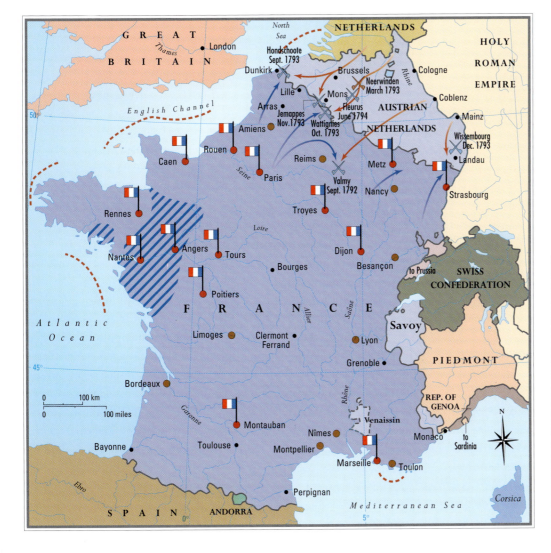

French Revolution
1789–95

→ advance of French revolutionary armies

→ attacks by Allied armies

✕ French victory

✕ Allied victory

--- naval blockade

major town where council was replaced by revolutionary committee

major town where council shared power with revolutionary committee

France in 1789

annexed by France in 1792–93

center of counter-revolution

Expansion and Settlement

Seizing power in a coup d'état in 1799, Napoleon Bonaparte proclaimed himself Emperor of France in 1804. Meanwhile, he acquired Louisiana from Spain in 1800 as the commencement of a French New World empire, but he sold it to the United States for fifteen million dollars, approximately 13½ cents per acre. He needed the money for renewed warfare in Europe.

Born in 1734, Daniel Boone typified the mythic, heroic frontiersman. Serving in the North Carolina militia, he marched with Braddock against Fort Duquesne (1755). He next traveled down the Ohio Valley to view Kentucky but continued to live in North Carolina. Eventually, he cut the Wilderness Road through the Cumberland Gap and was one co-founder of the failed colony of Transylvania.

Boone was constantly moving and settled his family in Spanish territory (Missouri). His wanderings took him to present-day Kansas and up the Platte River to the Yellowstone. His paths and trails became Highway 25-E and grew into the Santa Fé, Salt Lake, and Oregon trails.

Thus, Boone exemplified the restlessness of the pre- and post-revolutionary years. The population of America was regularly moving 10 percent of its people annually into the next state or adjacent territory. The major movements were from New England into upstate New York. Middle state movements were into the Pennsylvania interior followed by moves to Pittsburgh, down the Ohio River to Marietta and onward. Settlers from Virginia traversed the Cumberland Gap into Kentucky and Tennessee, following those who entered the region during the Revolutionary War. The first census (1790) showed 100,000 people there, whereas there had been only 12,000 in 1783. Kentucky became a state in 1792, followed by Tennessee in 1796. Ohio became a state in 1803. By 1800, 15,000 people were recorded in the Mississippi and Indiana territories.

The westward movement was made possible by the defeat of the Cherokees and Shawnees. Expansion was slower north of the Ohio because the Miami Confederacy was powerful. However, some Americans settled on Lake Erie. Wayne's campaigns against Little Turtle forced the northern Indians to the Treaty of Greenville in 1795. Also, 1796 witnessed the evacuation of Detroit and other posts by the British thereby strengthening American control over the Northwest Territory. After Wayne's victory, Connecticut settlers poured into the Lake Erie region; homesteads were found at Green Bay, Wisconsin; and trading posts existed on the St. Joseph, Kalamazoo, and Grand rivers in Michigan.

As with earlier settlers, new settlements saw the imposition of European agricultural techniques of forest and field clearance and fence building. The landscape was changed. New Englanders, leaving poor plots behind, engaged in Ohio Fever and replicated New England culture and architecture in this fertile land.

Westward migration had affected two other societies. Indians had their land taken or bought, and the territories ceded between 1784 and 1810 were immense. African Americans were taken west by slaveholders into Tennessee, Kentucky, western Georgia, and to

Expansion and Settlement
to 1820

- United States, 1783
- Louisiana purchase, 1803 (natural boundary)
- joint occupation with Great Britain
- ceded by the United States to Great Britain, 1818
- ceded by Great Britain to the United States, 1818
- ceded by Spain to the United States, 1819
- Spanish empire after 1819
- Spanish treaty line of 1819
- 1812 new state admitted with date

the Gulf Coast. Chesapeake African-American communities were broken up and some 100,000 people were moved west by 1810 causing social suffering and lifestyle changes when being removed to remote regions. Thus, all society was in flux with constant movement.

In the south settlers were pressing into Florida, which was a sanctuary for escaped slaves and a base for marauding Creek Indians. President Jefferson sought to buy the territory from Spain and met rebuttal. In 1810, while Spain was defending against a Napoleonic invasion, Americn settlers in West Florida rebelled, proclaimed a republic, and asked for U.S. annexation. President Madison agreed, after having allegedly been secretly involved in the coup d'état. A similar revolt further west failed despite American material support, so the United States did not gain Mobile. That town was seized from Spain during the War of 1812 because Spain was Britain's ally. Americans had to wait until 1819 when John Quincy Adams bought the remainder of Florida.

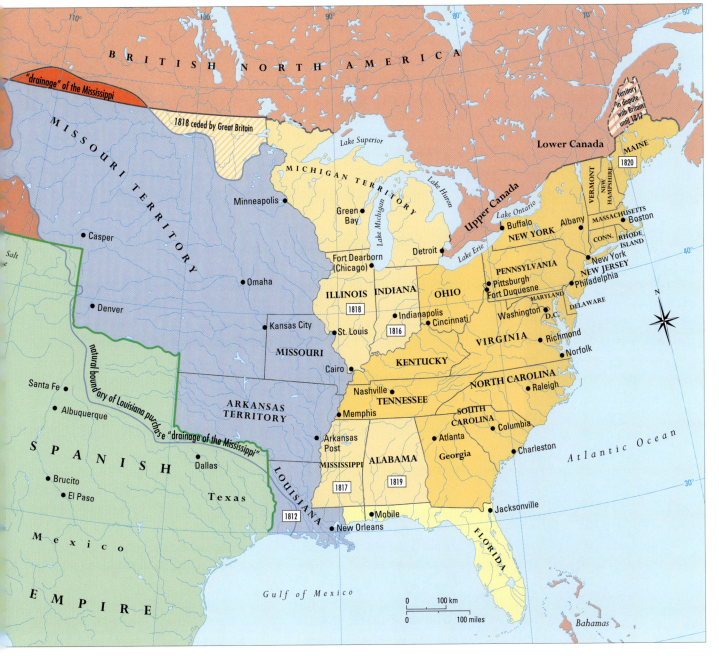

Opening of the West

18 November 1805:
Lewis and Clark
first sight the
Pacific Ocean

CHINOOK

COWLITZ

SPOKANE

Fort Clatsop

YAKIMA

PALOUSE

Columbia River

Pacific
Ocean

UMATILLA

WALLA WALLA

NEZ PERCE

Salmon R.

Lolo pass
Traveler's Rest

KLIKITAT

CAYUSE
YAKIMA

SHOSHONE

FLATHEADS

Cameahwait's
Shoshone village

120°

Camp Dubois

Madison R.

Camp
Fortunate

BANNOCK
CROW

115°

IDAHO

110°

BLACKFOOT

portage

R u p e r t

Lewis lived near Jefferson's Virginia home of Monticello and became his personal secretary, while Clark later became governor of Missouri and championed Native American causes.

In Europe, Napoleon dreamed of a new French Empire in North America, and in 1800 he coerced Spain into returning Louisiana to France, the region having been originally lost at the end of the French and Indian War in 1763. The treaty was kept secret and Spain continued to administer the territory. By this time, the Ohio and Mississippi valleys were being settled by Americans. Many relied on the rivers to transport goods to New Orleans where the goods could be stored prior to export. Thus, the city controlled a vital trade route. In 1802, the Spanish Intendant of New Orleans closed the Mississippi to American commerce and reneged on the Pinckney Treaty (1795) disallowing the storage of American goods.

Rumors abounded that Louisiana had been transferred to French sovereignty and Jefferson feared an aggressive, expansionist French regime on the American borders. Pressure for war grew among commercial interests so Jefferson sent James Monroe to France to negotiate the purchase of New Orleans. On his arrival in Paris, he learned that Napoleon was losing interest in the Americas. He had sent an army under General Leclerc to defeat Toussaint L'Ouverture in Haiti, an island considered to be an essential stepping stone to Louisiana. Leclerc and vast numbers of French troops succumbed to yellow fever. Although Toussaint was captured, this black revolution was not suppressed. Napoleon offered the United States not just New Orleans to Monroe but all of Louisiana for $15 million. The land transfer would comprise some 828,000 square miles, costing a mere 13½ cents an acre. This purchase meant that westward expansion could continue even though the territory's borders were not clearly defined. The land could be a home for eastern Indian bands when they were deprived of their former hunting grounds. Jefferson had brought America nearer to the Pacific coast and justified his acquisition of new territory as a presidential move to protect the nation. This satisfied the electorate in 1804 when Jefferson was granted a second term in office, winning every state except Delaware and Connecticut.

The American government required maps of the region and Jefferson had an interest in the Missouri. He sent his private secretary, Meriwether Lewis, and William Clark, together with nearly fifty compatriots, the Corps of Discovery, along the Missouri. Jefferson

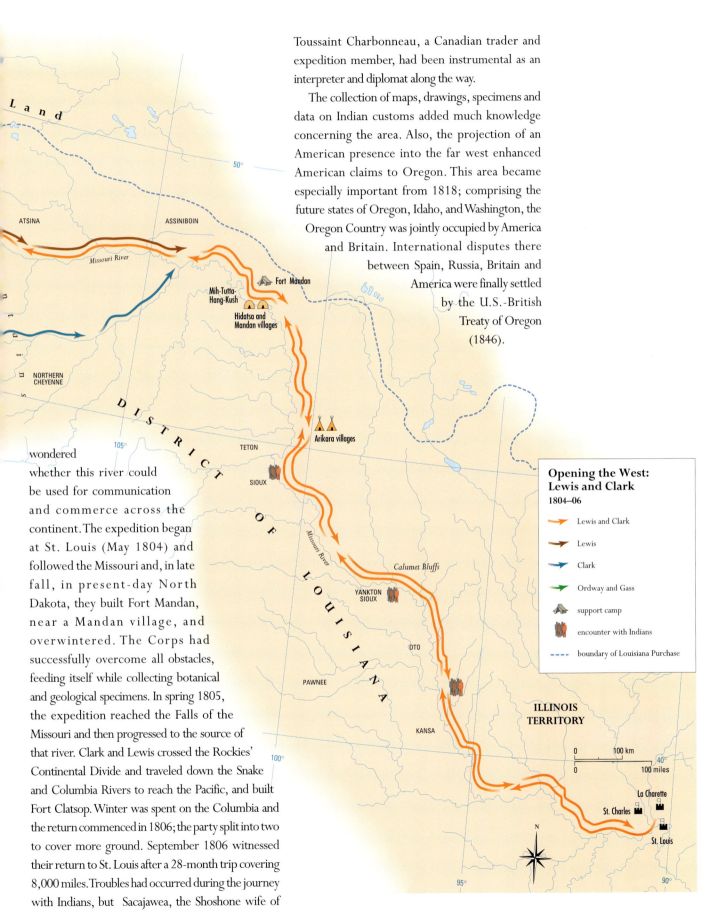

Toussaint Charbonneau, a Canadian trader and expedition member, had been instrumental as an interpreter and diplomat along the way.

The collection of maps, drawings, specimens and data on Indian customs added much knowledge concerning the area. Also, the projection of an American presence into the far west enhanced American claims to Oregon. This area became especially important from 1818; comprising the future states of Oregon, Idaho, and Washington, the Oregon Country was jointly occupied by America and Britain. International disputes there between Spain, Russia, Britain and America were finally settled by the U.S.-British Treaty of Oregon (1846).

wondered whether this river could be used for communication and commerce across the continent. The expedition began at St. Louis (May 1804) and followed the Missouri and, in late fall, in present-day North Dakota, they built Fort Mandan, near a Mandan village, and overwintered. The Corps had successfully overcome all obstacles, feeding itself while collecting botanical and geological specimens. In spring 1805, the expedition reached the Falls of the Missouri and then progressed to the source of that river. Clark and Lewis crossed the Rockies' Continental Divide and traveled down the Snake and Columbia Rivers to reach the Pacific, and built Fort Clatsop. Winter was spent on the Columbia and the return commenced in 1806; the party split into two to cover more ground. September 1806 witnessed their return to St. Louis after a 28-month trip covering 8,000 miles. Troubles had occurred during the journey with Indians, but Sacajawea, the Shoshone wife of

Opening the West: Lewis and Clark
1804–06

- ➡ Lewis and Clark
- ➡ Lewis
- ➡ Clark
- ➡ Ordway and Gass
- ⛺ support camp
- encounter with Indians
- --- boundary of Louisiana Purchase

King Cotton

The Revolutionary period demonstrated that slave-based agriculture was not particularly profitable, especially in the Upper South. By 1801, the cotton belt could be found in Virginia, the Carolinas, Georgia, and a small area in Tennessee. However, the old plantocracy, especially in Virginia, was debt-ridden and agriculture was mainly based on tobacco whereas the other states grew rice and indigo. Only the "sea-island" coastal area of South Carolina and Georgia, with their special climatic conditions, could grow profitable long-staple cotton. Other areas produced the short-staple variety that was replete with sticky seeds.

In the late eighteenth century, British demands for its textile industry required ever more cotton. The 1780s witnessed massive British imports of raw cotton and the subsequent export of manufactured cotton goods based upon the growth of the factory system in Lancashire, England. By 1820, cotton used 5 percent of the Manchester, England, work-force and comprised 7 percent of the British Gross Domestic product. By 1805, cotton constituted 42 percent of British exports which stimulated a range of ancillary industries. By the 1830s, cottons and woollens reached 80 percent of British exports. Consequently, an Atlantic economy developed linking Manchester and Liverpool to American ports as well as to British

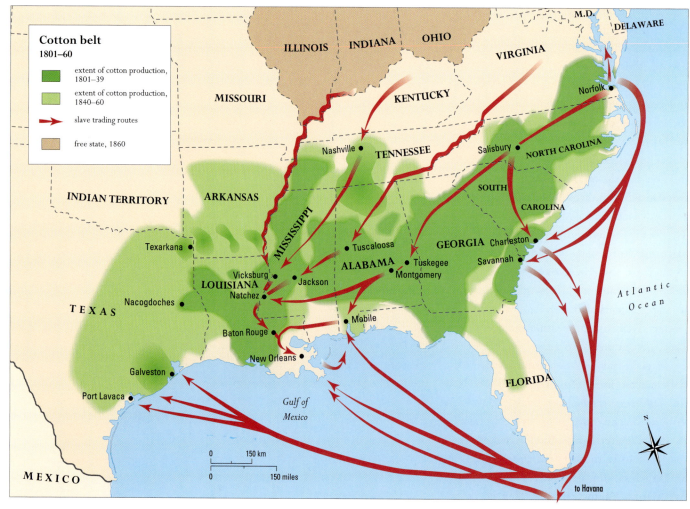

Asian market places. British profits from cotton manufacturers ended in commerce, railway construction, and American investment.

In response to this demand, thousands of Americans tried to produce short-staple cotton but were hampered by the sticky seeds. However, in 1793, Eli Whitney invented the cotton gin, which separated seeds from short-staple cotton and made commercial cotton growing possible on almost any soil, provided there was adequate rainfall and little frost. Cotton production, therefore, spread into the Piedmont of South Carolina and Georgia, then into the Alabama-Mississippi Black Belt and the Mississippi Delta, and eventually into Texas. Eastern production also increased in Virginia, North Carolina, and Tennessee. By 1825, the South was the world's major, if not dominant, supplier of cotton, and, by 1850, Britain imported 70 percent of its cotton from the South.

A consequence of increased cotton production was the revival of slavery, so much so that Southern regionalism brought a societal sectionalism. Alabama, Mississippi, and Louisiana (Gulf States) found more in common with the Atlantic littoral slave states than with New England and newer western states such as Ohio, Illinois, and Indiana. Large-scale agricultural production demanded slave labor whether the produce was cotton or other staples such as tobacco, sugar, rice, or corn.

The end result of the demand for slaves was their increase in number. The slave population doubled every thirty years, despite the legal banning of the slave trade in 1808. South Carolina acquired some 40,000 slaves between 1803 and 1807 to beat the approaching ban. Nevertheless, illegal importation continued, mainly from Havana acting as a transit station

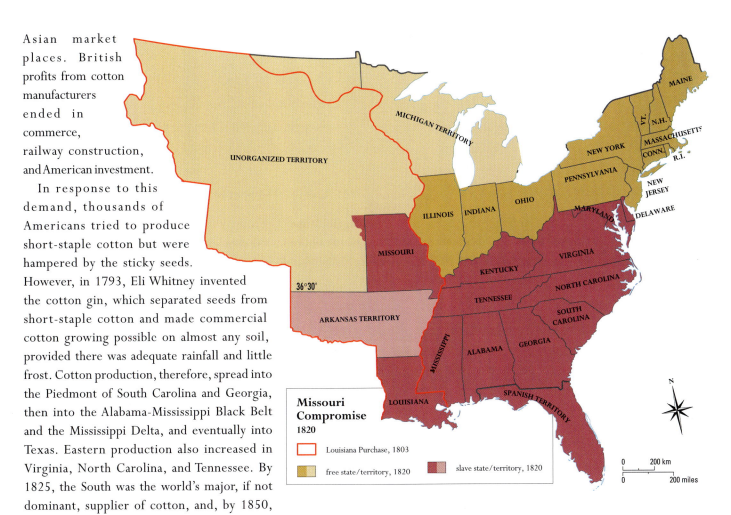

Missouri Compromise 1820

☐ Louisiana Purchase, 1803

◼ free state/territory, 1820   ◼ slave state/territory, 1820

from Africa to the West Indies; between 1808 and 1860, estimates suggest the illegal importation of some 200,000 slaves. The latter date saw some 4 million slaves in a Southern population of 12 million. By 1860, the distribution of slaves varied: in South Carolina and Mississippi, more than 50 percent of the population were slaves, while in Louisiana, Alabama, Florida, and Georgia, slaves comprised 40 percent. However, most slaves in new cotton states came from Virginia and Maryland, where soil fertility was depleted.

The existence of slavery also generated certain political issues of where slavery should be allowed. The 1787 Northwest Ordinance banned slavery from the new lands gained in 1783, and the 1820 Missouri Compromise banned slavery from the Louisiana Purchase for a while. The issue was to emerge with debates over the 1850 Compromise and the 1854 Kansas-Nebraska Act.

Selected Biographies

The following biographies refer mainly to the War of Independence and concentrate on involvement in that war.

ADAMS, JOHN (1735–1826)

Adams served in the Continental Congress and virtually ran the Board of War and Ordinance singlehandedly. With Jefferson, he joined the committee drafting the Declaration of Independence. Diplomacy followed from 1778 to 1783, serving alongside Franklin in Europe. His Constitution of Massachusetts (1779) became a model for the federal constitution. He served as vice-president under Washington and became the second president for one term in 1797.

ALLEN, ETHAN (1738–1801)

Allen and his Green Mountain Boys militia, with Benedict Arnold, captured Fort Ticonderoga (1775), and were involved in Schuyler's Canadian campaign. After capture and exchange between 1775 and 1778, Allen left combat and returned home to look after Vermont affairs.

ARNOLD, BENEDICT (1741–1801)

Arnold helped Ethan Allen capture Fort Ticonderoga (1775), helped besiege Boston, and unsuccessfully campaigned against Québec. Involved at Valcour (1776), he became a major-general and his audacious leadership in 1777 at Fort Stanwix, Freeman's Farm, and Bemis Heights ensured the failure of Burgoyne during the Saratoga campaign. In 1778, Arnold treasonably joined the British and carried out raids in Virginia (1780) and Connecticut (1781), capturing Fort Griswold.

BOONE, DANIEL (1734–1820)

American pioneer, explorer, and settler of Kentucky. Between 1776 and 1778, he fought the Shawnee and Cherokee in Kentucky, once being captured and escaping.

Constantly defending the frontier, he was involved in the American defeat at Blue Licks in August 1782 where 77 out of 182 Americans were killed, including Boone's son, Israel.

BRANT, JOSEPH (1742–1807)

Pro-British Mohawk chief who gained powerful influence over the Tuscarora and Oneida tribes, splitting the Iroquois confederation. Meeting Germain in London in 1776, he returned to America and cooperated with Johnson's and Butler's Loyalists in raids on New York and Pennsylvania. Unfairly blamed for the atrocities at the Cherry Valley massacre, Brant raided the Ohio Valley (1780), and in 1782, planned a 1,100-warrior raid in the same area. In England, he was painted by George Romney.

BURGOYNE, GENERAL JOHN (1722–92)

Serving under Gage in Boston, Burgoyne was appointed to command the British forces in Canada in May 1777. He marched south and captured Fort Ticonderoga before being defeated by Gates and surrendering at Saratoga (7 October 1777). This British disaster was a turning point in the war, winning America considerable foreign support.

BURKE, EDMUND (1729–97)

British Conservative politician who in parliamentary speeches in 1775 and 1776 claimed that parliamentary sovereignty could only be exercised over colonies with the latter's consent, for purposes recognized as being of mutual interest. After Saratoga, he foresaw that British force would not defeat the Americans.

BUTLER, WALTER (1752–81)

A Loyalist, fleeing to Canada, Butler joined his father's (John) Rangers and fought at Oriskany (1777). His father won the Battle of Wyoming (July 1778), but Walter was in charge at Cherry Valley (1778) and was eventually killed in 1781 in a raid sent out of Niagara.

CARLETON, GUY, 1st BARON DORCHESTER (1774–1808)

Appointed Governor of Lower Canada (Québec) in 1766, he was also placed in command of all British troops in Canada during the American War of Independence. He defended Québec in December 1775 against the Americans. In 1776, Carleton drove American forces out of Canada and defeated Benedict Arnold at Valcour on Lake Champlain. In 1777, Carleton was succeeded militarily by Burgoyne and, in 1782, resumed command of all British troops again while the British were evacuating America. As a reward, he was ennobled and made governor of all British possessions in Canada in 1786.

CLARK, GEORGE ROGERS (1752–1818)

Fought in the Northwest Territory during the War of Independence. He helped Kentucky settlers against Native American pro-British attacks, and, in 1777, he was appointed a Lieutenant Colonel in the Virginia militia. During 1778, he captured the British forts at Kaskaskia, Cahokia, and Vincennes (1778). He kept the British out of the region and defeated the Shawnee at Chillicothe. His control in parts of present day Illinois, Ohio, and Indiana allowed the United States to claim the area after the war and turn it into the Northwest Territory after 1787.

CLINTON, SIR HENRY (1738–95)

In 1775, Clinton fought at Bunker Hill and largely planned the successful British campaign taking New York after the Battle of Long Island (August 1776). In 1778, he took over British forces from Howe. He fought Washington at Monmouth in December 1799. He captured Charleston (May 1780) but

after Cornwallis surrendered at Yorktown (1782), Clinton became a scapegoat and was replaced by Sir Guy Carleton.

CORNWALLIS, CHARLES, 1st MARQUIS AND 2nd EARL CORNWALLIS (1738–1805)

In 1775, Cornwallis became a Major-General, taking part in the Battle of Long Island and campaigns in New Jersey. Washington defeated his troops at Trenton (December 1776) and at Princeton (January 1777), but Cornwallis won at Brandywine (September 1777), and occupied Philadelphia. Although intensely critical of Clinton, he remained in the Americas and commanded British forces in the South. He defeated Gates at Camden (August 1780), but Greene forced his retreat after the Guilford Court House action. Surrounded at Yorktown, Cornwallis surrendered in October 1781.

DEANE, SILAS (1737–89)

Sent to France in 1776 as America's first foreign representative. Joined by Franklin and Lee, he signed treaties with France (1778). He was instrumental in acquiring the services of Kalb and Lafayette.

FOX, CHARLES JAMES (1749–1806)

Fox was a Whig politician who, despite having supported the Boston Port Act when in office, defended the American colonies and advocated recognition of their independence. He recognized that war would affect the British economy and maybe destabilize the British Empire. He opposed using Native Americans to attack settlements. He considered that the American actions were part of a general conflict between liberty and royal absolutism. In 1782, he became foreign secretary under Rockingham and both men supported U.S. independence, but Fox soon resigned because of Royal opposition to his policies.

FRANKLIN, BENJAMIN (1706–90)

Statesman and scientist, Franklin was sent to France to borrow money, to issue letters of marque for U.S. privateers, and to oversee U.S. interests, including arms shipments and weapons for the United States. His friendship with French Foreign Minister Vergennes aided his task. He negotiated peace conditions with Britain and signed a preliminary peace treaty with Jay, Adams, and Laurens (30 November 1782) for the United States.

GAGE, GENERAL THOMAS (1721–87)

British colonial governor in America and military commander of Massachusetts, Gage raised tensions after the Boston Port Act and ordered British forces to Lexington and Concord. He was severely criticized for his attack on Breed's Hill and the pyrrhic victory at Bunker Hill (June 1775). October 1775 witnessed his resignation from his new status of British Commander-in-Chief of North America.

GATES, GENERAL HORATIO (1728–1806)

Commanding Fort Ticonderoga (1776–77), Gates succeeded Schuyler in 1777 and forced Burgoyne to surrender at Saratoga (October 1777). He tried to acquire Washington's command (Conway Cabal) and in 1780 was sent south. He was signally defeated by Cornwallis at Camden (1780), fleeing the campaign, traveling 340 miles in four days. Thereafter, he served under Washington.

GEORGE III, KING (1738–1820)

George III was convinced that his cause was just regarding America. His stubborn attitude and political support against the War of Independence meant that his ministers were blamed for military disasters. The King was the focus of criticisms in the Declaration of Independence, and he also became the target of Charles Fox, a Whig politician.

GERMAIN, GEORGE SACKVILLE, 1st VISCOUNT SACKVILLE (1716–85)

Lord George Germain served as Colonial Secretary from 1775 to 1782 and was responsible for British policy during the American War of Independence. His administration improved the American Department, but his conduct of the war was partially responsible for the Saratoga surrender. He was supported by intellectual inferiors and failed to prevent military-naval hostility. He basically misunderstood the American war and American commitment.

GRASSE, FRANÇOIS-JOSEPH-PAUL DE, COMTE (1722–88)

French admiral who commanded a squadron in the 1779 and 1780 campaigns in the West Indies and North America. In 1781, he sailed 27 ships-of-the-line to the Chesapeake joining in the entrapment of Cornwallis at Yorktown. On 5 September 1781, he drove off a British naval relief force at the Battle of the Capes. He was later defeated by British Admiral Rodney at the Battle of the Saintes (12 April 1782).

GRAVES, ADMIRAL THOMAS (1725–1802)

Graves helped blockade Rhode Island and engaged in the Battle off Cape Henry on 16 March 1781. His lack of activity on 5 September 1781 allowed de Grasse to leave the Chesapeake and prevent Graves from entering. This indecisive battle ensured a French naval hold over the Chesapeake, which was a factor in forcing Cronwallis' surrender at Yorktown.

GREENE, GENERAL NATHANAEL (1742–86)

After Lexington and Concord, Greene became a Rhode Island general and led his state's troops to the Siege of Boston. Greene was partially responsible for the loss of 3,000 men at Fort Washington (16 November 1776) telling

Washington that it was highly defensible. He saw action at Germantown, on the Delaware, and at Rhode Island (1778). Greene's military reputation was earned in the south (1780–82). Fighting at Cowpens and Guilford Court House and losing many actions, Greene nevertheless took all British posts in the South, ultimately winning the campaign.

HAMILTON, ALEXANDER (1757–1804)

Hamilton was commissioned as an artillery captain in 1776. He served at Harlem Heights and stood his ground, and then he helped cover Washington's retreat to the Delaware. He saw action at Trenton and Princeton and then joined Washington's staff until July 1781 when he served under Lafayette and launched a successful night attack on Redoubt No. 10 at Yorktown. He was discharged in 1782, wrote many Federalist Papers and worked for constitutional ratification. He saw more military service from July 1798 to June 1800, and returned to law and politics. This Founding Father was killed in a duel with Aaron Burr in July 1804.

HOPKINS, ESEK (1718–1801)

In 1775, Hopkins was appointed commander of Rhode Island forces and then Commander-in-Chief of the Continental Navy. In February 1776, his small squadron sailed to sack Nassau, Bahamas, but his vessels failed to take the outgunned HMS *Glasgow* on his return. In January 1778, Hopkins was dismissed from the service.

HOWE, RICHARD, EARL HOWE (1726–99)

British naval commander in North America (1776–78) and brother of William Howe. He commanded the Channel Fleet in 1782, defeated a Franco-Spanish squadron, and relieved the British Gibraltar garrison.

HOWE, WILLIAM, 5th VISCOUNT HOWE (1729–1814)

British Commander-in-Chief in North America (1775–78), he fought under Gage at Bunker Hill. Succeeding Gage, he won the Battle of Long Island, took New York, and won the Battles of White Plains and Brandywine. He failed to attack Washington at Valley Forge, remaining in Philadelphia. Criticism over such quiescence might have occasioned his resignation in 1778.

JAY, JOHN (1745–1829)

A politician during the early days of the war, Jay became minister to Spain in 1779. Failure there led him to join Franklin in France where he helped to negotiate and sign the preliminary peace treaty with Britain. After the war, he signed the Jay Treaty with Britain providing for British evacuation from posts in the Northwest Territory.

JEFFERSON, THOMAS (1743–1826)

In 1776, Jefferson helped draft the Declaration of Independence, was a member of the Continental Congress, and represented the United States in Europe (1784–89). He became the third President in 1801, acquired Louisiana in 1803, and, on ending his term of office (1809) retired to his estate at Monticello, Virginia.

JONES, JOHN PAUL (1747–92)

In 1775, Jones entered the Continental Navy and joined the *Alfred* eventually joining the *Providence* as Captain. His cruise destroyed Nova Scotia fisheries and took sixteen prizes. From 1777 to 1778, in the *Ranger*, he cruised in British waters causing much alarm and destruction. In 1779, in the *Bonhomme Richard*, he took the HMS *Serapis* off Flamborough Head in the North Sea. He spent the rest of the war in dockyard duty before accepting a post under Catherine the Great of Russia in 1788.

KALB, JOHANN DE (1721–80)

Silas Deane gave de Kalb a commission in December 1776. De Kalb commanded a division at Valley Forge and stayed in New Jersey and the Highlands from 1779 to 1780. In Spring 1780, he was sent to relieve Charleston but found it taken. Superceded by Gates, de Kalb held the American right-wing at Camden after Gates fled, and he fought on receiving eleven wounds from which he died on 11 August 1780, the day following the battle.

KOSCIUSKO, THADDEUS (1746–1817)

Arriving in America in 1776, Kosciusko joined Gates and chose the battleground where Burgoyne was confronted in the Saratoga campaign. In 1778, he helped construct the fort at West Point and, in 1780–81, served with Greene in the South. In 1783, he was rewarded with U.S. citizenship but returned to his native Poland to fight in its defense against Russia.

LAFAYETTE, MARIE JOSEPH PAUL YVES ROCH GILBERT DU MOTIER, MARQUIS DE (1757–1834)

Given a commission in the Continental Army (1777), Lafayette was wounded at Brandywine and fought at Monmouth. In 1780, he countermarched in Virginia, which helped lead to Cornwallis surrendering at Yorktown. He had held the field until Washington and Rochambeau arrived.

LEE, HENRY, "LIGHTHORSE HARRY" (1756–1818)

A brilliant cavalry commander, Lee's Legion took Paulus Hook, N.J. (August 1779). Between 1780 and 1781, he supported Greene in the Carolinas, seeing action at Haw River (February 1781), Guilford Court House, Ninety-Six, and Eutaw Springs. His discipline, mobility, and cavalry penetration were masterly. Ill-health caused his resignation in 1781.

LINCOLN, BENJAMIN (1733–1810)

Appointed major-general in 1776, Lincoln was given command of Continental forces in the South in 1778. He surrendered Charleston in May 1780 with approximately 7,000 troops. He participated in the Yorktown campaign after a prisoner exchange.

LITTLE TURTLE (1752–1812)

Becoming chief of the Miami, Little Turtle feared the incursions of American settlers more than the British and, therefore, supported the latter during the Revolution. After American independence, he defended Native American interests in the Ohio River country against the Northwest Ordinance. After the Shawnees defeated the Harmar expedition (1790), Little Turtle and Shawnee Blue Jacket crushed St. Clair's expedition (1791), before Wayne defeated them at Fallen Timbers (1794). He signed the Treaty of Greenville; kept faith with the United States, allegedly receiving bribes for quiescence; and crusaded, thereafter, against alcohol in his tribe.

MADISON, JAMES (1751–1836)

In 1776, Madison was elected to the Virginia Convention. From 1780 to 1783, he served in the Continental Congress. With his friend Jefferson, he formed the Republican (Democratic) Party. During constitutional ratification, he wrote many Federalist papers under the name, Publius. He was the principal author of the first ten amendments, ratified in December 1791 as the American Bill of Rights. He served as Jefferson's Secretary of State, 1801–09, and was elected fourth President in 1808 and served from 1809 to 1817.

MARION, FRANCIS, "THE SWAMP FOX" (1732–95)

A dedicated Southern Patriot guerrilla leader, Marion accompanied "Lighthorse Harry" Lee, and attacked Loyalists and small British outposts, thereby helping to frustrate British plans in the Southern states. Despite several defeats, he generally retired in good order, and disbanded his unit in 1782 when the British left Charleston.

MORGAN, GENERAL DANIEL (1736–1802)

Morgan accompanied Arnold on his unsuccessful Québec campaign, was captured and exchanged, and fought at Saratoga. He is best known for his outstanding victory at Cowpens, S.C. (17 January 1781).

PAINE, THOMAS (1737–1809)

Paine went to Philadelphia in 1774 with an introduction from Franklin. He demanded independence in his tract, *Common Sense* (1776), which facilitated a successful ratification of the Declaration of Independence, and then served with Greene as an aide-de-camp. He joined the Foreign Affairs Committee (1777–79). He travelled to France with Laurens and sent back money, clothing, and munitions. He later became involved in French Revolutionary events and wrote his famous *Rights of Man* (1791–92).

PICKENS, GENERAL ANDREW (1739–1817)

Best known for defeating Carolina Loyalists at Kettle Creek (1779), Pickens fought at Stono (S.C.) and against British Creek allies. His militia command at Cowpens (1781) ensured an American victory, and he then fought in a civil war against Southern Loyalists, particularly at Augusta (1781), eventually fighting at Eutaw Springs. Finally, Pickens successfully prevented the Cherokees (1781–82) from joining Loyalist-led raids against frontier hamlets.

PINCKNEY, THOMAS (1750–1828)

Joining the 1st South Carolina Regiment, he served in various forts. Involved in the 1778 campaign in West Florida, he then fought at Stono Ferry, Savannah, Charleston (1780), and Camden, and he joined Lafayette in the 1781 Virginia campaign. In 1795, he signed the Treaty of San Lorenzo with Spain. He served in the War of 1812 but saw no action.

REVERE, PAUL (1735–1818)

A skilled Boston silversmith, and maker of artificial teeth, Revere engraved an image of the 1770 Boston Massacre; took part in the Boston Tea Party (1773); and on 18 April 1775, with two others, rode towards Concord from Boston to warn of approaching British troops. Although his personal mission failed, a warning arrived in time. He became a militia major in 1776.

ROCHAMBEAU, JEAN-BAPTISTE DONATIEN DE VIMEUR, COMTE DE (1725–1807)

Sent to command a French army in support of the Americans, he was blockaded by the British fleet at Newport, Rhode Island, for nearly a year. He then marched South to join Washington in the investiture of Yorktown, which led to Cornwallis surrendering.

RODNEY, GEORGE BRYDGES, 1ST BARON RODNEY (1718–92)

British admiral who won many victories during the War of Independence. On 8 January 1780, he captured a Spanish convoy near Finisterre, followed by the defeat of Langara's Spanish squadron (18 January 1780) off Cape St. Vincent. He fought indecisive actions against French Admiral Guichen off Martinique in April 1780. In 1781, he seized the Dutch island of St. Eustatius, and on 12 April 1782 defeated the French at the Battle of the Saintes.

SCHUYLER, PHILIP JOHN (1733–1804)

Appointed a major-general in 1775, Schuyler ran the failed 1775 Canada campaign and was superseded by Gates in 1777. Nevertheless, he should be remembered for contributing to Arnold's successful delaying tactics at Valcour (1776) and to slowing down Burgoyne's advance in 1777. He retired in 1779.

STEUBEN, FRIEDRICH WILHELM VON (1730–94)

Arriving at Valley Forge (23 February 1778), Steuben improved the military organization and training of the Continentals. Becoming Inspector-General, he encountered great difficulties with Virginian Thomas Jefferson who pursued state rather than federal interests. Steuben commanded troops at Yorktown, and, through these, the British marched to lay down their arms.

SULLIVAN, JOHN (1740–95)

Brigadier John Sullivan commanded a brigade in July 1775, saw action at Bunker Hill, was involved in the Canadian campaign and was superseded by Gates. He fought at the Battles of Long Island, Trenton, and Princeton. Further action followed at Brandywine, Germantown, and Rhode Island. In 1779, Sullivan conducted a campaign against the Iroquois in the Finger Lakes region of New York state. He resigned the same year.

SUMTER, THOMAS "GAMECOCK" (1734–1832)

In 1776 Sumter first defended Charleston, then fought the Cherokee, and finally helped repel a Loyalist invasion from East Florida (1778). As a guerrilla leader, he attacked Southern British supply lines and suffered mixed fortunes, losing at Rocky Mount and Fishing Creek but winning at Hanging Rock and Fish Dam Ford. He aided Greene's campaigns by independently attacking enemy bases,

eventually aiding Greene at Ninety-Six. Sumter resigned in 1792.

TARLETON, BANASTRE (1754–1833)

In December 1776 Tarleton captured General Charles Lee. Participating at Germantown and capturing Forts Mifflin and Mercer, Tarleton is best known for his Legion and his cavalry tactics and guerrilla warfare against Patriot partisans. His victories included Monck's Corner (14 April 1780), Lenud's Ferry (6 May), Waxhaws (29 May), and Fishing Creek (18 August) before being smashed at Cowpens (17 June). His summer 1781 Monticello and Virginia raids displayed his tactical qualities, but his Legion was accused, with good reason, of butchery and no quarter.

TECUMSEH (1768–1813)

A Shawnee, born in the Ohio River Valley, Tecumseh took part in Little Turtle's pan-tribal Native American force, defeated at Fallen Timbers (1794). Constantly campaigning against land cessions to Americans, claiming that one tribal concession was illicit without pan-tribal agreement, he argued against white customs, values, and alcohol. With his religious visionary brother, Tenskwatawa, The Prophet, after being forced into Indiana, he attempted to build a new pan-Native American alliance against America, with British Canadian aid. In 1811 Harrison defeated Tecumseh's brother at Tippecanoe, while Tecumseh was trying to win Creek support in the South. Tecumseh was killed on 5 October 1813 at the Battle of the Thames, Ontario, while fighting on the British side in the War of 1812–14.

TOWNSHEND, CHARLES (1725–67)

British Chancellor of the Exchequer, Townshend passed the Townshend Acts, among which he levied the duty on tea. The resulting Boston Tea Party was a sign of the increasing hostility towards Britain, which was exacerbated by these Acts, leading to the War of Independence.

WASHINGTON, GEORGE (1732–99)

Became Commander-in-Chief of American armies in the War of Independence (1775–83). He regained Boston and proved himself a commander of great fortitude, and a capable officer who could choose accomplished subordinates when not forced to appoint for political reasons. He was responsible for the Yorktown campaign, which virtually ended the war. He was chosen President of the Constitutional Convention (1787) and was elected first President in 1789 and re-elected in 1792

WAYNE, GENERAL "MAD" ANTHONY (1745–96)

In 1776 Wayne commanded a Pennsylvania regiment, and he served at Trois Rivières, Canada; Fort Ticonderoga, and as Brigadier-General he fought at the 1778 battles of Brandywine, Germantown, and Monmouth, and achieved a successful, commando-style, bayonet attack at Stony Point (1779). Contributing to the British Yorktown defeat (1781), he eventually defeated the Tecumseh Native American confederacy at Fallen Timbers (1794), thereafter concluding the Greenville Treaty.

Bibliography

Anderson, M. S., *Eighteenth Century Europe, 1713–1789*, Oxford University Press, London, 1966

Anderson, M. S., *The Rise of Modern Diplomacy, 1450–1919*, Longman, London, 1993

Bailyn, B., *The Ideological Origins of the American Revolution*, The Belknap Press of Harvard University, Cambridge, MA, 1967

Bailyn, B., *The Peopling of British North America*, I.B. Tauris & Co. Ltd., London, 1986

Bailyn, B., *Voyages to the West. A Passage in the Peopling of America on the Eve of the Revolution*, Alfred A. Knopf, 1986

Bayley, C., (ed), *Atlas of the British Empire*, Hamlyn Publishing Group Ltd., New York, 1989

Black, J., *War for America. The Fight for Independence, 1775–1783*, Alan Sutton, Stroud, 1991

Blanco, R. L., *The American Revolution, 1775–1783: An Encyclopedia* (2 vols), Garland Publishing. Inc., New York, 1993

Brogan, H., *Longman History of the United States of America*, Longman, London, 1985

Brown, R. D., (ed), *Major Problems in the Era of the American Revolution, 1760–1791*, D. C. Heath & Co. and Houghton Mifflin, Boston, 1992

Calloway, C. G., (ed), *The World Turned Upside Down. Indian Voices from Early America*, Bedford Books of St. Martin's Press, Knoxville, 1994

Carnes, M. C., & Garraty, J. A. with Williams, P., *Mapping America's Past. A Historical Atlas*, Henry Holt and Co., New York, 1996

Conway, S., *The War of American Independence*, Edward Arnold, London, 1995

Cumming, W. P. & Rankin, H., *The Fate of a Nation. The American Revolution through Contemporary Eyes*, Phaidon Press Ltd., Oxford, 1975

Davies, P., *The History Atlas of North America*, Macmillan, New York, 1998

Davis, P. K., *Encyclopedia of Invasions and Conquests from Ancient Times to the Present*, ABC-Clio, Santa Barbara, CA, 1996

DeConde, A., *The Quasi-War. The Politics and Diplomacy of the Undeclared War with France, 1797–1801*, Charles Scribner & Sons, New York, 1966

Dickinson, H. T., *Britain and the American Revolution*, Longman, London, 1998

Draper, T., *A Struggle for Power. The American Revolution*, Little, Brown & Co., New York, 1996

Dunbar, W. F., & May, G. S., *Michigan. A History of the Wolverine State*, William B. Eerdmans Publishing Co, Grand Rapids, MI

Englander, D. (ed)., *Britain and America. Studies in Comparative History, 1760–1970*, Yale University Press, New Haven, CT, 1997

Gilbert, M., *American History Atlas*, Weidenfeld & Nicolson, London, 1985

Godechot, J., *France and the Atlantic Revolution of the Eighteenth Century, 1770–1799*, The Free Press, New York, 1971

Greene, J. P. & Pole, J. R., (eds), *The Blackwell Encyclopedia of the American Revolution*, Blackwell, London, 1994

Hamilton, A., Madison, J., and Jay, J., *The Federalist Papers*, Bantam, New York, 1982

Heale, M. J., *The American Revolution*, Methuen, London, 1986

Henderson, J., *The Frigates*, Adlard Coles Ltd., London, 1970

Henderson, J., *Sloops and Brigs*, Adlard Coles Ltd., London, 1972

Homberger, E., *The Historical Atlas of New York City*, Henry Holt, New York, 1994

Kupperman, K. O., *Major Problems in American Colonial History*, Houghton Mifflin, Boston, 1993

Larrabee, H. A., *Decision at the Chesapeake*, William Kimber & Co. Ltd., London, 1965

McNaught, K., *The Penguin History of Canada*, Penguin, New York, 1988

Maidment, R. & McGrew, A., *The American Political Process*, Sage Publications, London, 1986

Martin, J. K. & Lender, M. E., *A Respectable Army: The Military Origins of the Republic, 1763–1789*, Harlan Davidson, Inc., Arlington Heights, IL, 1982

Miller, J. C., *The Federalist Era, 1789–1801*, Harper & Row, New York, 1960

Namias, J., *White Captives: Gender and Ethnicity on the American Frontier*, The University of North Carolina Press, Chapel Hill, NC., 1993

Norton, Mary B.; Katzman, David M.; Escott, Paul D.; Chudacoff, Howard P.; Peterson, Thomas G.; Tuttle, William M. Jr. & Brophy, William J.; *A People and Nation*, Houghton Mifflin, Boston, 1995

O'Brian, P., *Men-of-War*, Collins, London, 1974

Palmer, R. R., *The Age of the Democratic Revolution*, Princeton University Press, NJ, 1964

Parish, P. J., *Slavery. The Many Faces of a Southern Institution*, British Association for American Studies, Keele University Press, 1979

Perdue, T., *Native Caolinians. The Indians of North Carolina*, North Carolina Department of Cultural Resources, Raleigh, NC, 1985

Powell, W. S., *North Carolina through the Centuries*, The University of North Carolina Press, Chapel Hill, NC, 1989

Quarles, B., *The Negro in the American Revolution*, University of North Carolina Press, Chapel Hill, NC, 1961

Symonds, C. L., *A Battlefield Atlas of the American Revolution*, The Nautical and Aviation Publishing Co. of America, Inc., 1986

Vanderbeets, R., (ed), *Held Captive by Indians. Selected Narratives, 1642–1836*, The University of Tennessee Press, 1994

Wright, D. R., *African Americans in the Colonial Era: from African Origins through the American Revolution*, Harlan Davidson, Arlington Heights, IL, 1990

Index

Figures in *italic* are map references.

Map Name Index